howard stern
KING OF ALL MEDIA

ALSO BY PAUL D. COLFORD

The Rush Limbaugh Story

howard stern

KING OF ALL MEDIA

THE UNAUTHORIZED BIOGRAPHY

PAUL D. COLFORD

ST. MARTIN'S PRESS 🕮 NEW YORK

A THOMAS DUNNE BOOK.
An imprint of St. Martin's Press.

Design by Scott Levine

Library of Congress Cataloging-in-Publication Data

Colford, Paul D.
    Howard Stern :   the king of all media :   the unauthorized
    biography of Howard Stern /   by Paul D. Colford.
        p.   cm.
    ISBN 0-312–14269-2
    1. Stern, Howard, 1954- . 2. Radio broadcasters—United
States—Biography. I. Title.
PN1991.4.S82C66   1996
791.44'028'092—dc20
    [B]   96-6073
                                                           CIP

First Edition: July 1996

10 9 8 7 6 5 4 3 2 1

CONTENTS

ACKNOWLEDGMENTS

Howard Stern declined to be interviewed for this book. To the best of my knowledge, however, he issued no all-points bulletin urging people from his present and past to ignore my inquiries. As a result, only a few individuals turned down my requests for interviews. These few included his father, Ben Stern, who called me one day to politely explain that he did interviews only if Howard asked him to (and clearly Howard did not want him to speak with me).

Mel Karmazin, the president of Infinity Broadcasting Corp., who probably has a terrific book of his own to write about managing growing companies and handling star talent, was consistently accessible during the eight years that I wrote *Newsday*'s radio column. This time he said: "Howard asked me not to cooperate. Howard works for me and I respect his wishes." And I continue to respect Karmazin, whose role in Stern's extraordinary success has gone largely unnoticed outside the radio industry. My disappointment at Karmazin's turndown was offset by the knowledge that a great deal of the Infinity story could be learned from documents squirreled away in the courts, the Federal Communications Commission, and other public agencies. I also had eight years of my own reporting to draw on.

Although a few potential sources quaked at the notion of speaking about their encounters with Howard, hundreds of others shared information and stories with an eye toward helping me chronicle his life thoroughly and accurately. I also am indebted to those (you know who you are) who helped open doors to sources who otherwise would have been reluctant to cooperate with me.

Lucky is the writer who has friends, colleagues, and family members to assist him in his task. I wish to thank Verne Gay, *Newsday*'s enterprising television reporter, for his invaluable support during my research and for his editorial suggestions. Also, my sincerest thanks to Jerry Agel, prolific author and friend, who generously gave of his time and counsel when I started to turn a sprawling manuscript into finished goods. Special thanks, too, to my friend Michael Barson, who was the first to recognize that a book on Howard Stern had merit; to my big brother, Dr. Joseph E. Colford III, for being there; and to my parents, Joseph and Catherine Colford, for their unfailing support.

Susan Brenna, the best newsroom neighbor in the world during the years she worked at *Newsday* and one of the best writers I know, listened patiently to tales of the book in progress and helped in the clutch. *Newsday* columnist Dennis Duggan invariably provided a welcome lift in the form of his bountiful Irish laughter. Two other *Newsday* colleagues, Thomas Maier and Thomas Curran (now at *The Star-Ledger*), gave aid at key points in the research. The editor of *Newsday*, Anthony Marro, generously approved two leaves from the paper that enabled me to complete the task.

Christine Baird, a dogged researcher at *Newsday* (and now with *The Star-Ledger*), moonlighted a second time on my behalf and continued to show that she knows what you're looking for even when you haven't asked for it.

My research also profited immeasurably from the resources of several fine libraries, especially the New York Public Library for the Performing Arts (at Lincoln Center) and the greatest of them all, the Central Research Library of the New York Public Library (on Fifth Avenue at 42nd Street). The accommodating professionals at the Long Island Studies Center at Hofstra University and at the University of Georgia's Hargrett Rare Book and Manuscript Library also were extremely helpful. In addition, after years of being aided on *Newsday* stories by William Asadorian, of the Queensborough Public Library's Long Island Division, I am pleased to be able to credit him publicly for his help with some of the historical research that went into this book.

Thanks also to Peter Kanze, a walking library of radio lore; my literary agent, Jane Dystel; associate editor Jeremy Katz, and my book editor, Thomas Dunne, who clearly listens to the radio. Thanks, too, to my friend John Williams and to Andy Edelstein, *Newsday*'s radio and TV editor.

Finally, if time and patience are the most precious gifts shared by the parents of young children, then I owe my wife, Jane, more than I could ever repay. She endured my frequent inaccessibility without complaint and never asked that most guilt-inducing question, "When will it be done?" I am blessed by her support and sustained by her love.

Catherine, age seven, and Liam, five, understood once again that the closed door meant "Dad at Work." I hope they will forgive me for my absences.

Finally, this book is dedicated to the memory of Ben Kubasik, *Newsday*'s late TV columnist and the sweetest person who ever toiled in newspapers, and to my fellow workers on the paper's New York edition, *New York Newsday*, which was closed by Times Mirror Corp. on July 16, 1995, after a valiant decade of setting the highest standards.

INTRODUCTION

A few months before completing this book, I unexpectedly took another step in my effort to understand Howard Stern and how he has transformed the radio industry. After twenty years as a newspaperman, I was invited by WOR-AM, the New York news/talk station, to be a substitute host. The instructions from program director David Bernstein were to be informative and "to have fun."

At *Newsday* (and the now defunct *New York Newsday*), I had covered the radio industry for eight years. I also had written a biography of the radio commentator Rush Limbaugh. I knew that it took a lot of lively talk to energize, let alone fill, even one radio hour. Yet despite my clearheaded understanding of the process, and two decades of interviewing people for print, "to have fun" so that the listeners had fun proved a formidable challenge.

During an overnight program and many evenings of filling in for the veteran talk personality Barry Gray, myriad interviews (politicians, authors, journalists, and academics) and calls from listeners constituted the raw material of my broadcasts.

Howard Stern, on the other hand, has become one of the most influential personalities in the history of broadcasting largely because he *abandoned* the fixtures of the radio trade. Over the past ten years he purged most of the rock music from his show, as well as the traffic reports, time checks, and weather forecasts. He set off, unanchored, in his own raging stream of consciousness. Although he has continued to call himself a disc jockey, he now presides over a talk show that echoes only the ambient rhythms of his own psyche. He weaves his offbeat and often vulgar ruminations about sex, politics, and pop culture into long, ever-curious riffs. He tells all. When he is not drawing from his own imagination, he presents tales of the dysfunctional family consisting of those who work with him inside and outside his New York radio studio. Part of Howard's genius is to expose his insecurities, plus those of his cohorts, and to have people identify with them. The relatively few guests invited to visit his show are mere foils.

The format of "All-Howard, All the Time" is no match for many of the more traditional music and talk programs with which he competes. At the end of 1995, he was drawing around four million listeners a week. He was earning about $8 million a year from radio deals with New York's WXRK-FM, Los Angeles' KLSX-FM, and his two dozen other affiliates around the country. The self-proclaimed "King of All Media" was receiving millions more from sidelines such as his two published books and a nightly show on the E! cable channel.

In addition, early in 1996, it was announced that he would star in a movie version of his book *Private Parts*, that he had signed a new, five-year radio contract with Infinity Broadcasting Corp., and that he planned to launch the Howard Stern Radio Network as part of a grand design to extend his morning program into many more markets.

Howard Stern: King of All Media seeks less to explain his extraordinary appeal than to paint a detailed portrait of the man on and off the microphone and to chronicle his jagged yet determined path to the top of his profession. He is a ranting scourge of the Federal Communications Commission and a contemplative practitioner of Transcendental Meditation, a man who would be governor of New York and a family man who prefers no place over his own home, a foul-mouthed pariah to those in genteel circles and a ratings superstar who has made Wall Street cheer. He is a mass of contradictions who appalls and enthralls.

—Paul D. Colford, March 1996

I'm going to send Howard an autographed picture and I'm going to write on it, "Howard: Enjoy the show, just don't get arrested in L.A."

—Judge Lance Ito, responding to Howard Stern's on-air remarks during jury selection in the O. J. Simpson trial

Howard Stern is a geek. He's the guy in the carnival who ate the live chicken. . . . He stands there with blood dripping down his chin and feathers in his mouth. How could anybody do that?

—Garrison Keillor, host of public radio's *A Prairie Home Companion*

It is true that talk radio is entertainment, but let's not kid ourselves. Entertainment can take us just so far. At the core of the modern talk-radio *phenomenon* is that elusive component known as *trust*. (Hey, this concept even applies to Howard Stern, whose radio persona is one of the most consistent and credible in the history of the box.)

—Michael Harrison, editor and publisher, *Talkers Magazine*

I always wanted to be on the radio. I think I can relate to a mike better than I can to people. I feel more comfortable around it, which is maybe sad. But the mike doesn't talk back.

—Howard Stern

ONE

Day after day, a man identifying himself as Mr. Howard called. He sounded unduly mysterious, skipping all pleasantries and asking to speak immediately with one of the saleswomen. Word around the real estate agency, which sold expensive homes on the North Shore of Long Island, New York, was that Mr. Howard wanted to move elsewhere in the area, because unwelcomed people had discovered where he lived. Too close to the road, he said.

One prospect—described to him as a partially built home in the woods, far removed from neighbors, far removed from the main road—made him curious. Before he would see the place, he insisted that his interest and visit be absolutely confidential. He agreed to meet the saleswoman at a time when her colleagues planned to be away from the office at an open house and no other clients would be around.

When the appointed hour arrived, a limousine pulled up in front of the real estate office and out stepped Howard Stern and his wife, Alison. For all of the hush-hush preliminaries, the secretive, lanky, six-foot-five "Mr. Howard" wore a conspicuous red bandanna around his head, and a limousine hardly deflected stares.

He had traveled only a short distance from his home, but radio's most famous shock jock also had come a long way.

* * *

When Howard Stern was growing up on Long Island, he had started out about twelve miles and several income levels south of the North Shore—in Roosevelt.

The square-mile community had been known as Greenwich Point until the turn of the century, when the addition of a local post office prompted residents to change the name in honor of former New York governor Theodore Roosevelt, who was then vice president of the United States and had a summer home in nearby Oyster Bay. After the Second World War, the availability of open land in Roosevelt, and its proximity to Manhattan twenty miles away, made the community a natural choice for housing development.

Howard Stern's father was among those who went looking to buy.

Born in Manhattan in 1923, Ben Stern was the son of Froim and Anna (Gallar) Stern, natives of the former Austria-Hungary who eventually settled in the South Bronx. In August 1943, he was inducted into the army, serving first with the 1222nd Service Command Unit, at Camp Upton on Long Island, and later with a communications outfit, the 2nd Signal Service Battalion, at locations in California. He rose to the rank of Tec 4 (technician fourth class) before being discharged in March 1946 and beginning work as a radio broadcast technician in Manhattan.

Living at the time on East 156th Street in the Bronx, Ben became serious about a spirited woman with an infectious laugh on nearby West Farms Road. The young woman, Ray Schiffman, an office clerk, who was born in Manhattan, was also the child of emigrés from Austria-Hungary, Sol and Esther (Reich) Schiffman.

Ben and Ray were married by a rabbi at the Imperial Garden, a kosher catering hall in the Bronx, on May 17, 1947. Ben was twenty-three; Ray, nineteen.

Their first child, Ellen, was born in the Bronx two years later, on September 12, 1949, and the family moved to another of the city's outer boroughs—to the Jackson Heights section of Queens, where they resided when their son, Howard Allan, was born on January 12, 1954.

In 1955, Ben followed thousands of other veterans in search of greener spaces farther east of the city. The house that he and Ray selected was one of the new single-family dwellings in Roosevelt. The population of Long Island—1.4 million—had grown by five hundred thousand since 1950. In the effort to erect affordable housing in these suburbs, uniform styles of construction became common. On the Sterns' side of Conlon Road, the shingled split-levels with attached garages were known as Hausch houses, named for a Nassau County builder, John Hausch, who was active in transforming much of the area, including Hausch Boulevard and the two-hundred-unit Hausch Manor, into a tree-lined suburb of homes priced below $20,000.

On a street of well-tended properties, the Sterns' rectangular piece of suburbia was spacious; the 70-by-120–foot lot included both a front lawn and backyard. But what made Roosevelt unusual on predominantly white Long Island was the community's integrated population. When the builder William J. Levitt mass-produced homes and developed all-white Levittown after the Second World War, the charms of Roosevelt were advertised by its home builders in black-oriented publications and on billboards in Atlanta and other southern cities. By 1957, an estimated 20 percent of Roosevelt's residents were black. A decade later, when fifteen thousand people lived there, the number of black residents was 60 percent. A coalition of church, fraternal, and civic groups went so far as to unite in an effort to discourage white residents from moving elsewhere.

The campaign failed. In the late 1960s, Roosevelt experienced a radical case of white flight—an exodus hastened by exaggerated fears of middle-class blacks, who were buying into formerly all-white neighborhoods, and by the influx of other blacks who were receiving public assistance and renting available properties. White flight also was spurred by mounting concerns that the public schools had to cope with the remedial needs of welfare recipients (at the expense of other students) and by escalating disputes over school desegregation.

Although Howard Stern went on to exercise comedic license about Roosevelt, describing a more menacing level of decline in his immediate neighborhood than was supported by the facts, there clearly was more social upheaval in the community as a whole, particularly in the public schools, than he ever related in his radio broadcasts.

When Howard Stern was nine years old, in 1963, the local board of education implemented a plan to end racial imbalance at an elementary school whose enrollment had become almost all black. The board later rescinded the plan, setting in motion a series of school boycotts and other community protests led by the local chapter of the National Association for the Advancement of Colored People.

By the fall of 1965, when Howard was in the sixth grade, Long Island experienced its biggest school boycott: 1,235 students—one-third of the enrollment in Roosevelt's five public schools—stayed home during a two-day NAACP protest against what the civil rights group considered de facto segregation in the elementary schools. Washington-Rose School, which Howard was attending, was a notable exception; its enrollment of around 650 was divided almost fifty-fifty between white and nonwhite students.

"The truth is, it was an extraordinary time to grow up in Roosevelt," recalled Jerry Dikowitz, Stern's boyhood buddy. "When most of our families moved into the town, in the 1950s, it was perfectly integrated. Our parents were free thinkers and forward looking, so it was a great town in which to see all the changes taking place. Later on, Martin Luther King was a big topic of conversation. There were marches and parades and demonstrations. There was even an element that went around posting handbills saying that Martin Luther King was a Communist. I can remember picking up *Newsday* [the Long Island daily] as a thirteen-year-old and looking for [a] Roosevelt [dateline], because we were making news in those days."

Howard's liberal parents talked liberally about the civil rights movement even during his preteen years, when he was barely able to grasp its significance. In marked contrast with them—especially his mother, Ray, who was known for her gregarious manner—young Howard confronted with shyness the changes swirling in the community. Although Howard's sister, Ellen, has recalled that he used humor to soften their parents when they were angry with him, he is remembered by former neighbors in Roosevelt as a gawky kid who mostly kept to himself—no doubt an easy target for his rowdy peers. "Whenever you're on the outs, you want to be in," Howard explained to *New York* magazine in 1985. "Being Jewish is a pain in the ass sometimes. I was totally out of my culture. I wanted to be black in the worst way then."

Eleanor Wexler, who grew up near the Sterns and became a local schoolteacher, remembers the startling difference between Ray Stern and Howard. "Ray was very verbal, very involved in the family," she said. "But when I see Howard on TV now, you wouldn't believe it was the same shy person from back then."

Despite an introverted mien, Howard offered early glimpses of his radio personality, revealing youthful creativity and mischievous instincts. Instead of making ordinary crank phone calls, the kind in which the prankster asks a store owner if he has Prince Albert in a can ("Then you better let him out, ha ha"), Howard pretended to be TV game show host Gene Rayburn and used a tape recorder given to him by his father to capture the reaction of the unsuspecting people he dialed. "I'd put the microphone on the phone . . . and give away prizes," he told a reporter. "I'd do insane stuff like that and then tape it and make it part of the shows I'd do when I was a little kid."

In these make-believe radio shows, Howard also presented daffy moments with marionettes and dummies, including an expensive replica of Jerry Mahoney, the round-faced character that often appeared on TV in the hands of the ventriloquist Paul Winchell. Howard also was drawn to the antics of Clownie, the wisecracking puppet on *Terrytoons Circus*, a nightly cartoon show on New York's WOR-TV hosted by the "ringmaster" Claude Kirchner.

Impressed by Howard's interest in putting on puppet and marionette shows, Ben built him a stage. Ray liked to see her son

5

play with puppets, because she believed that they would help him become a more sensitive man. She saw them as substitutes for war toys and certainly better than dolls.

Howard would maintain a lifelong interest in puppets at home and on his radio show. Through them, he was able to act out and to express darker imaginings. His parents were unaware that little "Howie," as many of his friends called him, was treating his pals to simulated sex shows with the puppets. "I took something so innocent and beautiful and really just ruined it," he later confessed. He turned the puppets into alter egos. (In a similar fashion, he would develop a shocking radio personality to articulate the uglier views of the quiet and responsible family man that he really was.)

The Sterns' basement became a performance space for Howard and his puppets. It also served, in effect, as his first radio studio. Ben, a radio engineer, equipped the area with a reel-to-reel tape player, microphones, and turntables that enabled Howard to cue up records like a disc jockey. The professional arrangement allowed Howard and his friends to invent and record commercials for use when they played radio. Howard created an environment much like the glassed-in studios where he later would release his manic energy onto the airwaves.

It was in the basement, too, that Howard's rock-and-roll group, Electric Comicbook, sometimes practiced. The band featured Jerry Dikowitz on drums and Robert Karger on guitar. Howard sang lead on original tunes such as "Silver Nickels and Golden Dimes" and "Psychedelic Bee." Howard also played an electric keyboard unlike any on the market; his father had wired the keyboard to an amplifier. The guests who attended Dikowitz's bar mitzvah heard what would be Electric Comicbook's only public performance. It was an event that assumed such importance that in 1994 he playfully likened the Comicbook's musical "reunion" on the radio to a reformation of Cream, the British supertrio famous during Howard's Roosevelt days.

"When Howard talks about Roosevelt on the radio, I'm transported back to our childhood," Dikowitz said. "He remembers things about my life that I had forgotten. Like the silly little fact that my younger brother Bernie kept his tonsils in a jar. I'll think to myself, Why does Howard remember this?"

For all of the youthful high jinks that Howard engaged in outside his parents' line of sight, Ben Stern unwittingly did much more than simply equip his son for diversions in rock music and puppetry. In his own professional life, Ben went a long way to influence his son's choice of a career and on-air persona.

After the war, Ben worked as a technician at New York radio station WHOM-AM, which was owned by the Pope family, whose holdings included *Il Progresso*, an Italian-language daily newspaper published in New York. The WHOM schedule ranged from Italian broadcasts during the day to Spanish variety shows performed live in the radio studio during the early evening to shows from Club Baby Grand in Harlem late at night.

When Howard was a youngster, Ben was a co-owner of Aura Recording Inc., on West 52nd Street in Manhattan. Of the many sound studios operating in the city, Aura was known for superior acoustics. It did a steady business in the taping of advertising agencies' commercials, which included the voices of top disc jockeys, such as Dan Ingram and Ted Brown. Aura also laid down the audio tracks for television cartoons. Don Adams, a comedian who entertained in nightclubs and appeared frequently on Ed Sullivan's television show, was the unadvertised voice of the sarcastic penguin Tennessee Tuxedo, a Saturday-morning children's fixture on CBS from 1963 to 1966. On *Tennessee Tuxedo and His Tales*, the penguin plunged into complicated situations that invariably overwhelmed him but, at the same time, subtly taught him about space travel, underwater life, history, and other matters. Adams and others gathered in a quiet studio and "cut" the sound track, usually doing three half-hour shows in a session. The cartoonists then used the recording to complete the animation. (Starting in 1965, Adams starred as Agent Maxwell Smart in the TV sitcom *Get Smart*.)

The actor Wally Cox, who had popularized small-town science teacher Robinson Peepers in a hit television show of the 1950s, *Mr. Peepers*, visited the Aura studios in the mid-1960s to record the voice of "Underdog." In this cartoon spoof of Superman, a hound named Shoeshine Boy transformed himself into Underdog in order to protect the nation's capital and his girlfriend, Sweet Polly Pure-bred, from the dastardly deeds of Simon Barsinister.

For Howard, these were fascinating encounters—observing popular performers at work in his father's studios, absorbing the imaginative uses of a soundproof room, and, perhaps most impor-tant of all, seeing that such fun was honorable work for a serious gentleman such as his father. The recording sessions stirred an early desire to become a radio entertainer. He thought that Don Adams and the rest of the stars "had the coolest job in the world."

It was during a visit to his father's studio that the Sterns, father and son, recorded an exchange that would sound hilarious years later when Howard discovered the tape and, of course, played it on the air. A painfully somber Ben asked Howard, then around seven years of age, if he believed that the United States should remain in the United Nations. Howard said yes, then followed with a child-ish remark about "the Japs," complete with his own simulation of machine-gun fire. Ben scolded his son, saying, "I told you not to be stupid, you moron." In another moment an exasperated Ben screams, "Shut up! Sit down!" (Ben later said that he and President Richard M. Nixon should have done the same thing: burned the tapes.)

Because Howard was a fanatical reader of *Mad*, in the late 1960s his father took him to see off-Broadway's *The Mad Show*, a fast-paced revue based on pieces from the irreverent humor maga-zine. During the many car trips with his father between Roosevelt and Manhattan, Howard sampled a lot of radio programming, such as all news, that bored him enough to hunger for a more sponta-neous alternative—the kind that he himself would provide in due time. He remembered those rare moments when a blooper or an announcer's unexpected remark to someone else in the studio with him went out on the airwaves, breaking the monotony.

"I've had the same concept since the beginning," Howard later told an interviewer. "I'd watch my dad commute, and when he was stuck in the car, he'd just sit and listen to CBS News. And I thought, Wouldn't it be great if he was laughing? If every once in a while he heard a disc jockey say something funny, something that made him glad he was there?"

The image of Ben Stern, trapped like millions of others who battled their way in traffic in order to reach work, all the while with the radio on, locked in Howard's mind as the picture of the typical listener. In Howard's words, the "average schlub" at the wheel was the one he wanted to make laugh.

"Even at an early age, I remember wanting to be on radio, wanting to do a show, as opposed to sitting there and playing records," he recalled in an interview with *Playboy*. "My father bought me a tape recorder and I would sit in my room and do radio shows—but not like what I heard on the radio. I would do hours of sketches and voices and all kinds of shit. I wanted to have fun and entertain people."

He also hoped that radio would make him so famous one day that everyone in New York would know his name.

After leaving Washington-Rose School at the end of the sixth grade, Howard faced a bleak situation at Roosevelt Junior-Senior High School. Because of the dramatic influx of disadvantaged blacks into the community, the school's enrollment had come to exceed capacity by more than one thousand students. "We need a massive shot of adrenaline to help these youngsters start achieving what middle-class youngsters come to school already achieving," Robert R. Spillane, Roosevelt's superintendent of schools, pleaded to New York State education officials. So much time and energy was being expended in remedial instruction that the more advanced youngsters, such as Howard, lacked a challenge.

By the end of the 1968–69 academic year, when Howard was completing the ninth grade, more than three-quarters of the four thousand students in Roosevelt's schools were black and one-third were in families receiving welfare assistance. In order to address the needs of much of the student body, the Roosevelt school district called on the state to offer even greater financial aid to pay for the costly remedial programs. Superintendent Spillane charged that the Nassau County Department of Social Services was allowing too many welfare families to settle in Roosevelt, thereby adding to the school district's burden (and frightening white homeowners into moving out). When voters twice rejected the proposed school budget, the board of education instituted austerity measures, which included the suspension both of interscholastic sports and the purchase of new library books, Spillane refused to cut a school lunch program, because he feared "the youngsters just wouldn't eat."

By this time, most of Howard's pals had left Roosevelt; friendships waned, because the boys were not old enough to drive to visits with one another. In addition to the discouraging school situation, longtime residents were unsettled by local crime. A spring night in 1969 turned particularly ugly; violence at the Roosevelt Youth Center was followed by a rampage along the main commercial thoroughfare, Nassau Road. An estimated two hundred black youngsters attacked whites and damaged property. One person was shot, two others were stabbed, and three businesses were destroyed.

White flight became so widespread that, records show, almost every house on Conlon Road and adjoining streets changed ownership in the late 1960s. There was a near total transformation during Howard's last few years in the neighborhood. As the broadcaster told *Newsday* in 1983, "almost every white person, every beautiful liberal white person, moved out. My parents felt that they didn't want to run. They talked it over with me. I said yeah, I definitely would like to remain in the community. We did that whole trip."

His tone was conciliatory: "It was a very tough time. Blacks were really finding their own identity, their own music—I was into the Beatles, I had fights—but it wasn't so much with the black kids as with lower-class white kids." He added: "Yet it was definitely a good experience." Other times Howard also has insisted that growing up in Roosevelt had helped to liberate him.

In the 1990s, he embellished his descriptions of Roosevelt, no doubt for theatrical effect, so that his nastier recollections were studded with details of black-on-white menace and a weakling's fears. At times he claimed to have been the only white kid in a black neighborhood—an exaggeration that his own mother scoffed at— and he belabored memories of his early teen years, declaring that he had been repeatedly intimidated and assaulted in junior high school by tough black students, who forced him to hand over his lunch money. These far more dramatic tales replaced his 1983 claim that most of his fights had been with "lower-class white kids."

Nevertheless, Howard held with a martyr's fervor to the belief that he had been enlightened by how others reacted to fear. Recalling the changes in his neighborhood, he decried the "phony white liberals" who fled Roosevelt without trying to live in integrated surroundings. He claimed that they had imparted a lesson in hypocrisy.

No group observed the turnover in the neighborhood with greater puzzlement than the black newcomers. Many of them were from New York City. They had chosen to purchase on Conlon Road and surrounding streets in order to have their own single-family home and leafy piece of the suburban—and the American—dream. More than a few of those new black home buyers of the 1960s still lived in those same houses, in the Sterns' old neighborhood, in 1995.

"The way people took flight was amazing," remembered Christina Evans, a black nurse who moved from Queens to Roosevelt's Hausch Boulevard with her husband and children in 1968. "You'd be talking with them one evening and they'd be gone without a word the next day. It was like we were the plague or something. Many people moved away because their friends had moved, but many of these same people clearly couldn't afford another mortgage because there were homes that they sold for nothing."

These sellers, who had bought their homes new in the 1950s for around $16,000, typically had asked $28,000 to $30,000 a decade later but settled for $20,000 to $23,000. Black families who moved into the Conlon Road area were further confused because they themselves—an accountant, a policeman, a doctor, a teacher—were as middle class as, or perhaps even more prosperous than, the whites who were selling and fleeing. Although the immediate neighborhood's racial makeup changed dramatically, it remained a well-kept and relatively tranquil enclave amid deterioration. It did not become a slum, as the sellers of the 1960s feared.

Ben Stern acknowledged, in his words, that it "really wasn't that bad." For example, his house was never robbed. His friendly wife went out of her way to compliment new neighbors, such as the nurse Christina Evans, for taking better care of their greenery and property than the previous homeowners. What's more, Ben and Ray were upset when some of their white neighbors became panicky. The Sterns voiced a moral obligation to avoid the herd mentality exhibited by the people fleeing Roosevelt. They attended meetings at which blacks and whites encouraged one another to stick together and not to give in to hysteria.

Yet for all the nodding agreements expressed at these sessions, some owners sold their homes as swiftly as they could. Some of Howard's friends who moved did not come by later because of parental fears, he told *Rolling Stone*. "I had one or two black friends, and that was it," he said. "My parents could pick and choose. They would go and meet some of the more middle-class, upscale black people. They'd get in their car and drive and go see their white friends. They had a nice life. I, on the other hand, was in a prison every day."

When recalled sentiments such as these prompted a woman to call Howard's radio show and accuse him of promoting racism, he fired back: "I'm promoting racism? Hey, I lived this."

Ben and Ray Stern have suggested that they remained in Roosevelt as long as they could. They were swayed to leave by Howard's reports of being beaten up at school. According to Howard, he had cracked under the stress and begged his parents to move.

"It got to a point where you couldn't fight anymore," Jerry Dikowitz, Howard's buddy, recalled. "People were so determined. 'We have to stay, we have to stay.' But, as parents, they saw that it had become too dangerous."

In June 1969, at the end of Howard's first year at Roosevelt Junior-Senior High School, the Sterns bought a house in nearby Rockville Centre. "We just felt it was time to leave," Ben Stern said. Less than three weeks later, the Sterns sold their home in Roosevelt to a black woman.

"Howard was the only one of us who had it on the line," Ray told a reporter. "Our black friends told us, 'You gotta leave.' Finally, we did. I felt a tremendous defeat. But I don't regret what we went through. All the kids who left Roosevelt found that the experience left its imprint."

Howard disagreed with his mother's assessment. "When my father pulled the car away from Roosevelt that day, I never looked back," he told his listeners.

In practical terms, the social laboratory that Roosevelt had become during Howard's formative years paid off handsomely. It enriched his comedy. The experience emboldened him to press the envelope of racial humor much farther than most white performers had dared—and to get away with it. "I love it when I get called a racist for doing black dialect," he said to an interviewer. "The fact is that some people *do* talk like that. *I* talked like that."

Howard came to use his harsher, negative view of growing up in Roosevelt as a springboard for attacks on "phony" white people who preached racial tolerance but resisted any contact with blacks. His up-front exposure to black sensibilities gave him the confidence to engage in outrageous antics with and about African Americans.

As O. J. Simpson awaited trial in 1994 for the slaying of his former wife and one of her friends, Howard did street-corner radio interviews with blacks to see if they shared his conviction that the former football star was guilty. To one man, an emigré of Ghana, he asked: "What's the main export of Ghana? Gonorrhea?" As seen on that night's televised playback on cable television's E! channel, the man laughed at the question. He laughed even harder when Howard asked him if he had ever been snagged in Africa by the kind of trap that hooks a foot and yanks a person upside down. To the next man, who identified himself as an immigrant from Jamaica, Howard inquired if he had any rolling papers. Yes, indeed, the man admitted with a sly smile.

Although his use—and abuse—of black stereotypes often stirred immediate protests from his sidekick, a black woman, Robin Quivers, he would have his listeners believe that he knew all too keenly that most blacks took no offense. He said that he experienced none of the fears that other white people had when discussing black people, because he once lived among them: "I happen to know that black people are not as uptight as the average white man thinks they are."

Try repeatedly as he did to distance himself from Roosevelt, saying on a broadcast that a return visit to the community would make him nauseous and give him the shakes, he let it slip that deep down the old neighborhood exerted an unbroken attachment. He asked a camera crew from his show on E! to get footage of the house on Conlon Road, "so I could see what it looks like."

It was still there, he told his audience. Painted a strange shade of yellow, too.

He *could* go home again—if only through videotape.

TWO

The Sterns' home in Rockville Centre was barely two miles west of his Roosevelt address, but the new environment felt foreign to young Howard. Rockville Centre was four times larger than the square-mile Roosevelt, and its population of more than twenty-seven thousand was greater by around ten thousand people. In addition, Rockville Centre was whiter, more sedate, and noticeably richer than Roosevelt. The stage legend John Barrymore, the comedian Alan King, the baseball pitching great Sandy Koufax, and the jockey Eddie Arcaro had lived there. The absence of shopping malls in Rockville Centre allowed a tidy commercial district of small stores to prosper. The village, countrified on some streets by porch swings and New England–esque clapboard, was comfortable and settled—in marked contrast with the deterioration and poverty the Sterns had escaped only minutes away.

Like the house in Roosevelt, the Sterns' new home had six rooms and an attached garage, but it stood on a smaller piece of property and on a more densely developed street. However, what Rose Lane lacked in spaciousness and architectural variety—gable-roofed homes of brick-framed construction predominated—it offered in stability and affluence. Around the time of the Sterns' arrival, in the summer of 1969, Rose Lane and its immediate environs were rated a high-income area by *Cole's Directory*, a published sales reference that based its annual assessments on U.S. Census data, property valuations, and canvassing of blocks. *Cole's* was designating Conlon Road, in Roosevelt, low income.

There was another important difference between the communities. Even though Rockville Centre had a large number of Catholic residents and was the seat of Long Island's Roman Catholic archdiocese, centered at St. Agnes' Cathedral, nearly all of the Sterns' new neighbors in and around Rose Lane were Jewish. Nevertheless, in a snub outrageously close to home, Jews were not welcome to play golf at the country club around the corner. That is, even among neighbors with whom Howard might feel comfortable, he remained an outsider.

Happy as Howard was to be out of Roosevelt, the transition proved difficult. Fifteen was an awkward age at which to be transplanted into an unfamiliar setting. Harder still was Howard's experience at South Side Senior High School. The student body of more than one thousand students had divided itself into cliques in Rockville Centre's junior high and local elementary schools before Howard arrived. "I met Howard because I was also a new kid in town," classmate Marty Getraer recalled. "I found him sitting alone in the cafeteria."

After Roosevelt, Howard later told an interviewer, "I went to a school with all the blond hair and blue eyes, and I was very freaked out." Although anti-Semitism among teenagers did not arise in the form of ugly displays, except during name-calling incursions made by tough Italian kids from adjoining South Hempstead, everybody knew who was Jewish and who was not. Howard and his friends recognized that Jewish girls would date non-Jewish boys, but Jewish boys did not draw much attention from non-Jewish girls. He says he felt like a misfit both in Rockville Centre and among many of his teenage peers. He also considered many of the other students and teachers disconnected from real life as he had experienced it in hostile Roosevelt: "To me, it was the same kind of crap all over again. All the teachers were like, 'Let's talk about the black experience, what it's like to be black in America.' . . . It was so hypocritical. I was so angry with the whole phony liberalism."

Only fourteen blacks were pictured in the yearbook among the more than three hundred students in Howard's class. The black families in Rockville Centre lived mainly in the west end, a section that underwent glacially slow urban renewal, causing the agonizing relocation of some longtime black residents. Urban renewal also pitted those whose homes were slated for demolition against the municipality and prompted critics of the plan to complain that it was designed to decrease the village's black population. More than five years would pass before a blighted area that once totaled about 150 homes was fully transformed into a community of garden apartments and town houses for several hundred low- and middle-income families.

In response to the hypocrisy that Howard said he saw all around him, he decided to be silent in class. He built a protective shell around himself. "I became a total introvert," he said. He became so introverted, so inconspicuous, despite his long hair and height of more than six feet, that between his arrival in 1969 and graduation in 1972 he left only the dimmest impression among most of his classmates and teachers. As late as 1995, many still had no idea that the infamous radio personality had been a member of their high school graduating class until they were contacted during the research for this book. Only the few close friends that he made during his three years at South Side seemed to remember him at all.

Howard's lone student activity was an early involvement with the Key Club, which set up recycling programs and worked with underprivileged youngsters. Despite his uneasiness at South Side, he managed to talk his way through the interviews conducted by club members and win their vote of admission. But Peter Bralower, who lived down the street from Howard, was in the same grade, and became president of the Key Club in his senior year, retained no memory of Howard. It was only after hearing that Howard had mentioned him on the radio that Bralower learned of their common past.

This would have been Howard's reference to a car pool. Bralower recalls that he was a passenger in a short-lived ride-sharing arrangement covering the mile between home and high school, but he does not remember if Howard climbed in for the trip. Howard, for his part, suggests that he knows why Bralower and others would have forgotten him:

"Ma, when you drove the car pool in high school, didn't you see that the other boys weren't talking to me?" he once asked his mother on the radio. Mrs. Stern countered that Howard was never shy, as evidenced by the many times that he left his bedroom to greet his parents' guests. This remark only caused him to explode: *"In the house, Ma! In the house! There's a difference between the house and school!"*

Rejections and embarrassments did not lose their sting: "Everyone in my high school was smarter than me, but I did better than all of them," he said later.

Lawrence Waxman, who in 1969 joined the South Side faculty to teach drama and public speaking, had an icebreaking exercise that required each student to face the class and do something silly, such as humming the National Anthem while standing on one foot. According to Howard, his assignment was to stand and sing "Row, Row, Row Your Boat," but he proceeded in such a low, mortified tone that Waxman urged him to project more, compounding the misery. Howard wanted to repay this anguish years later by nominating Waxman to be the first civilian shot into space.

The teacher says he does not recall the "Row, Row" incident. Howard had slipped so completely from Waxman's mind that he, like Peter Bralower, drew no personal connection to the Howard Stern whom he occasionally listened to on New York's WNBC-AM a decade later. Only when one of Howard's classmates described Stern's growing radio fame did Waxman dig out a 1972 yearbook and search for a graduation picture. The photograph dusted off Waxman's memory of a kid who was, in the teacher's words, "a personalityless character who sorta looked like a goofy-looking drug freak." Nothing else. "There were many far more outrageous kids who were memorable for their blatant drug abuse or for being more talented or funnier than Howard."

Robert Ruesch, who taught English literature, remembers that "Howard basically slept through my class. It's one of the great ironies that you had this very quiet person who went on to become an outrageous star."

In the American history course taught to juniors by Richard Caproni, the students were expected to discuss developments in foreign policy, economics, women's rights, and other areas, often in response to articles in *The New York Times*. However, whether the topic was the Vietnam conflict or the struggle for racial equality, Howard participated hardly at all. Caproni said: "South Side was a happy place, but none of the kids was about to reach out and include a new youngster in the group unless you brought something to the table. For someone new to the school, it was doubly tough to make friends unless you joined an activity." But joining was not for Howard.

"Something must have been going on behind those eyes," Caproni added. "He clearly was absorbing things, considering all the times he's talked about South Side on the air. He just never allowed us to get a glimpse of the real Howard Stern. As far as I was concerned, he just kinda passed through."

It's the belief of some students who went to South Side with Howard that he has exaggerated for radio purposes the slights and follies that he claimed to have experienced in high school. "When I hear some of the things he says, I just think it makes good copy," said Michael Horn, a fellow graduate. "It was different for him, obviously, being new to Rockville Centre and all. But still, those of us who remember Howard, we scratch our heads at some of his stories."

In high school, Howard saw himself as a geek, "too tall for the world," a "big, ugly, Tiny Tim–looking bastard." His jeans would slide down his bony hips because, he would say, "I have no butt."

He also fretted over the size of his penis. It was meager. Years later he would turn his paltriness into shtick, especially in the company of reputed ladies' men such as singer Tom Jones, to whom he confessed being "hung like a pimple." In high school, however, when hormones rage and teenagers fear the taunts of their peers, the towering Howard acted particularly self-conscious when it was time to wash up with other boys after gym class. On at least one occasion he was observed showering in his underpants; other times he skipped the suds and simply put on his street clothes over his sweaty body. Those who knew of Howard's "shortcoming" saw that he was Ninja-like in his concealment. Joking repeatedly on the radio years later about his woeful proportion may have been a defense mechanism, as if he were trying to laugh away an infirmity.

"When Howard moved into Rockville Centre, he was very quiet and incredibly uncoordinated," recalled Scott Passeser, who became one of about a half dozen boys who hung around with him. "Even though he was one of the tallest guys in our class, he couldn't dribble, shoot, or jump in basketball. We called him 'Gunkard,' or 'the Big Gunk,' because he was so big and gunky. He didn't like the name."

But "Gunkard" fit. In a basement game of Ping-Pong, Howard whacked a point-scoring shot and was so thrilled that he jumped up—banging his head into a ceiling light and bending everyone around him into pains of laughter.

"Being a passenger with Howard was funny because he couldn't drive," Passeser said. "He was physically uncoordinated, his depth perception was all off, and you'd be terrorized that he would hit another car."

Horn added: "Howard was just a tall, skinny, nerdy kind of guy, but he had a subtle sense of humor. For example, our conversations in the back of the classroom would involve making fun of the teacher up in the front." Howard referred to a teacher with a skin discoloration as "Blueberry." He was unafraid to step into put-down duels. Eric Davis, another member of Howard's group, remembered "one of the basketball players started to get into a rank-out contest with this overweight guy, and he ended up brushing off the guy by calling him fat. Howard didn't stand for that. He cut the guy down, saying something like 'You think basketball is such a big deal,' then he made believe he was taking a basketball shot in this funny, affected way. The basketball guy was stunned that Howard would rip into him like that. I don't think Howard liked being mean, at least not back then. He prided himself on having a pretty good wit, and he thought that calling a guy 'fat' was too low a blow. Howard had his standards."

Friends say that Eric Davis possessed the most biting sense of humor in their group and was an influence on Howard. Davis, whom Howard called "Big Davis," was quickest with a put-down if he didn't like someone, and he was hard to top with a comeback line. "If we could have predicted which of us would become a comedian, it would have been Eric," said Keith Firestone, another one of their circle. "Howie wasn't expected then to come back with a mean joke to put you down."

There were hardly any hints of the outrageous personality that Howard would become.

"Howard was quite a bit different from who he is on the radio now," said Jonathan Weiss, whose father used to put the boys to work, on Saturday mornings, unpacking boxes and sorting pipe fittings at his Brooklyn plumbing supply company. "He had a pretty wry sense of humor, with a lot of sarcasm, but on the whole he was retiring. When he made it big on the radio, I was surprised by his persona, because in real life he had been so much shyer than that."

Added Bob Komitor, another of Howard's friends: "No one would have thought that any of us would have gotten to the level that he has. He was not a standout."

A decade later, when a funny new disc jockey on New York radio named Howard Stern was recommended to Marty Getraer, he, too, listened for a long stretch without realizing that he knew the fellow. Only afterward, when a mutual friend made the connection for him, did Getraer tune in again and, flabbergasted, realize that Howard and Howie were the same guy. Who would have guessed?

Getraer, Weiss, Passeser, Komitor, Firestone, and the few others who made up Howard's network of friends were Jewish, upwardly mobile (three became lawyers, one a physician), and content to pass much of their free time playing basketball, table sports such as pool and Ping-Pong, and card-slapping games of seven-card stud. They have since scattered around the country—and, for the most part, out of one another's lives—but unanimously agree that Howard lived a Rockville Centre life as happily uneventful as their own. They have strained their hindsight to identify clear signs that America's most notorious shock jock was lurking within the teen-ager they knew so well. They can point only to his ready sense of humor and to the few moments when he shed his outward reticence to reveal a restive spirit.

Howard loved rock music, especially Grand Funk Railroad, the popular heavy-metal band of the early 1970s. He blasted the group's albums on an old record player, its arm weighed down by a coin to keep the needle from skipping. The former member of the Electric Comicbook in Roosevelt also liked to play rock with friends in Rockville Centre. He pounded a tambourine and sang "covers" of the Doors' "Soul Kitchen" and the Jimi Hendrix Experience's version of "Hey Joe." He also could sit down at a set of drums and with wide-eyed exuberance punch out the signature riff that opens the Rolling Stones' "Honky Tonk Women."

Poker games occasionally unraveled into disgusted howls when Howard carefully held a match at his rear end and farted the light into a gaseous blast of flame. He sought out racy movies in theaters such as Grand Avenue Cinema in nearby Baldwin in hopes of catching at least a glimpse of naked flesh. One such outing in the early 1970s was to see *Myra Breckenridge*, which starred a boda-cious Raquel Welch in novelist Gore Vidal's story about a trans-sexual. Although *Myra* failed to deliver a topless Raquel, as Howard had expected, he was so wound up that he emerged from the thea-ter, ripped off his shirt, and started bellowing—drawing the stares of all around him.

The young women of Rockville Centre did not share Howard's wild side. "Girls never, never noticed me," he has said, "and when they did, they noticed I was ugly."

But he did try to meet girls. One way was through a group of friends affiliated with the local B'nai B'rith Youth Organization, ostensibly a social service group and a common link among Jewish teens in Rockville Centre. Howard's interests centered on the weekly meetings in members' homes, the basketball games at the Wilson School, and the coed parties and dances on weekends. "But I'd bet five dollars that nobody in my high school had sex with Howard before we all went to college," Passeser stated.

"We all wanted to have girlfriends," Firestone remarked. "Most of us did not." The boys fantasized about the desirable girls in their class; because they were not the most popular guys among the opposite sex, however, it was easier for them to ridicule the girls in the resentful though defensive belief that the beauties did not know what they were missing.

Another opportunity for meeting girls—and a broadening experience all around—was summer camp in the Catskills. Before and after moving to Rockville Centre, Howard went for part of the two-month school vacation to Camp Wel-Met, in Narrowsburg, New York, in the Catskill Mountains north of New York City. The sprawling facility was one of three upstate sites affiliated with the Metropolitan Jewish Welfare Board (the name Wel-Met was an abbreviation of sorts), but the nonprofit camp operated independently to serve middle-class and low-income Jewish youngsters from the New York City area. Six hundred, or even more, would occupy rustic cabins and pitch tent sites at Wel-Met. They were supervised in an unpretentious, nature-intensive program by counselors who were studying to be social workers, educators, and psychologists. Because of what one board member described as Wel-Met's "classic liberal point of view," the fees that parents paid to give their youngsters a six-week stay in the country were tapped by the camp to provide camp scholarships for inner-city youths from New York who integrated the outdoor experience. This aid also qualified Wel-Met for government surplus food of such limited variety that campers were challenged to create lunchtime combinations out of American cheese, peanut butter, white bread, and

23

ketchup. Although Wel-Met emphasized hiking, swimming, softball, crafts, and other organized activities, the camp also unwittingly allowed by now horny Howard to steal away from the group and seek his first sexual adventures with girls who would have him. It was easier to be daring in the Catskills.

Howard was a respectful son. Moreover, he drew such affection from Ben and Ray, that in an ironic way his happy family life may explain why this outwardly self-conscious "geek" would become confident enough to let it all hang out in public, via the radio—and would sometimes sink to a level of vulgarity that most sons never would display in private to their parents or anyone else. Although the personality quirks of Ben and Ray Stern later formed bottomless wells of radio material, from all accounts the couple were so devoted to their son and so supportive that they may have laid the foundation for his broadcast exploits. "Stop worrying about me," he said to them benevolently when they expressed concern about his comings and goings during high school. And there was a looseness between them; Eric Davis recalls watching Howard assume the guise of a science-fiction monster and make grunting noises to fend off an order given by his father—and his father played along with the ploy, addressing the monster by the name Howard was using and telling him to listen to his mother.

Confident of his parents' love, Howard later could talk graphically on the radio about bodily functions and the sexual appetites of his guests, perhaps because he was not dragging a yoke of scruples about how Mom and Dad were reacting as they listened at home. His parents appeared to tolerate his outrageousness on the radio because they knew the loving son behind the blue humor; besides, he was never vulgar with them. They were able to separate Howard from the star of *The Howard Stern Show* in the same way that a Hollywood director distinguishes the actor from the ghoulish character he plays in a horror movie.

Bodily functions? We all have bodily functions, Ray Stern would say. Why get uptight just because Howard talked about bathroom habits on the radio? His older sister, Ellen, also accepted what he did on the radio, stating, "He says what most people are thinking."

Howard said of his parents: "They've always been supportive of my career and letting me do what makes me happy."

Ray occasionally professed shock at Howard's bawdy treatment of women who visited his studio and at his more wicked condemnations, such as wishing the death of a Federal Communications Commission official, but she always rose above such maternal concerns on the strength of knowing that her son was respectful to his parents and remained close to them. What mother wouldn't be proud? she asked.

How many guys came home on visits from college and insisted that their mother accompany them on shopping trips to help pick out new clothes? Ray would suggest to Howard that he was big enough to go by himself, but he dismissed the thought. He knew that she enjoyed the outings; besides, he added, "I don't care what anybody says."

Ray told him on the air: "I raised you good and I'm very satisfied." She saw Howard as sweet and sensitive, hardly vulgar.

"His fans see beneath the facade, see the real Howard and, as outlandish as the jokes are sometimes, I always say give people a laugh," she told *The Washington Post*. "Some people take life so very seriously they forget how to be childlike, and Howard is a child. That's the beauty of Howard."

The usually serious Ben saw himself as something of a goof artist, one who used to rib others—short of offending them, that is. He did not think Howard went over the line on the air because, the father said, words were basically meaningless, even when propelled to a vast audience by powerful radio transmitters. According to Ben, actions were what counted.

Howard told *The Washington Post* that his parents "understand that . . . I focus on the funnier aspect of our relationships, but it's a good relationship that most people would be envious of. My father yelled at me, yes, but I see that he cared about me. It wasn't done to harm me, but to better me. With my mother, it's a true unconditional, unselfish love, and when you have that kind of love, things do go right in your life."

Besides being exposed to his father's New York recording studio and his tales of working with broadcasting figures such as Symphony Sid, the legendary jazz disc jockey, Howard developed an interest in radio during the many hours he spent listening to the box. Music radio—as it was presented by the chime-sounding, echo-chambered Top 40 disc jockeys who ruled the New York airwaves in the 1960s—turned him off, however, because the format seemed so artificial. Among the myriad air personalities on the New York dial, he warmed to talk-show hosts Alex Bennett and Bob Grant. Although they broadcast, respectively, from the liberal and conservative ends of the political spectrum, both men mainly stood out because of their iconoclastic styles. When Howard's own radio show became enormously popular in the late 1980s, he often insisted that everyone else of consequence in radio was stealing his act, including Bennett (by that time working in San Francisco) and Grant. He was loath to acknowledge what the two veterans knew from their own encounters with Howard in his aspiring years—that they had been major influences.

"One day I made the mistake of saying to my father, 'Gee, I want to be on the radio. I'd like to be a millionaire,'" he told *People*. "He yelled, 'You idiot! You don't know anything about money! You never worked a day in your life!' But that's just his way of relating. I never felt unloved. I just felt like an idiot."

"That's what Howard said he wanted to be—he wanted to be *on the radio*," Ray recalled on his show. "That, Howard always said that."

But he didn't always say *that* outside the family. In his late teens, when Howard was passing a few weeks in the mountains at Wel-Met, other campers heard him speak openly and assertively about wanting to become a famous disc jockey. Until then, his friends knew little about his radio aspirations, except that he wanted to attend Boston University because of its comunications program.

"*I* was the comedian in our group," his friend Marty Getraer said. "I would tell jokes at lunchtime. There was no sign of anything brewing with Howard. Except for this one time."

Close friends remember that Howard, using the microphone on Jonathan Weiss's tape recorder, said something into it like "I am Stern, master of the universe!" and ad-libbed a routine. This may have been the earliest version of the bit he later developed into a radio trademark, calling on "God" to give the day's weather forecast.

Looking back on that moment, Getraer recalled: "We were all a little goofy, but there was something there."

All of the boys had laughed out loud. It was a start.

THREE

Howard turned down an acceptance to Elmira College, in upstate New York, and chose Boston University because of its reputation in teaching broadcast communications. However, his indifferent grades at South Side Senior High School denied him immediate admission to BU's School of Public Communications; for the first two years in Boston, he had to park himself in the College of Basic Studies, a name that all too clearly labeled the preparatory program as a holding pen for less than stellar students, some of whom derisively referred to the setup as the "thirteenth and fourteenth grades." At the end of the sophomore year, those in Basic Studies either matriculated into the general population of BU for their junior and senior years or transferred to other colleges.

"In those days, Howard had long hair and he looked like he weighed no more than a hundred and ten pounds—so skinny that his jeans always hung off his butt," recalled Ellen Fuchman, who became a friend in their freshman year. "He was really, really lanky. And his hair wasn't just long, it was the thinnest, most unruly long hair you ever saw." He sometimes stuffed his locks into a hairnet before going to bed at night.

Added another classmate, Kevin Goldman: "You have to understand how ugly Howard was. Take away that long, flowing hair that he has now [in 1994] and give him real scraggly hair and a geeky mustache. He was really unattractive, and he hung out with these grungy people who looked like the rock group Blue Öyster Cult."

Considering that Howard displayed his frightening scarecrow look on a six-foot-five frame, it was no wonder that he repulsed more women than even he hoped would share his dormitory room bed in the sexually permissive seventies. To further isolate his thrown-together appearance, many students at Boston University favored the slick uniform of the so-called beautiful people. The men wore their shirts open and their jeans pressed—the early version of a sleek style that would be widely popularized by John Travolta in the 1977 disco movie, *Saturday Night Fever*.

Quaaludes were the recreational choice among the beautiful people, whereas Howard's small circle of hippie types preferred pot. "We were into having a good time," Fuchman said. "We were all screw-offs, we were all smoking pot."

It was early in Howard's stay at BU that he developed a serious interest in the mystical and embraced Transcendental Meditation. TM draws on ancient Hindu techniques, especially the repetition of a chosen word, or mantra, to help a practitioner turn inward and calm the spirit. The method had come into international vogue in 1967 when the Indian founder of TM, the berobed Maharishi Mahesh Yogi, became a spiritual adviser to the Beatles. Other show-business personalities, such as the actress Mia Farrow and Mike Love of the Beach Boys, also took up TM. A framed portrait of the maharishi was posted in his bedroom in Rockville Centre. And as he took his first steps into radio at college, TM became a valuable tool of preparation.

WBUR-FM, a station that drew listeners throughout the Boston area, operated out of studios in the university's School of Public Communications but offered limited hands-on work to BU students. Most students who wanted broadcast experience had to settle for campus station WTBU, which was to big-time radio what a college newspaper was to the *Boston Globe*. WTBU's low-powered signal barely reached all the BU buildings.

Howard hooked up with WTBU in his sophomore year and got the chance to spin records and read the news. For fifteen minutes to a half hour before a show, he prepared by meditating—a routine he

29

has followed to this day. He also teamed with three older students at WTBU to put on comedy. Their show, *The King Schmaltz Bagel Hour*, was loosely named after a nationally syndicated rock concert broadcast, *The King Biscuit Flour Hour*. As Howard later boasted, "We said whatever the fuck we wanted. It sounded just like what I'm doing now." But their equal opportunity swipes at religious, ethnic, and racial groups, especially during a sketch called "Godzilla Goes to Harlem," unnerved the station manager, who fired the quartet during their very first show—and kicked off a career-long series of clashes that Stern would have with radio management.

Not that Howard short-changed schoolwork in his hope for radio success. The College of Basic Studies operated like a small high school within the mammoth university—around twenty students per class. He applied himself and received high grades.

As the two-year program neared an end, he and the 274 other sophomores had to complete an ambitious team assignment known as "the Utopia Project." A year spent studying the utopian ideas of Plato, B. F. Skinner, the Shakers, and others culminated in a period without scheduled classes during which the sophomores were supposed to test their concepts of a perfect society. The groups of about five students each were advised to spend several weeks away from campus, sampling such pursuits as kayaking, meditating, and living together in the country. The experiences were then to be described in book-length papers for a final grade.

"Needless to say, we goofed off for two months and then decided we would write the whole thing in one weekend," Kevin Goldman remembered. His group of five, including Howard, retreated to a hotel in Concord, Massachusetts, with the intention of living in seclusion and producing a creative utopia. As Goldman reported in a piece about the Utopia Project that appeared in *The New York Times*, "Howard Stern, one of the sophomores, feels the decision-making process is more important" than the final paper and oral examination. An oh-so-serious Howard was quoted as saying, "Here is a project where we compromise over policies and learn how people would act placed in our society."

Not reported in Goldman's article was that the men reserved only two rooms at the hotel in Howard's misguided hope that the shortage of beds would force Ellen Fuchman into his clutches atop one of them. Nothing doing. She and the other woman assigned to the group got a look at the arrangements and insisted on claiming one of the rooms for themselves. This forced the hapless Howard, Goldman, and a third man to make do in a room that had only one bed and a pull-out couch. Out of the weekend came a rambling, team-written paper describing their utopian community of Ataraxia. It was good enough to pass review during an oral presentation at Boston University so that Howard gained admission to the School of Public Communications, starting in the fall of 1974.

During the intervening summer of 1974, Howard returned to the fold of Camp Wel-Met, not as a grunt or a kitchen steward, but as a staff counselor on a six-week trip to Yellowstone National Park and other points west. As he helped to supervise about three dozen younger teenagers, he seemed no less a juvenile himself. Wearing a silly-looking round hat, his Adam's apple bobbing at the throat of his impossibly gawky frame, he played disc jockey on the odyssey, holding the bus microphone to a cassette player armed with rock music.

The twenty-year-old Howard, whom everyone called "Howie," displayed the same interests and level of maturity that he would popularize on the radio. "He was obsessed with his phallus, which he called his 'schween,'" recalled Kary D. Presten, who was among Howard's charges. "He'd say things like 'This oatmeal was sexually abused,' and he had a ritual of 'phallicizing.' He'd pick out things that looked like a penis, such as a cucumber or even a jet airplane. He's really never grown up, if you ask me. He sounds on the radio now like the same person he was on that camping trip in 1974."

In keeping with the nature-loving spirit of Wel-Met, the group camped out every night of the trip. They gazed at Mount Rushmore and rose at sunrise to hike the Grand Canyon. In addition to the panoramic views, his companions also never lost sight of Howard's by now outspoken intention to succeed as a disc jockey. When not commandeering the bus microphone, he talked often about radio. "He was hell-bent on a career," Presten remembered. "We'd say, 'Take the needle out of your arm, Howie, you're hallucinating.'

"One morning while he was shaving, he stopped and said to me, 'I'm gonna be the biggest deejay in New York. You wait and see.' He was a goof, but he was passionate about it."

At BU, Ellen Fuchman had a similar encounter with his ambition to break into the medium. As the two of them relaxed in a student lounge, Howard explained that he planned to study for the technical exam that he had to pass in order to obtain a first-class radio-telephone operator's license from the Federal Communications Commission. The goal reflected impressive discipline and a lofty desire to master engineering technospeak so as to improve his employment prospects; it was hard enough for the average radio wannabe to pass the much easier test for a third-class permit, then the sole prerequisite for on-air work.

Howard further impressed Fuchman: he wanted to do "something different" in radio. "He knew that disc jockeys were a dime a dozen, and he said, 'I have got to do something different and outrageous in the business,'" she recalled. "We agreed that most stuff on the radio sucked, but he was determined to succeed at it. 'If you're going to make money,' he said, 'you've got to go out and do something different.' Howard knew where he wanted to go, and he had drive."

Meanwhile, Howard's self-esteem received a badly needed lift. He met Alison Berns through a mutual friend in their junior year. Four months younger than Howard, Alison came from nearby Newton Centre, a leafy and affluent village within Newton, a suburb of Boston. She'd grown up in a handsome brick house on a circular drive not far from Commonwealth Avenue and attended Newton North High School. Her father, Robert Berns, was president of Pullman Vacuum Sweeper Company, in Boston. She was studying social work.

"Alison thought I was the biggest asshole in the world," he later told *Rolling Stone*. But after more than two years of flunking romantic relations, and given beautiful Alison's willingness to converse with the loser that he felt himself to be, Howard became determined to get something going between them. First, as part of a class assignment—Howard was enrolled in the broadcasting/film division of the School of Public Communications—he convinced Alison to appear in a movie he was making about Transcendental Meditation. Later, she agreed to join him on a date, going to see the movie *Lenny,* in which Dustin Hoffman starred as Lenny Bruce, the tortured stand-up who (like Howard himself years later) had faced repeated government censure as he sought to extend the boundaries of comedic taste. Howard and Alison clicked—a romance was born. After they graduated in 1976, Howard returned home to Rockville Centre and Alison went to Columbia University, in New York City, to pursue a master's degree in social work. It was clear that they had a future together.

Among the radio stations that Howard contacted for a job after college was WRNW-FM, a rock outlet in Briarcliff Manor, a suburb of New York City, in northern Westchester County. Donald Jay Barnett, who doubled as general manager and program director, interviewed him and liked what he heard on his tape. Besides Howard's college training and first-class FCC license, he had had brief professional experience at WNTN-AM in Newton. Barnett filed Howard's tape toward the front of his preferences for future job openings.

When Barnett called to offer work not long afterward, Howard cited other commitments and declined. Privately Howard was unsure of his talent and uncertain about the radio business. In making the rounds of radio stations in search of a job, he had come across has-beens from New York radio who now toiled in out-of-town obscurity. He submitted to this insecurity and took a couple of safer positions, including an entry-level opportunity with the New York advertising agency of Benton and Bowles. Only after

Alison and his parents noticed what he himself felt gnawing at him—that he had made a boneheaded detour from the radio career he wanted—did Howard reverse himself and phone Barnett for a second chance.

Howard got the chance to prove himself when Barnett needed another broadcaster. As Christmas 1976 approached, Barnett agreed to host WRNW's morning show on the holiday itself so that the regular host could spend the day with his family. But New York station WKTU-FM, where Barnett was a part-time disc jockey, asked him to broadcast there on Christmas morning. What to do? WKTU,* a union shop, paid much better than WRNW, and Barnett believed that he would undermine his standing if he turned down the Christmas shift. "I went to my list of people [for WRNW], and Howard was first on the list," Barnett recalled. "I called him and he jumped at the chance to come in that day."

It was a stressful initiation. As Barnett was broadcasting in Manhattan on 92.3 FM, and Howard was trying to do the same in Briarcliff Manor on the distant dial position of 107.1 FM, the inferior equipment of WRNW failed him soon after he went on the air. He was unable to turn off the microphone, which also meant that he could not easily cue up the records he wanted to play without putting those sounds on the air as well. Like an inexperienced pilot calling the control tower for emergency instructions on how to land the rickety plane, the panicky Stern phoned Barnett at WKTU. "I tried to suggest what he might do to cut the mike, but he was unable to restore the speaker in the studio, so then I told him to call the chief engineer at home," Barnett remembered.

The Christmas near disaster was not held against him. Barnett found the twenty-two-year-old Howard to be reliable and professional. He followed instructions and spared management much aggravation by obeying the annoying law that required broadcasters to

---

*WKTU, a soft-rock station that called itself "the Mellow Sound," evolved two years later into "Disco 92" and eventually became WXRK, or "K-Rock," Howard's home base since 1985.

note on the program log the precise minute that each commercial aired. "Some people became hard to control, but I don't ever recall having a problem with Howard," Barnett said. He gave Stern a steady amount of work, at the farm-league rate of four dollars an hour, or ninety-six dollars a week (before taxes). Howard did a standard four-hour air shift six days.

WRNW was "a three-thousand-watt FM toilet bowl," Howard said later. But WRNW became an extremely rare and valuable radio environment. He was encouraged to be inventive. He also vented some of the adolescent obsessions that would help earn him a large and receptive audience in the years that followed.

FOUR

In the sixteen years that WRNW-FM (now WRGX) had been on
the air in Westchester County, the station moved its base of operations from Mt. Kisco and tried several music formats before settling on rock and roll. Crowded studios and offices were cobbled
out of a house at 55 Woodside Avenue in Briarcliff Manor that simul-
taneously sheltered a travel agency and a contracting firm. Later, a
hairdresser squeezed into the space.

Conditions did not come much more primitive than what
Howard encountered when he started work at the end of 1976.
Some station employees knew enough to bring their own toilet
paper to the office. On paydays staffers raced to the bank to cash
their checks out of fear that the last on line might find the account
depleted. Poor ventilation drove disc jockeys to raise high the windows on hot days, letting in a breath of air and the bark of a neighbor's dog, which was so loud that puzzled listeners sometimes
asked if WRNW was broadcasting from a farm.

The owner and licensee of WRNW was Lake Champlain
Broadcasting Corp., four men whose main business interests were
in Manhattan real estate. Although they held on to WRNW as an investment, the station operated in the tall shadows of New York
City's album-rock giants, WNEW-FM and WPLJ-FM, and was hardly
a cash cow. Indeed, Donald Jay Barnett, the general manager and
program director, remembers that the electric company several
times threatened to cut off power owing to lack of payment. The

transmitter, if it was to deliver better reception and a more competitive signal throughout Westchester, required the kind of costly overhaul that was not made.

At the same time, the Spartan setup exerted its own funky charm. The remote location was in a countrified setting, and having such distant owners meant that the laid-back operation would not be saddled with commercial imperatives. In other words, the choice conditions allowed a bunch of enthusiastic long-hairs to enliven the airwaves with an eclectic assortment of rock sounds. The disc jockeys were into the Ramones, the Sex Pistols, and other punk bands long before the New York City stations caught on. On one "blue Monday," the staff agreed to play nothing but the blues, performed by Buddy Guy, Paul Butterfield, and other greats. A silky vocal by Joni Mitchell might segue any day of the week into a freaky jazz cut by Sun Ra. Live concerts, put on the air from a local recording studio, featured Tom Paxton, David Bromberg, Jim Dawson, Aztec Two-Step, and other folkies of the period. A weekend broadcast done from the station's porch drew dozens of beer drinkers to the grounds to catch such acts as ZZ Top and Patti Smith live.

"If you had talent, you had a place at 'RNW to experiment with it, and that builds confidence," recalled John Vidaver, host of *The Porch Show*. "You didn't have to stop. You were able to push it as far as you wanted to go."

Vince Cremona, who worked at the station briefly in the mid-1970s, said: "I think all of us were into the art, as opposed to the business, of running a radio station."

The atmosphere was so open to musical exploration that WRNW spun off a long list of well-known alumni. Some of the air personalities even backstepped to the Westchester outpost after New York's WQIV-FM ended its brief incarnation as an album-rock outlet in the mid-1970s. Besides Vidaver, the WRNW ranks included Meg Griffin, Al Bernstein, Dan Neer, Harris Allen, Donna Donna, Lisa Karlin, Bob Marrone, Thom Morrera, and Joe Piasek. Known as "Joe from Chicago," Piasek was a beloved radio guru, a controlled anarchist in his on-air style. He inspired the timid Howard to loosen his approach and take the first steps toward developing the crazed persona who would uncork and share with the audience his vulgar obsessions and abundant neuroses.

"Howard was a mellow jock. He didn't understand humor on the radio," Joe said. "He hadn't mushroomed. He would say, 'Here's Joni Mitchell,' in a shy, almost tentative way." He seemed repelled by the brash punk favored by some of the other jocks. His whispery presentation made him sound like a parody of an FM disc jockey.

"Howard was quiet, unsure of himself," recalled Ted Utz, who was hired as a disc jockey around the same time as Howard. "He really didn't show any of the characteristics that we now know. The devil was still hiding inside of him."

Piasek teased Howard, saying, "'How-weird,' get weird. It's in your name." Howard disliked the nickname but came to see that his muted approach on the air was a dead end in a business overpopulated with disc jockeys who did little more than announce song titles and weather forecasts. "He knew he had to do something new, otherwise he would fall into the big, faceless mass of deejays," Barnett said. "The standouts are the ones with the balls to do something different."

One way that Howard stretched was to drag visitors into on-air conversations. "You always risked the possibility of being put on the air by Howard," said Kevin Trotta, a WRNW salesman. "One day I went into the studio to put a commercial into the rack, and I signaled him to leave me alone. But he called on me anyway, and my voice cracked when I responded, as if I had just reached puberty or something. He picked up on this and started to tease me, all over Westchester."

Live exchanges with salespeople, other disc jockeys, even janitors, heralded the kind of radio that Stern would build around himself as his popularity soared in larger markets afterward—it boosted his popularity. That is, he played it straight at WRNW until someone else was available to serve as a comic foil. He leaned more toward being a ringleader than a stand-up comic. As one WRNW colleague put it, "He needed someone to play off of." (Robin Quivers, Fred Norris, and Jackie Martling would fill that role within a few years.)

Another outlet in which Howard invested his nascent creativity was in the delivery of live commercials and the production of recorded spots. Robert Komitor, his friend from Rockville Centre, was driving through Westchester and heard a disc jockey cleverly playing around with the copy he was reading for the Crazy Eddie electronics stores. The commercial was memorable because of the jock's goofing. The broadcaster identified himself as Howard Stern.

"Howard worked really hard for our clients," said Barbara Freeman, who was employed in WRNW's sales and traffic departments. A local bakery expressed its thanks by making Howard Stern cannoli, iced and decorated to depict him accurately with eyeglasses, curly hair, and big nose. The Cheese Wheel responded to his use of the owner in the store's commercials by sending over spreads of bagels, lox, and cheeses. "We ate very well because of Howard," Freeman added.

Still, these were baby steps in Howard's development. The more daring radio was being practiced by Joe from Chicago, who hosted the show that followed Howard's midday shift. "Joe had Coney Island of the mind, a surrealist's take on the world," said Jeff Levenson, who wrote and produced many of the station's commercials. One of the absurdist lines that Joe posted around the station read: "Time Is Rubber." Another colleague described him as a grown child.

Joe looked on during a broadcast interview with Al Jarreau as the singer gave a dazzling display of percussion by patting out a rhythm on his own kneecaps. Joe crafted audio theater out of his wide choices in music, comedy recordings (such as those by the Firesign Theatre), and studio sketches. There were dramatizations of the weather forecast; Joe played a robot that pondered meteorological readings supplied by weatherman "Phil Rodent" (newsman Ted Bonnitt), who pretended to be speaking from a wind-torn mountaintop or while being swept away by the Gulf Stream.

"Howard would enter the studio and ask, 'How do you guys do that?'" Bonnitt recalled. "He was still in his pupa stage. He was still finding himself."

Howard watched because Joe stuck out. He wanted to stick out, too.

The impressionable side of Howard gave management the sense that he could be turned into a stabilizing influence among his more rebellious peers. After Lake Champlain Broadcasting announced a plan in June 1977 to sell the station for $450,000, the company released Barnett, who had hired Howard. Joe from Chicago became the new program director. However, after the sale was closed in the fall, the two new owners, doing business as WRNW Inc., sought to attract a wider audience by imposing a tighter rein on the music format than they thought Joe could implement. Because Howard did not display a burning passion for WRNW's progressive rock sound, he seemed a more pliable choice for the mission.

Howard also got along with Yube Levin, the Israeli-born sales manager who survived the transfer of the station, becoming general manager under the new owners. "I wanted to make the station more profitable," Levin recalled. "That hard-rock format was not the way to go. It was successful for kids, but at one point I couldn't take it anymore. Howard and I were along the same line about that. He was not a burned-out, rock-and-roll type. I got along with him very well because he wasn't like the others. He knew exactly what I wanted."

Joe was axed, and Howard succeeded him as program director, graduating to a $12,000 annual salary.

Howard's colleagues point to the sale of WRNW as the beginning of the station's end as an outlet for progressive rock. Unanimously recalling how much they liked Howard personally, they also cite his elevation to program director as evidence that he was essentially colorless and noncombative, in Jekyll-and-Hyde contrast with the radio personality of today. In 1977, he simply was the best choice to help the new owners guard their investment and broaden the station's appeal. Howard himself has said that he did not care about the music. He saw the program director's job as a great opportunity. None of his colleagues seemed to blame him for being a willing tool in the ouster of Joe from Chicago.

"We had caused a ruckus to make an impact," Joe said. "But the new owners wanted to follow a predetermined format. Howard didn't have strong feelings about it one way or another. He was not entrenched at the station, he was not a programmer per se, nor did he have a powerful show. He was a mellow jock."

On one key point, however, Howard and Levin disagreed. Howard wanted to remain on the air even though, according to Levin, "he sounded horrible, horrible, horrible! I didn't see any potential for him whatsoever." Levin relented only because Howard insisted on retaining an air shift before he would accept the programming job.

While continuing to do a four-hour show each day—for a time Howard took over the morning program, but mainly he held the midday stint—he steered WRNW toward softer rock. "You still had some freedom to choose, but instead of the Sex Pistols or the James Gang, you now were playing Seals and Crofts, Carole King, and the other singer-songwriters," recalled Bruce Figler, a disc jockey who worked in the wee hours. The hard sounds of the Who and the Rolling Stones were all but eliminated.

And Howard started to come across like an ever-so-serious program director and cheerleader. "There has been a complete void in covering any kind of local issues, everything from local government to happenings in the schools—just taking calls, speaking to people, finding out really what Westchester's needs are," he told a local freelance writer for *The New York Times* in 1978. "That's our edge, that's the difference."

He identified WRNW's role: providing information and entertainment. "We want to have a definite sound," he said. "We want people to turn on WRNW and know right away, 'That's WRNW, that's my station, I like it.'"

Fred Schreier, one of the new owners, found Howard to be "one of the most capable young men on the staff, very pleasant and always very cooperative." The right man for the job.

A few months after Howard became program director, a description of the station in *Radio Guide*, a bimonthly publication, reflected the station's more serious demeanor: "WRNW is a sophisticated Rock format with a musical mix that includes the best in contemporary music as well as a combination of outstanding albums of the past [sic]. Local news every hour. Services and announcements geared to the New York suburban area throughout the day." Howard's midday show was defined in broad terms: "Howard broadens the musical spectrum with emphasis on rock from Oldies to new wave and sprinklings of jazz, soul, funk and folk."

He tempered his direction of WRNW's overall sound. He did not interfere with the other jocks. The ones who asked him for input were told, "You sound great, don't worry about it."

Howard and Alison had been dividing their time between the Upper West Side of Manhattan, where she was attending Columbia, and his place on Bronx River Road in Yonkers, which was closer to WRNW. As Alison completed her master's degree in social work, the pair planned their wedding. In marked contrast with the equal opportunity offenses against religions that Howard later would commit on the radio, the choice of setting could not have been more reverent and traditional. Temple Ohabei Shalom (which means "Lovers of Peace" in Hebrew), founded in 1842, was the first Jewish congregation in Massachusetts and the second oldest in New England. Located on Beacon Street in Brookline, a short distance from where Alison grew up, the Reform temple was distinguished by its beautiful domed edifice, built in an imposing Byzantine-Romanesque style said to have been modeled after the great synagogue at Florence.

On June 4, 1978, Howard and Alison entered the temple under an inscription that reads "My House Shall Be Called a House of Prayer for All People." They were both twenty-four years old.

Maybe it was the love in his life, but Howard gained confidence as his programming stint progressed. Barbara Malmet, hired as news director in 1978, became his first "Robin Quivers" as he commented on stories in her newscasts during the morning show they did together. Colleagues recall his broadcast from the Westchester premiere of *Sgt. Pepper's Lonely Hearts Club Band,* the movie version of the Beatles album, which starred the Bee Gees, Peter Frampton, and George Burns. Although only a few people turned out to see the widely panned film, Howard stirred them to such a whooping frenzy that it sounded to WRNW listeners as if there were thousands.

Off the air, Howard was as likely to mock some of the music that WRNW was playing and to join in the kind of naughty humor being given wider cultural license by NBC's *Saturday Night Live.* He also began to share with a few of his associates an excessive and unembarrassed interest in vulgarity that offered a clear sign of where he was heading.

Long accustomed to bending his six-foot-five height through doorways, a giant among smaller people, he took advantage of WRNW's cramped quarters by reaching out and pinching other men's nipples when they had to squeeze past him in tight spaces. He also joked about flatulence, especially his own. Years later he reveled in the memory of the time that two women from the station fled his farts at a local motel during the night that he and several other staffers split the cost of a room during a snowstorm. What's more, Howard bragged about the hefty size of his bowel movements, going so far as to leave the toilet unflushed and insisting that production director Jeff Levenson go peek at his output.

"He was always engaged in some form of self-denigration," said Levenson, who collaborated with Howard on many commercials. "He seemed wildly uncomfortable in his own body."

Disc jockey Meg Griffin: "To see him back then was like seeing a *Beavis and Butt-head* nerd kind of guy. He had thick glasses and was much heavier. His short hair was like Brillo. It was a real unfortunate look."

Gross as some of Howard's gestures were, he may have dwelled on them in order to lance larger anxieties about his physical awkwardness. He was like a comedian who secretly cries behind his laughter. His keen interest in his plumbing system may have been his unconscious way of jettisoning heavier baggage so that he could more easily struggle with managerial responsibilities. "He was an anxiety-ridden guy," Levenson added. "Life made him anxious, whether it was the boss coming in today or the commercial reading he had to do at two o'clock—all sorts of things made him nervous."

Stern had yet to figure out a way to package his neuroses and sell them on the radio, but he had learned how to cope with stress. He continued to do so in a manner that could not have been more different from boasting about his bowel movements.

Howard practiced Transcendental Meditation as faithfully as a monk says his morning and evening prayers. He was never too busy to drop everything and do it, usually once in the morning and again in the afternoon. Early in his stay at WRNW, he retreated to the parking lot before his show and meditated for about twenty minutes in his car. Later, his colleague Barbara Freeman would give him the keys to her home near the station so that he could meditate in a quiet environment. "He liked his 'alone' time," she said. "It was a very private thing with him."

Private, but not always out of view. Seated on occasion in the production studio, eyes closed as he silently repeated a mantra, he appeared to some as if he had nodded off to sleep. "He looked like someone's grandmother taking a nap," Levenson recalled. "It was almost as if the meditation were Howard's pendulum swinging back in the opposite direction from some of the grosser things that he would dwell on."

Howard was so impressed by the stress-relieving power of meditation that he discussed the psychic possibility of being able to levitate himself and others. "He and Alison once threw a party, and I remember that he talked about whether it was possible to levitate his mother," Barbara Malmet said. Joe from Chicago would ask, "How's the levitating going?" Howard's interest in this heady area affirmed Joe's choice of nickname, "How-weird."

Reflecting in 1994 on his experience at WRNW, Howard said: "I used the place, I made a living, I wanted to make money. . . . I hustled, I hustled, I showed my employer how good I was, and they kept finding new things for me to do because they wanted *me* in charge."

But after two years at WRNW, an eternity in the gypsy world of small-market radio, Howard wanted to move on and up. An opening for a wacky morning man at WCCC, a powerful station in Hartford, Connecticut, prompted him to seek the job. The first thing he needed was a tape of his antics that would reveal his qualifications. It was no small chore: Howard had hardly distinguished himself as the wackiest jock on the dial.

One day, though, he veered in that direction, possibly to prepare himself or to capture on tape a few morning riffs that might impress WCCC. As Bruce Figler drove home from doing WRNW's overnight show, he listened to Howard, who had traded shifts that day with the station's regular morning man. Neil Young had released a new album, *Comes a Time*, which contained a standout tune, "Four Strong Winds." Although the song was a wistful take on time passed, Howard told his listeners that "Four Strong Winds" was about flatulence. "Here it was between six and seven in the morning, and Howard's doing farting routines on the air," Figler recalled. "I wondered if he had gone off the deep end."

Figler added: "I think he had heard of the opening in Hartford, arranged to work in the morning, and sent them a demo tape of that show. He knew that none of our bosses would be listening at that hour."

Whatever tape Howard put together reached WCCC program director Bill Nosal. "It was nothing special," Nosal said. "The tape was mainly time and temperature oriented, but there was something about him that I liked. And Howard was persistent. He kept calling and calling. I finally had him up for an interview and an audition. What I liked to do was put a guy in a production studio with an armful of records and have him record a thirty-minute show for me. If I recall correctly, his show was quite mediocre and I wasn't interested in him. But he kept bugging me so that I had him back for a second taping. He wore me down and we hired him."

Most of the WRNW staffers were sorry to see him go. "He was the nicest guy I ever worked for," Figler said. "I don't remember him getting mad at anyone. He was a sweetheart of a guy."

Keeping track of Howard's subsequent career through stories in radio trade publications, most of his WRNW colleagues were unprepared for his stunts and pranks elsewhere. The mellow "Howweird" they had known did not seem to harbor a grand ambition to be an outrageous air personality. "What was surprising is that he parlayed so successfully the kind of off-the-air, juvenile, adolescent, bathroom humor that most of us had used and left behind," Barbara Malmet said.

On closer examination, it was easy to see that the freewheeling, often anarchic, and always colorful world of WRNW had been a unique breeding ground for Howard's latent outrageousness. "He was not yet confident or courageous enough and/or dopey enough to reveal that side of himself [on the air]," Jeff Levenson said. He used those two years to explore parts of himself that he thought would fly professionally, thereby establishing a connection between the scruffy station and the radio superstar he would become.

FIVE

If Howard was going to stand out on Hartford's radio dial, it had to be on the strength of his own creativity and self-marketing. His employer operated too frugally to promote him into stardom on the two stations that simulcast his morning program in competition with rock outlet WHCN-FM.

WCCC-AM, which broadcast only from sunrise to sunset, and the twenty-thousand-watt WCCC-FM, which simulcast most of the AM programming, were the sole radio properties of Greater Hartford Communications Corp. Its president, Sy Dresner, also served as the stations' general manager, chief engineer, and jack-of-all-trades. A child of the Depression, he ran WCCC with a hands-on manner and a small staff, as if he feared that the stations would perish on someone else's watch. He stocked the soda machine himself, disposed of the empties, and fixed the antiquated equipment. He exercised such control, especially when it came to spending money, that during his vacations routine purchases were put off and COD deliveries were not accepted until he could approve them personally.

Howard had graduated from sleepy Westchester to the capital of Connecticut, thrilled by the prospect of working at a far-reaching station located halfway between New York and Boston. "It was probably the best move I ever made," he later told *Newsday*. "I didn't want to be a program director anymore." Nevertheless, at

WCCC he was being paid the same miserly salary of $12,000; he had to be on the air six mornings a week; he had a weekend public affairs show to prepare and do, and he had more commercial work to complete than ever before.

He awakened in darkness and drove from the apartment that he and Alison rented in suburban Bloomfield to WCCC's downtown studios, at 11 Asylum Street. His sign-on was 6:00 A.M. The operation was so lean that he had no one else to pull records, field phone calls, or rip and sort the reams of news stories that continually spilled out of the Associated Press machine during his show. After four hours on the air, he often dialed around Hartford to apprise the other media of his antics. "He was always on the phone to the local TV stations and the newspaper reporters," Nosal said. "He was the world's best self-promoter."

What Howard gave Hartford, starting in early 1979, was a much tamer and far less bawdy version of the show that would turn him into a giant years later. Dresner and Nosal, for example, encouraged him to use the phones to interact with his listeners. During a springtime period of gasoline shortages, Howard invited his audience to call in their reactions to a local chain letter urging people to fight back against the oil industry by making an example of Shell. The callers sounded so angry that before long Howard took up the war cry, proclaimed, "To hell with Shell," and advocated a two-day boycott of Shell products. Representatives of the oil company urged the station to call for gasoline conservation instead of a boycott, but Dresner allowed his morning man to sustain the heat. Howard instructed motorists to drive with their lights on to further protest the high cost of gasoline. The drum beating got Howard news attention—and that lifted the twenty-five-year-old disc jockey out of radio obscurity for the first time.

Seizing on a news story that medical schools were facing a shortage of bodies for research, Howard held a "cadaverthon" to recruit specimens. (There were no pledges.) In a routine that he would repeat in other cities, he called on leading public officials to declare his birthday, January 12, a holiday. Connecticut's governor and Hartford's mayor dismissed him, apparently failing to see the humor in the ridiculous request. However, after hearing Howard gripe about the brush-offs, Dennis Schain, the enterprising press secretary for State Senate Minority Leader Joseph I. Lieberman, saw it as a playful way to obtain some favorable exposure for his boss. "We really gilded the lily," Schain recalled. An official proclamation, worded in florid language and signed by Lieberman, declared that January 12 would be an important date "for the rest of eternity." Schain delivered the document to Howard, and the disc jockey praised Lieberman on the air. (Lieberman, who recognized the power of radio broadcasts long before many politicians, was elected Connecticut attorney general in 1982 and United States senator in 1988.)

In January 1980, when Paul McCartney was arrested in Tokyo for possession of marijuana and jailed, his incarceration dragged on for ten days (before he was released without charge). Howard seized the opportunity to seek contact with the former Beatle and to protest his treatment to whomever else he could reach on the phone. At one point Howard called Tokyo and ended up speaking with one of McCartney's prison guards. The situation in Japan, where McCartney had gone to do a concert tour with his band, Wings, inspired a song that Howard and some station mates recorded for his morning show: "Don't Clip His Wings, Let Him Fly."

"I'm a lifelong resident of the Hartford area, and there's no question that Howard brought something special to local radio," Nosal said. "He had balls. He wasn't afraid to try things." In a world of homogeneous morning shows, Howard began to stand out.

Lacking a newsperson to play off, Howard brainstormed ideas for his four-hour program during nightly phone conversations with Nosal. The program director, who also did the midday shift after Howard, believed in doing bits, bits, and more bits to entertain the wake-up audience. Howard also enlisted the help of a nighttime disc jockey at WCCC, Fred Norris.

Norris, whose real name is Fred Nukis, worked at WCCC while pursuing a degree in speech and theater arts at Western Connecticut

State University, in Danbury. He had a distant manner that struck some at the station as unfriendly. He also had a facile way with voices that enabled him to impersonate celebrities, such as nasal-toned sportscaster Howard Cosell, when the morning man needed an extra player at short notice. He and Howard formed a creative bond that would endure all but continuously.

For all of the bathroom humor that Howard displayed, and the gross obsessions he would share with his listeners years later, he achieved a level of consistency at WCCC that translated into an even-tempered disposition off the air.

"Howard's affect was rather gentle, and thoughtful, and at odds with the culture of rock radio," said Colin McEnroe, a columnist with the *Hartford Courant* who at that time counted the city's radio beat among his duties at the paper. "He was, on and off the air, a mannerly guy, so that when I heard years later about all the appalling things he was doing, I made a few inquiries to be sure it was the same Howard Stern."

McEnroe added: "It's fair to say that he wanted me to know about what he was doing, but he was never obnoxious about it. He'd call up and say, 'Here's something you might want to know about.'"

When Nosal left the station with a bad case of radio burnout, early in 1980, Howard accompanied him to the unemployment office and in the days that followed demonstrated concern by keeping in contact with his former boss.

In the company of the overnight disc jockey, Hal Lichenbaum, known on the air as "Lich," Howard took up racquetball. They played late afternoon games at Rollout, in Rocky Point. Although Howard has maintained that WCCC was an intolerable slave pit, Lich remembers that he and Howard were so passionate about the radio business that they endlessly discussed ways to improve the station. "We talked about it as if it were our home, and how we wanted to set it apart in the market," Lich said.

As far as the rival WHCN was concerned, Howard had succeeded in setting himself apart. The proof was in the ratings. After trailing WCCC in several ratings periods, WHCN tied its rival in The Arbitron Company's April–May survey of 1979. However, in the October–November ratings, a surge in Howard's numbers (to a 3.2 percent share of the morning listening audience during a so-called average quarter hour) helped WCCC to pull far ahead of WHCN once again.

Howard was generating a buzz and earning salable ratings. "He was not kicking ass in Hartford, but he was a master at getting press and creating a stir," said Bob Bittens, who was then WHCN's overnight disc jockey and later the station's program director. As a result, WHCN took steps to remove Howard from WCCC—even though Howard was none the wiser.

"If you've got a guy who's hurting you in some way, it's standard operating procedure in radio to hire him away from the competition or find him a job out of town," Bittens said. WHCN's own morning man, Michael Picozzi, was doubling as the station's program director. As a result, WHCN chose not to hire Howard for its own morning show, but to steer him out of the market so he would no longer pose a threat.

"As the overnight jock at 'HCN, it was my job to start recording Howard's show after finishing my own shift," Bittens explained. The tapes and assorted newspaper clippings about Howard were given to Burkhart/Abrams & Associates, a leading radio consulting firm whose roster of clients included WHCN. As Howard tells the story, he desperately wanted to flee WCCC and made the jump to WWWW-FM in Detroit after applying for an advertised opening and impressing the general manager. Ample evidence, however, indicates that Howard's exit came about because he was a pawn in a tactical plan carried out by several people.

The tape supplied to Burkhart/Abrams was given to a member of the firm, Dwight Douglas, who was consulting WWWW at the time. "You move fast in the consulting business, so maybe you don't listen to a tape as closely as you'd like," Douglas said. "But I drove around with Howard on the tape player and I found myself sitting in the parking lot, even after I had turned off the motor, still listening so that I could hear the entire tape. I thought, Isn't this what we want the listeners to do—to keep listening? I thought Howard was pretty funny. This guy was going to make it."

Douglas thought Howard sounded like "Alan Alda on acid." He forwarded the tape and news clippings to Dick Hungate, WWWW's program director.

Hungate had worked in programming and as an air personality at WMMR-FM, the dominant album-rock station in Philadelphia, one of the country's largest radio markets. His rock credentials were strong—and WWWW needed as much. When Hungate joined the station in January 1980, five months after Shamrock Broadcasting Company had bought the struggling property from Starr Broadcasting Group, WWWW was locked in a three-way battle for Detroit's rock audience. The station's biggest challenge was to overcome the loss of its comic morning team, Jim ("J.J.") Johnson and George ("the Bruiser") Baier, who had defected the previous July to WRIF-FM. WWWW tried to compete with the funny men it had lost by presenting a music-intensive wake-up show, but an exodus of fans loyal to Johnson and Baier enabled WRIF to pull farther ahead in the ratings. In their first ratings period together at WRIF, the new morning team scored a 6.0 percent share, compared with the station's 3.9 before their arrival.

Hungate decided that WWWW needed something totally different in the morning—something outlandish yet topical, something not previously heard in the Motor City. Reviewing the tape sent by consultant Douglas, he became convinced that the morning man from Hartford would be perfect. At a time when many FM rock stations featured either the stoned tones of hippie disc jockeys or the brassy projections of personalities who had risen through the echo-chambered ranks of Top 40, Howard sounded on the radio as Hungate had imagined he spoke off the air: whiny, but natural. Howard's way of enlivening weather forecasts also appealed to Hungate; he skipped the rigid meteorological script and put the details in his own words, telling Hartford listeners, for example, that they were going to see sun later in the day and then it would probably rain, period.

The staff at WWWW was hearing whispers that Shamrock wanted to quit Detroit's rock wars and switch to country music— the popularity a few months later of the movie *Urban Cowboy*, with John Travolta and Debra Winger, would suggest that even urban Detroit might dig two-stepping tunes. But Hungate and the general manager, Wally Clark, pushed ahead, deciding to make Howard the morning quarterback of their rock team. Their hunch was that Howard would hook a growing number of listeners, who would remain tuned to WWWW the rest of the day.

Hungate and Clark flew to Hartford and at dinner offered Howard the morning show at a salary of $28,000 a year—more than double what he was making at WCCC. If Howard had doubts about taking the job, he hid them from his suitors. But he gave his colleague Lich the impression that he still had plenty of thinking to do. Perhaps the weakening insecurity that briefly had blocked him from entering the radio business after college had returned. Another possibility: He feared following in the path of Steve Dahl, who had left Detroit radio for Chicago two years earlier and had become an audible influence. (Howard was being wooed to the job at WWWW that Dahl had once held.)

The wild and crazy Dahl, then broadcasting on Chicago's WLUP-FM, had generated considerable news coverage in the summer of 1979 when he led an organized rally against disco music at Comiskey Park. As the Chicago White Sox waited to play the second game of double-header with the Detroit Tigers, he exploded a bunch of disco records, and there ensued a free-for-all which caused such destructive mayhem on the field that the White Sox had to forfeit the nightcap. On the air, Dahl tweaked Chicago institutions and berated callers. He recast the Knack's big hit, "My Sharona," into "Ayatollah." *Animal House* pranks included dropping things out a station window to see what kind of reaction he would get from passersby below. Dahl was among the popular radio personalities (Alex Bennett in New York was another) who presented an audio form of TV's *The Dating Game*—in which a bachelor or bachelorette questions interested callers, then selects one of them for a date.

Howard had had his own dial-a-date routine on WCCC and was all too familiar with Dahl's shtick, because he used to listen to tapes of Dahl's shows in Hartford. Lich received the recordings from a friend in Chicago. "Howard and I used to listen to the tapes while sitting in my car after playing racquetball," Lich stated. "He didn't say much about them, but looking back, you can tell that Dahl was the catalyst for what Howard later ended up doing. . . . I know Howard would never admit that, but he took what Steve Dahl was doing and took it to the next dimension."

Respect for Dahl's style, never disclosed by Howard or reported by the media, would give way to unforeseen competition in Detroit between the two morning men before long (and an even nastier rivalry would flare more than a decade later, when Howard's show was being syndicated in Chicago).

After returning from a visit to Detroit with a job offer that Hungate and Clark had sweetened to $30,000, Howard finished a morning broadcast and went to explain his situation to WCCC owner Sy Dresner. "I remember that day vividly, because I could hear the shouting coming through Sy's door," Lich recalled. "Sy was livid. Nobody had the foresight to see what would happen, that Howard was destined for bigger things. Sy had this thing about loyalty. He wanted loyalty and dedication."

Although Howard's version is that WWWW laid down a fat check that allowed him to kiss off WCCC without a moment's hesitation, Lich recollects that his friend had serious doubts about the move and would have remained in Hartford for an additional forty or fifty dollars a week. The problem was, not only did Dresner rarely part with a raise, but he was the type to resent being pushed to the wall by a competing offer. "I don't think Howard went in there with a take-it-or-leave-it attitude, but Sy felt squeezed," Lich said.

Howard was denied a raise—in 1995 Dresner remembered only that he believed "Howard was looking for a bigger market"—and decided to leave. He never got the chance to say good-bye to his listeners, because impacted wisdom teeth sidelined him in the last two days he was scheduled to work. "I felt terrible about that," he told the *Courant*. "Hartford was a great place to work, and I feel sad about leaving. This offer was just too good."

Fred Norris graduated from college soon after Howard headed off to Motown. They would be together again sooner than either of them could have expected.

SIX

After broadcasting from an old house in Westchester County and depressing studios in downtown Hartford, Howard did not expect that his giant step up would place him in another former dwelling. WWWW was incongruously situated on East Jefferson Avenue, in a forlorn industrial part of Detroit. The station was newly owned by a major corporation (the principal shareholder in Shamrock Broadcasting was Roy E. Disney of the Walt Disney Company), and Detroit was the big time. Not only was the center of the American auto industry a large radio market, but the birthplace of the soulful Motown sound also boasted a thriving rock-and-roll scene. Detroit produced the lusty shouts of Mitch Ryder and the heavy-metal anger of the MC5 during the 1960s and now claimed aggressive rockers such as Bob Seger, Ted Nugent, and Iggy Pop. Hot-ticket concerts were plentiful. Rock clubs flourished. Howard said that Detroit was "the rock-and-roll capital of the world," while personally shunning the chemical and late-night excesses of the local rock scene that appealed to many of his broadcast colleagues.

Although disc jockeys were still years away from saying "That sucks" or using the word "penis" with impunity, Howard assumed greater license to talk and act dirty than he had in Hartford. Irene DeCook, a leather-wearing costumer for the Romantics, a local rock band, became the Leather Weatherlady on his show, spicing her segments with talk of dark pleasure and pain. When Debbie Beller, the morning newscaster, mentioned on the air that she wanted to visit a nudist colony, Howard invited his audience to help her prepare for the ambiance—prompting two male listeners to strip naked and climb atop the WWWW marquee, with Howard in pursuit, live microphone in hand. Howard wrestled women outside the studios and held a Halloween costume contest that drew a man "disguised" as a giant penis. Howard interviewed hookers, including a set of identical twins. He asked if they provided sex together, and with the same man, and in the same bed. He urged his listeners to identify the most outrageous places where they had had sex, then recorded the confessions for playback. He had no use for those who professed ignorance of his show when he called them on the air, asking, "Don't you know who I am?"

His top-rated competitor, WRIF's Jim ("J.J.") Johnson, argued in 1995 that Howard went largely unnoticed on WWWW because the station was floundering as a rock outlet. Indeed, the ratings during Howard's stint in Detroit show that his program underperformed or tied the station as a whole as he earned percent shares of 2.3, 3.0, and 1.6 (in October–November 1980) of the morning audience. Nevertheless, Howard was laying out provocative fare for Detroit in 1980, especially alongside J.J. and the Bruiser's broad comedy. Although Howard did not reverse the fortunes of "W-4," he generated enough of a response and a buzz in the market to keep him focused on creating the wild radio personality that would make him famous and rich.

"I learned that I had to be more aggressive and let more of myself come out in Detroit," he later told *Newsday*. "I was still one of those happy guys: no matter what was bothering me, I was happy on the air. I still sounded like an FM announcer. It finally dawned on me that what I was doing was all wrong—it wasn't going to work.

"I decided to cut down the barriers and just go into being myself on the air. Strip down all the ego. I mean, what prevents an announcer from talking about the fact that he has hemorrhoids? Because he has an ego. Well, I thought, let's strip that away and be totally honest."

Some of the listeners hated him, because he did not shut up, but they stuck with his show to find out what he would do next. In place of a music-driven morning program, Howard's yakking left room for as few as two or three songs an hour, even though some of his talk *was* just plain silly.

While impersonating President Jimmy Carter—badly—Howard took a call from a woman wanting to know why the federal government didn't address its financial woes by using lottery money. "They make over a million dollars a week," she said.

"They do?" the "president" replied. "Gee, no one told me about that. I figure the only one making that kind of money was my brother, Billy, off the Libyans"—a reference to Billy Carter's controversial lobbying.

Not yet a full-blown shock jock, Howard had made it to blunt jock. He ridiculed a new album by Peter Frampton while a representative of the rock star's record company was on the show. When the visitor later gave a high score to a listener who sang in that morning's talent contest, Howard remarked: "You liked that? I gotta be honest with you, I didn't like it. I thought that was lousy."

On a station that aired artists such as Journey, Ted Nugent, and Tom Petty and the Heartbreakers, Howard still was maintaining—publicly, at least—that the music filled a vital role on his program and in his life. "I think competition is healthy," he told Detroit's WXYZ-TV. "Every time there's a morning show on that sounds good, the Motor City is getting a lot more entertainment, a lot more rock and roll, and you have that much more to choose from, and competition is always healthy. You can get on the air and do just about anything you want as long as you're playing rock-and-roll records, because that affords you the opportunity to get on the air and go crazy, go nuts, because rock and roll is that kind of inhibitionless medium. It's fantastic."

In Howard's own recollections during the early 1990s, he repeatedly bemoaned his stay in Detroit. "It sucked," he said. But speaking to WXYZ-TV six months into his stay, he sounded exuberant: "On any given weekend you don't have one or two major acts, sometimes you have three major acts in an area, plus you have local clubs that are supporting bands that are terrific. There's so much music, so much excitement, I can't handle it. After milk and cookies, I should be in bed at night, but I'm out, you know, cruising the clubs there and finding out what's going on. It's incredible the amount of music that's going on here, and it's all supported."

However, unlike the radio and records people who partied with the rockers passing through Detroit and indulged in ready supplies of cocaine, Howard tended to limit his "cruising" to those events he was obligated to attend on behalf of WWWW. "He looked like he fit in with the rock-and-roll crowd, but he didn't," Beller recalled. "He wasn't into the drinking and the drugs."

He continued to seek peace through Transcendental Meditation. TM remained vitally important and helped him channel his energy into devising radio shtick. "He was not the person you heard on the air," Beller added. "That's the *character* he is. He's really a conservative guy from Long Island. I used to call him 'Jacob Javits.'" (Javits, the United States senator from New York, was far more liberal than most of his colleagues, but still an Establishment politician and a Republican.)

As the months passed, it was becoming clearer to people in the radio industry, but not necessarily to Howard, that WWWW would continue to falter. Competition was strengthening. Shamrock Broadcasting was tempted to seek more lucrative opportunities with country music. In addition, an insurrection among disc jockeys and other staffers who chafed at program director Hungate's rule led to his ouster by Shamrock in May 1980. The broadcasters voted overwhelmingly to form a union, as part of the American Federation of Television and Radio Artists (AFTRA); there was suspicion among the supporters that Howard had cast one of the dissenting ballots. His annual salary was beyond his starting wage of $30,000 (reaching $50,000 before he moved on).

The stiffer competition included Steve Dahl, who returned to the Detroit morning wars in June. Dahl's *Breakfast Club*, originating from his home base at Chicago's WLUP-FM, was picked up by Detroit's WABX-FM as part of a networklike arrangement. While working at WWWW years earlier, Dahl had enjoyed great popularity because of his often inspired bits. Howard now was up against the fellow whose tapes he had studied in Hartford.

A fourth rock station also crashed into the field. The launch of WLLZ, Detroit's "Wheels," further fueled speculation that the end was near for WWWW's rock format.

Howard insisted that his station was not giving him adequate promotion in the form of bumper stickers and other displays—a sign that management was saving its marketing dollars for another morning man or a new format. His ego was expanding, as was seen when the Republican National Convention moved into Detroit that summer to nominate Ronald Reagan for president. A discussion on air about the need to ratify the Equal Rights Amendment led to a bra burning outside the station. When a news photographer covering the convention asked Beller to be in the pictures, Howard became furious. "He let me know that he was the star of the show," Beller recalled.

For all of Howard's frustrations, he continued to express the belief that he could hit the top of the ratings. On the December morning after John Lennon was shot to death outside his New York home, Howard condemned the alleged killer, Mark David Chapman. Unlike most grieving fans and rock jocks, he hammered at the slaying itself more than he joined other stations in mourning the former Beatle's death. That night, over dinner, he bragged to Dwight Douglas, the consultant who had led him to WWWW, about his approach to the Lennon story. Douglas argued that Howard should switch to a more secure, successful station, but Howard wished to stay in Detroit. He was developing an effective act and wanted more time to work on it. "He was in his own tree," Douglas said. "He focuses on what he has to do." Howard held on to the conventional wisdom that it takes a year or more for a new morning show to catch on in a big way.

Even as Howard laid out his ambition to achieve glory in Detroit, Shamrock was preparing to silence the rock at WWWW. The last straw was the release in early January 1981 of the October–November ratings. The new rock station, WLLZ, had come out of nowhere to score a 4.6 share of the listening audience, behind WRIF's 4.7. WWWW—and Howard's show—had sunk to a miserable 1.6.

On January 18, a Sunday morning, Howard awakened to hear that his station had gone country after all.

For a few days he went to work and grudgingly played the records he had to. Toward the end of one program, he opened up his microphone, signaling to the others in the studio with him that they should be quiet, and said: "That was Waylon Jennings. My man Waylon. Y'all know Waylon, don'tcha? Y'all like to fuck sheep now, don'tcha?"

His colleagues froze, until they realized that he had not adjusted the microphone so that the listeners could hear him. A practical joke on his colleagues and the music. "I have no tolerance for country music," he later told a reporter. "I mean, the Judds remind me of Nazi women. I feel they would kill me."

The other Detroit stations showed no serious interest in hiring him. "I thought Stern was trying to copy Dahl," said Al Wilson, who was then general manager of WABX, the local outlet for Dahl's program. When Howard suggested to Wilson at a party that maybe they should talk about working together, the executive politely agreed, then turned to his wife and said, "That guy's not so hot."

Howard hunkered down at his home in Southfield and considered his next move. Douglas plotted to put him on the station he had programmed several years earlier and now was consulting, WWDC, in Washington. The rock outlet, known as "DC-101," had a new program director, Denise Oliver, and a new general manager, Goff Lebhar. They wanted to launch an attention-grabbing morning show.

"Denise and I had dinner with Goff about a week after 'W-4' went country," Douglas recalled. "It was a marathon dinner—the whole point was to convince Goff to hire Howard. He had never even heard Howard's tape. He finally said yes about eleven o'clock."

Lebhar had to offer only $40,000 a year, far less than a top morning man earned in those days. After broadcasting in Detroit for nine months, Howard agreed to take the job, principally because Washington was closer to his ultimate destination—New York.

A farewell party was held in the Detroit suburbs. It was a sedate gathering mainly of conservatively dressed people who were Howard's real friends in the area. Those rock-and-roll station mates who customarily arrived for a bash no earlier than 10:30 or 11:00 P.M. walked into a party that was breaking up. Entertainment was provided by a magician—geez, how square, the rockers snickered. His final trick was to cut up a newspaper so that it was opened up to read: Good-bye and good luck, Howard and Alison.

SEVEN

Launching Howard Stern at Washington's "DC-101" left only one key detail in solidifying the station's new morning show: hiring Robin Quivers as newscaster.

Program director Denise Oliver had a tape of Robin presenting the news at Baltimore's WFBR-AM with Johnny Walker, the station's irreverent morning man. Walker joked and Robin responded with a rich, jolly laugh. Oliver shared the tape with consultant Dwight Douglas, and he thought the laugh was wonderful.

In addition, Robin was black. This would make her a bonus in a regulated industry that routinely sought to head off government concerns about minority employment by having at least a few persons of color in on-air positions. She also could serve as an effective counterweight to Howard's often racially charged antics. Management liked the idea of pairing the controversial Jewish guy from New York with the black woman from nearby Baltimore.

Howard warmed to the prospect of working with Robin when he heard her on tape, but she played hard to get. She seemed unwilling to leave her native Baltimore after bouncing around the country and settling into her third radio job in a year. Robin deflected Oliver's entreaties until the program director played her a tape of Howard in action. Robin was impressed with his inventive style. "It was obvious it was not rehearsed or scripted," she recalled later. "I took the job to meet him."

Her decision to join Howard gave added kick to his show and would catapult her out of obscurity.

Robin Ophelia Quivers was born on August 8, 1952. She grew up in an integrated neighborhood in the Pikesville section of Baltimore. Her father, Charles, was a steelworker. Her mother, Louise, was a homemaker. She had three brothers. The household also swelled to include foster children taken in by her parents.

"Don't ask me about my parents," she remarked on Howard's show. Another time, when Howard was being scolded by his mother on the air for calling Ray "a Hitler," he said: "Boy, that's nice compared to what Robin calls her mother."

Robin withheld details about her childhood from the audience until the publication in 1995 of her autobiography, *Quivers: A Life*. She graphically accused Charles Quivers of sexually abusing her as a child and said that her mother frequently berated and hit her. The allegations shocked the listeners, who were accustomed to a show that seemed to expose all secrets. Few had known the scope of Robin's unhappiness as a youngster and the loss of self-esteem that it caused her as an adult.

"Kids would say to me, why do you laugh so much? What is so funny?" she explained to the *Amsterdam News* in 1984. "And I would tell them, why shouldn't I laugh? I suppose it has a lot to do with nervousness. It's a nervous reaction in some instances."

Unlike Howard, who aspired to a radio career as a teenager, Robin entered the business by a circuitous route. She enrolled in the University of Maryland and decided to major in nursing, because the field seemed to offer the promise of security. Her first position after graduating in 1974 was at Maryland Shock Trauma, the shock trauma facility of the Maryland Institute for Emergency Medical Services System (and a medical setting depicted in episodes of the NBC series *Homicide*, set in Baltimore). The patients, some of whom were flown to the unit after accidents around the state, suffered from spinal injuries, neurological damage, and other severe conditions. "I was a shock-trauma, intensive-care kind of nurse, so I saw unpleasantness all the time," she said.

As Robin sized up her situation, she was bothered not so much by the bad hours and the lack of appreciation she experienced as a nurse as by the sameness of her surroundings. Restlessness spurred her to seek opportunities farther afield. "I was *still* in Baltimore, so I decided to let the air force show me the world," she told *Vibe* magazine. "I said, I can use my nursing degree to become an officer, and they will fly me all over the world and I will see everything, and everything will be wonderful."

She joined the United States Air Force Reserve in July 1975, appointed a second lieutenant during a period when the Pentagon was increasing the number of women in all branches of the military. Active duty began on January 11, 1976. She was assigned to the staff of a huge hospital serving military personnel throughout the Midwest—the United States Air Force Medical Center at Wright-Patterson Air Force Base, near Dayton, Ohio.

The setting hardly fulfilled her wish to be a world away from Baltimore, but it led to a meaningful discovery. "Six months into the air force, I realized it was *nursing* I didn't like, not Baltimore," she recalled. "So now I had two years of air force time to be able to start a new career. . . . I *hated* the air force."

Despite her attitude, six months into active duty she was promoted to first lieutenant. Her stint at the sprawling facility earned her no decorations or awards but resulted in still another elevation, to the rank of captain, in June 1978. The next month she was discharged (although military personnel records show that she remained a member of the U.S. Air Force Reserve, with no active duty, until 1990).

After Dayton, Robin drifted to San Francisco, where she became involved in a self-awareness group called Summit and ended up in a telemarketing job that put her in touch with radio stations and gave her a pleasant taste for the medium. In 1979, she returned to

Baltimore and decided to attend a local broadcasting school, where she met Denise Oliver.

Robin took a news position on "WIOO-AM, a small station in Carlisle, Pennsylvania. Soon afterward, she moved to nearby Harrisburg, where she worked for the capital city's WCMB-AM, a springboard to WFBR's news department back home in Baltimore. Her specialty on Baltimore's well-established Top 40 station was "Coping in the '80s," a series of consumer-oriented reports in which she advised listeners on topics such as buying a car, managing credit cards, and caring for children.

"She tackled serious subjects, people-related issues," recalled Rosearl Julian, a newsroom colleague.

"She really worked hard on her research," said Mike Golden, another WFBR associate.

Julian, Golden, and other co-workers were surprised when Robin left a serious job in news to hook up with the wacky Stern. Their unanimous recollection of Robin's bubbly personality and sparkling giggle touched on elements that the newly formed team at "DC-101" may have considered even more important than her news-gathering abilities. To equip her further for the role with Howard, she had experience doing news reports at WFBR during the wake-up show of Johnny Walker, whose talent for double entendre and insult outraged Baltimore officials who were targets of his barbs and earned him high ratings.

Robin's ability to interact with a controversial personality would serve her well.

EIGHT

On paper, Howard fit the description of a transient radio broad-caster: he was twenty-seven years old and starting his fourth job in five years. But unlike other disc jockeys laying over in Washington en route to a better gig, Howard emitted a jolt of electricity on a dial unaccustomed to his brand of pranks and foolishness.

During his first broadcast at WWDC-FM and WWDC-AM—March 2, 1981—he called the office of Mayor Marion Barry and loudly ordered the assistant who answered the phone to explain what kind of man called himself Marion. "That's a girl's name," Howard insisted. He suggested that there be a local parade to welcome his new morning show.

On the second day, he rang a suburban high school and proposed that students be given the day off to celebrate his arrival. His premiere week also included mockery of President Ronald Reagan, whom Howard accused of greasing and coloring his hair, and turns of phrase that were bold for the times. In phone conversations with women about men, he asked, "Did you score?" There was also something about the president "playing with Nancy's gun."

"Sure, I'm a little crazy and a little weird," he told the *Washington Star* during his first week. "But I think a listener can identify with being a little weird. I don't think this area has experienced a morning rock-and-roll radio program that has something more to say than just being an electronic jukebox. So that's what I have to offer."

Howard's give-and-take on the phone, his dismissive hang-ups on those who annoyed him ("Ah, your mother"), his caustic opinions about the president on down gave his program the hook of unpredictability in an otherwise predictable medium. If he recalled for a moment the emotionless, sterile programming that he'd had to endure on those distant mornings when Ben Stern took him to his recording studio in Manhattan, the contrast would have seemed especially satisfying. He saw himself as a free spirit among his contemporaries in rock radio. "They think a nontalking, nonthinking disc jockey is all listeners will stand for," he said. "But I think that's nothing but robot radio. It doesn't relate and it's dishonest."

Helping him make the proceedings sound less robotic was Robin Quivers. "I just thought that I would come in and do the news and that he [Howard] would come in and be this crazy guy on the air and he would attract listeners and it would be a great showcase for me, because all those people would listen and hear me," Quivers later explained to an interviewer. "But it wasn't that way. He wanted much more than that. He wanted someone to play off of. Howard wanted a real live person there with him. But out of it, there was this wonderful chemistry that developed between us."

Howard became comfortable with Robin from their very first show together. He dispensed advice on picking up women from a book written by a man who had slept with thousands. One of the author's suggestions was to wear tight pants, which prompted Quivers to ask: If the guy managed to bed thousands of women, when did he have time to wear pants?

Howard loved her reaction. Their partnership clicked. Listeners recognized that she was much more than Howard's news reader. She became his "laugh track," a *Washington Post* reporter observed. "A genuine, sincere hilarity pulsates over the airwaves when she and Stern start exchanging commentary."

As Robin saw it, the show's loftier purpose was to make listeners think twice about their words and deeds. Blacks in the Washington audience "told me they liked the idea that white people were hearing exactly what they sounded like to black people—because they never listen to themselves, and they might not like what they hear," she said.

In the theater of the mind that is radio, Howard sometimes described Robin as a tall blonde. He loved to see listeners' shocked reaction at promotional appearances when a short black woman stepped out of the van.

The cast of the show also included the "Think Tank," a changing trio of local men Howard gathered from time to time to converse with him and play along with quizzes and gags. In the beginning, Howard invited listeners to phone in the answers to rock-and-roll and TV-trivia questions. Part of the show's insanity came in the form of dim-witted responses. A correct answer allowed the listener to pose a question to the Think Tank.

Harry Cole, a communications lawyer, used to dial between stations while driving to his Washington office. One morning he stayed with Howard's show, amused by the "three normal bozos" schmoozing with the host. "It was a very funny bit," he recalled, and he wanted to participate. Program director Denise Oliver, a friend of a friend, invited Cole to the station. Howard sat him down in the studio and was impressed when Cole knew the answer to a listener's question: How old was guitarist Mike Bloomfield when he died?

"I said he was thirty-six," Cole remembered. "I read it in *Rolling Stone* the weekend before."

Howard brought Cole back every two weeks or so, and the Think Tank became an increasingly cohesive unit, supplying ideas, trivia questions, and roundtable voices. Besides Cole, the unpaid trio came to include Steve Kyger, the manager of a record store, and Steve Chaconas, a salesman who had a knack for impersonations and often let out an infectious cackle that made a hyena sound shy. Chaconas, who also did stand-up comedy at local clubs, gained admission to the Think Tank after phoning in a deft impersonation of Curly ("nyuk, nyuk, nyuk") during a Three Stooges segment.

Invited to the studio, he showed up with a Stooges script that he had written, playing Curly to Howard's Moe. Other voices in Chaconas's repertoire allowed him to do multiple roles in spoofs of *The Match Game*, the television game show.

"Back then, Howard still played a lot of records, maybe five or six an hour, and there were all the commercials, too," Cole recalled. "So there was a lot of time during his show to brainstorm ideas about what we might do next. After the show, it was not unusual for us to go out and eat and talk some more."

Although members of the Think Tank contributed a lot of material and madness during their hours on the air—at no charge to the station or to the host—Howard skillfully quarterbacked the players by reviewing the ideas they submitted and maintaining the momentum of his show. He sometimes ruthlessly axed written dialogue, explaining, "This is garbage."

"He knew exactly what to do with us and when to cut us off to make good radio," Chaconas said. "We would be talking among ourselves while a record was playing and then he'd put us on the air in midconversation, as if the listeners were now eavesdropping on what we were saying. Other times, he'd cut away from us in the middle of something and go to a song. He always knew when we went on too long."

The sometimes lazy conversation between records represented a giant step in the show's evolution to an all-talk format. Howard and retinue would pass great spans of time discussing their personal lives, weekend plans, whatever. In Washington, Howard picked up the morning newspapers and ruminated on the air about what he had read. Reviewing the TV listings one morning, he said: "I don't know, man . . . Ted Knight actually has a TV show, believe it or not, and I don't know anybody who's ever seen it. *Entertainment Tonight* has a profile of actor David Soul. That guy's got a terrific career, huh? It's a good thing he dropped out of *Starsky and Hutch* to get better roles. Was he Starsky or Hutch?"

It was Howard's whiny, unaffected manner of speaking, so different from those of the scripted and polished broadcasters who predominated in radio, that gave his show an attitude that was both refreshingly direct and immensely entertaining. Howard clearly recognized that regular guys sitting around talking helped deliver the kind of natural feel and sound that he was looking for. "I get energy from having people in the room with me," he said.

The give-and-take with the Think Tank became doubly important to Howard. Even though he was honing his talent for quick lines and wicked commentary—such as his feigned call to Air Florida in January 1982 to ask the price of a one-way ticket to the 14th Street Bridge, where an improperly deiced plane had plunged into the Potomac River, killing seventy-eight people—his show relied heavily on prepared elements. Among the song parodies and comedy creations was "Out-of-the-Closet Stern," whom he brought to full, over-the-top, homosexual flamboyance at "DC-101." A spoof of *Family Feud*, the TV game show, featured host Richard Dawson smooching a contestant who had herpes. There also was "Kung Stern: The Movie," with Howard as "an easygoing disc jockey and a master of Kung Fu."

Howard was especially proud of his morning-long "coverage" of Prince Charles's wedding to Lady Diana Spencer, in July 1981. He submitted taped excerpts to *Billboard* in hopes of winning a second radio award from the magazine. *(Billboard* had named him personality of the year, in the album-oriented rock format, for his stint in Detroit.)

As Big Ben rang in the background, Howard made it seem that he was partying with the newlyweds and their guests, dining on Spam-in-a-blanket and listening to a dance band reconstruct an old Beach Boys tune: "Be true to your *shul* / Attend Hebrew school." Robin was said to be broadcasting alone from the studio on Connecticut Avenue.

"That's why I mentioned [actress] Susan George," she said to Howard during a newscast. "Because she used to be the prince's girlfriend, and she's the only thespian who was invited to the wedding."

Howard: "It's hard to hear you, Robin, did you say something about a lesbian?"

"Thespian, thespian."

"Yeah, there are a lot of lesbians over here in England."

Later, speaking to "Charles," Howard remarked that it must be hard for the prince to settle down when he could have any woman he wanted.

"Charles," speaking in a ridiculous Cockney-esque accent, replied: "Right, right. Anyway, I still have them, you know. I just don't tell Lady Di, right?"

Howard: "What do you mean? You say you're going to be with other girls even though you're married?"

"Of course. What do you think I'm going to do, stick with this one broad the rest of me life?"

A shrill-voiced "Di" later responded: "Well, you don't expect me to stick with this bloody thirty-two-year-old virgin all me life, do you?"

"God" also joined the wedding cast. Years earlier Howard had called on "Him" for weather forecasts; in Washington, God supplied forecasts and wisdom. Now, in a thunderous voice, the deity addressed the royal couple: "I would like to offer Lady Di a present. Lady Di will give birth to twelve beautiful children. . . . Barefoot and pregnant, that's the way I like to keep 'em."

Howard's bawdiest bits on "DC-101" sound quaint compared to his purposely shameful behavior more than a decade later, when he would spank women over the air and incur the wrath of the Federal Communications Commission for indecency. However, in the nation's capital, he revealed in subtle ways that he was still testing how far he could go. Sometimes he pulled back in fear that he might go too far.

Harry Cole wrote "50 Ways to Rank Your Mother," sung by Howard to the tune of Paul Simon's "50 Ways to Leave Your Lover." Cole's version gathered a litany of schoolyard put-downs about a sexually promiscuous mother, but Howard tinkered with the opening verse to soften its edge.

Cole had written: "My friends have all enjoyed your mom, they said to me / She was so generous, she does so much for free / Until they found out that she gave them all VD." But Howard changed "VD" to "social disease," even though the line no longer scanned. "He believed that 'VD' might be too offensive or graphic," Cole recalled. "Howard had a sense of limitations, whether he agreed with them or not, and he believed it was important to ensure those limits." A seven-second delay was installed in the radio studio to make certain that no questionable language slipped onto the airwaves.

But Howard's show in Washington was more uninhibited for its era than the New York morning program that he later syndicated to cities around the country, in the estimation of broadcasters who competed with him in the capital and afterward. "He was a lot tamer then, compared to today, but for that time period he was revolutionary," said Jim Elliott, who did a popular Washington morning show with Scott Woodside that moved from WPGC to WRQX ("Q-107") during Howard's stint at "DC-101." "He came in and set the market on its ear. Washington had never heard anything like it before. Howard's idea was to piss people off; ours was to hug ladies and babies."

Acquaintances of Cole often told him how gross they thought Howard was, then added, "Did you hear what he said yesterday?" People were talking about the morning guy on "DC-101." In a medium that usually builds a morning franchise over several years, Howard Stern's rise in the ratings was meteoric. In a business where a small improvement in the ratings is considered successful, he inherited a show with a 2.6 percent share of the morning listening audience and immediately increased it to a 5.2 share, in the spring of 1981, then to a 5.6 in the summer. It was clear that he would do even better as the months passed.

In addition, advertisers responded to what was happening—on the air and in the ratings. Some of them, such as a local food-store chain, pulled commercials, because they found Howard's program distasteful and feared a consumer backlash from the association with him. Other sponsors, impressed by Howard's numbers, were only too eager to tap into his following. "The United States Army came in and gave us very strong rates [payments] because they knew that young men were listening," said Don Davis, who succeeded Denise Oliver as program director in September 1981.

Howard's rapid success in Washington earned him a significant reward.

Weeks after Davis joined "DC-101," Howard lobbied to add to his show someone who could help with production and lighten his dependence on drop-in assistance from others, including disc jockeys at the station. Howard's choice was his old pal Fred Norris, with whom he had worked in Hartford. Although general manager Goff Lebhar argued that the budget was too tight, Howard made it seem that Fred would be his lucky charm—it was extremely important that he be hired. Lebhar finally gave in.

Fred not only was a production wizard, who helped Howard with many of the mechanical chores during the hours the show was on the air, but he brought creative weight to the performance. He played guitar, he had a keen ear for music, and he did voices better than most. He specialized in an off-center humor that perfectly complemented Howard's own. "To me, comedy is hostility," Fred later explained to an interviewer. "Henny Youngman says, 'Take my wife, please.' I say, 'Take my wife, please—and while you're at it, stick a coat hanger up her nose.'" He succeeded a staffer of more limited abilities known as "Earth Dog Brent," so Howard dubbed him "Earth Dog Fred." The name stuck.

Fred let loose on the air; off the air he was quiet and shy. All who observed him at work recognized that he craved none of the spotlight for himself and never threatened to upstage the star. His loyalty to Howard was unquestioned. "I believe Fred would do anything for me except let me visit his apartment," Howard said later.

One of their bits together was "Dueling Rooneys," a ridiculous spoof of Andy Rooney. Between Fred's guitar riffs from the hit instrumental "Dueling Banjos," the two of them alternately parodied the *60 Minutes* curmudgeon:

"Do you ever wonder about fish?" Fred whined. "They swim in the same water they go to the bathroom and make love in—and you swim in it, too!"

Howard: "You know, I got to thinking the other day: The only article of clothing you can wear two days in a row is your watch."

Among the recurring features that involved Fred were "Beaver Breaks," demented episodes in the life of the Cleaver family, known to TV audiences from *Leave It to Beaver*, which was popular during Howard's childhood. Sometimes the plot lines for the "Beaver Breaks" were hatched on weekends when Howard, Fred, and Steve Chaconas of the Think Tank sat around watching television, including reruns of *Leave It to Beaver*. They turned off the sound and inserted their own warped dialogue, putting the collaboration on paper afterward. In one of the Stern installments, Ward Cleaver, the understanding father in the innocent family sitcom, was portrayed as a raging transvestite.

Howard's success in Washington had a long-term impact on the radio industry. It opened broadcasters' eyes to the revelation that a high-energy personality could work in an FM format long wedded to music. The man whose once breathy delivery had made him sound like just another rock jock now was helping to reinvent the format. Howard appealed to the same young men that "DC-101" and other album-rock outlets traditionally targeted, and his show added listeners who might not have sampled the station.

"One of the biggest battles I ever had with Howard was over the number of records per hour that he played," Davis said. "He wanted to do shtick more and more of the time. I had to remind him that it was still a rock station. Looking back, I realize it was silly of me. We [management] were reacting to our upbringing in the business."

Howard had to air songs by Bruce Springsteen, Pat Benatar, Squeeze, and other artists of the moment, but he played around with this requisite, too. "I love Van Halen," he said one day. "Good band."

He opened the phone lines to listeners who had seen the group in concert the night before.

"Did you see Van Halen?" he asked one man who was making no sense. "Then why are you calling, you creep?"

Clunk.

No one else suffered the kind of drubbing that Howard reserved for Goff Lebhar. That Lebhar also happened to be Howard's boss raised this abuse to the level of civil war. Not that Lebhar was unfamiliar with tough guys. He was, after all, the son of Bertram Lebhar, Jr., a multitalented man who had excelled as a broadcasting executive, a tournament bridge player, and a sportscaster. The elder Lebhar had cut rich advertising deals as sales manager and later general manager of New York's mighty WHN (later WMGM), the popular radio outlet during the 1940s and 1950s for broadcasts of the New York Giants football team, the New York Knicks, the New York Rangers, and the Brooklyn Dodgers. One of his tactics was to keep his office at an ungodly frigid temperature, explaining that he had a throat problem; all the while, he was trying to wear down those who came to negotiate with him by freezing them to death. As a highly competitive bridge player, he won two national titles during the 1940s and as an administrator of member organizations he helped to advance the game.

To tens of thousands of New York radio listeners, he was known only as Bert Lee, the name he used as a cohost, along with the fabled Marty Glickman and Ward Wilson, of WMGM's *Warm-up Time* and *Sports Extra*. These two argumentative programs, respectively, preceded and followed Red Barber's play-by-play coverage of the Brooklyn Dodgers' games and by many years presaged the opinionated all-sports formats followed by New York's WFAN and other stations around the country. Glickman and Lee also cohosted *Today's Baseball*, fully describing the day's best games, complete with sound effects. (At times Lee became so enthusiastic and expressive in piecing together games he had not even seen that he ran past the show's allotted quarter hour.)

Goff—the nickname was short for his given name, Godfrey—also lived in the shadow of his athletic brother, Bertram Lebhar III, whose high school football games were carried by their father's radio station and who later emerged as a sportscaster on radio and TV, calling himself Bert Lee, Jr.

By the late 1950s, their father had left New York to co-own and operate radio and TV stations in West Palm Beach, Florida—and Goff, the bulky, ruddy-faced son, joined him. Goff first became a salesman under his father, who was one of the best salesmen in radio, then proceeded to make his own way on the management side of the business.

One theory about Lebhar's relationship with Howard holds that the general manager felt as if the disc jockey had been forced on him by both Denise Oliver and consultant Dwight Douglas. He was said to be uncomfortable with the morning man from the start. On the other hand, Lebhar supposedly was charmed by success and wanted some of Howard's mounting fame to rub off on him. According to this second view, when Lebhar's name was excluded from most of Howard's media coverage, the executive's disappointment put him in no mood for the insults hurled at him from the studio.

As Howard caught on in Washington, he was able for the first time to lash out at a superior from a position of strength. With ratings building, he knew that the station's commercial revenues were increasing as a result of his performance. The problem for Howard was that he had nothing in common with Lebhar, no middle ground of mutual respect.

Money, of course, became a major flashpoint. Howard had joined "DC-101" on a handshake. As earlier noted, his $40,000 salary was modest for a morning personality in a major market. Lebhar, who had taken over the station shortly before Howard arrived, was known to have cut an especially choice deal for himself. What's more, as Howard hungered for a larger salary, Lebhar's suburban home struck the morning man as a showcase of garish excess, particularly a foyer sculpture of a naked figure that issued water into a fountain from its penis.

By the summer of 1981, only a few months after Howard's arrival, Lebhar was blown away by the ratings and pushed his new star to sign a contract sooner than lose him to another station. Howard wanted the security of a long-term agreement, but Lebhar refused to be committed beyond one year. "Goff was so stubborn," recalled Jeffrey Southmayd, a Washington attorney retained by Howard to help him negotiate. "But Howard realized that if he did well, he could market himself. That's why he swallowed the pill and signed for a year."

It turned out to be a shrewd decision. Howard's growing success stirred other interest in his services, and even Lebhar recognized his own shortsightedness. When the fall 1981 ratings (released in January 1982) showed further extraordinary gains in Howard's numbers (he now had the second-highest-rated program in Washington), Lebhar approached him about signing a long-term deal after all. With seven months remaining on his contract, which was to expire on July 31, 1982, Howard made it clear that he saw no reason to rush into a new agreement. "Goff's initial offer was bullshit," Southmayd said. "And then, NBC called us—and NBC represented a real choice."

The attention of the National Broadcasting Company was focused on Howard by Jerry Nachman. A hard-bitten New York newsman who had chased stories for WCBS "Newsradio 88" and WCBS-TV, he was now general manager of WRC-AM, a moribund Washington news/talk station owned by NBC. "I got there in November of 1981, and I started to monitor the other stations in the market," Nachman recalled. "I turned on 'DC-101' and between the Molly Hatchet records I hear this guy who's outrageous at times and other times brilliant."

Nachman was especially impressed with what Howard did after the Soviets cracked down on Poland's independent labor union, Solidarity, arresting its leader, Lech Walesa, and declaring martial law. "The talk stations and the news stations were giving the same old stuff about the secretary of state and saber rattling by diplomats," Nachman said. "Howard, in the nascent character of Fartman, called the Soviet embassy and between farts into the phone was complaining about the situation in Poland. It was coarse, sure, but it also was a response in closer touch to the emotion of the moment than anything that the conventional coverage was providing. It was coarse with moments of real brilliance."

Nachman asked Howard to lunch, the first of several they would share in the next few months at Germaine's, a pan-Asian restaurant. Between bites of fish and vegetables, Howard found the street-smart Nachman as affable as Lebhar was imperious. Eventually, Nachman asked Howard to work for him at WRC-AM. "He hated playing records, and he felt unappreciated and underutilized at 'DC-101,'" Nachman said. "We informally agreed to do a deal to get Howard to anchor mornings on WRC."

Nachman's strategy for jump-starting WRC with the comic Howard represented a radical departure from the somber and serious demeanor of radio's news/talk format, which had yet to lighten up by adding humorous commentators such as Rush Limbaugh. But Nachman was ready to hire Howard at a station whose most popular show was a humorless political exchange between the conservative Pat Buchanan and the liberal Tom Braden.

Lebhar had no idea that Howard was entertaining another offer. As Southmayd saw it, Lebhar seemed to believe that no one else was interested in his morning man except the listeners.

Robert B. Sherman, a radio newsman's son who was then the forty-year-old executive vice president of NBC Radio, was known in the business as "the man who brought Imus back to New York." On accepting his previous position as general manager of WNBC-AM, Sherman recognized that the only profitable year the station had enjoyed in recent decades was after the comic Don Imus joined in 1971. He quickly ended Imus's exile on WHK-AM in Cleveland, where he had gone after being fired by WNBC as part of a 1977 music-format switch, and restored the gonzo broadcaster to WNBC's morning show in 1979. The return of Imus, coupled with Sherman's overhaul of sales and promotions, led to a swift and profitable turnaround within months.

When Nachman called Sherman, his boss, to rave about Howard, the executive became interested. He flew to Washington on business and planned to sample Stern's radio act the following morning. "I was more intrigued than shocked or appalled by what I heard," Sherman remembered. "I thought his humor was a little young and scatalogical for my tastes, but I heard a compelling personality, though not one without problems."

First, Sherman scratched Nachman's plot to bring Howard over to WRC, denying Washington the chance to hear the shock jock and Pat Buchanan on the same station. Instead Sherman considered Howard's act with an ear toward bringing him to WNBC-AM in New York. Placing Howard in the afternoon-drive slot would give the station another renegade besides morning man Imus and additional muscle against the continued exodus of listeners from AM to the FM band. "We all knew that an aberrant AM station would do well over time," Sherman said. Hiring Howard also would get him out of Washington, where research seen by NBC was said to have shown that he was drawing black listeners away from the network-owned WKYS-FM, the urban-oriented music station that was home to the popular morning man Donnie Simpson.

Sherman, whose success at WNBC had given him wide license to cut deals quickly, arranged a meeting later that day at WRC with Howard and Southmayd. The contrast in impressions that the two sides took away from the session heralded the disagreements that would arise before long.

"Howard appeared to be a nice young man—a bit overweight—and his lawyer appropriately took charge of their side of the table," Sherman added. "I talked about the kind of company we had and how we liked to manage our people and exercise authority on form and content. My guess is that he was amenable to what I was saying, or else his silent attitude was: Yeah, we'll see."

Southmayd sensed that Sherman and WNBC general manager Domenick Fioravanti were skeptical about working with Howard. "I thought they were two slick NBC New York guys who came to see who this foul-mouthed kid was that Nachman had been raving about," Southmayd recalled. "They did the whole New York schmooze and then said something like 'You interested?'"

Howard was *very* interested. "I left the room agreeing to have a contract drawn up," Sherman said. It called for a starting salary of $150,000. By the time the agreement was signed months later, it was to pay $1 million over five years.

"Once the word got out that Howard was available, we got a lot of tire-kicking calls," Southmayd said. Steve Kingston, then program director of WPGC, a local station that was among the original Top 40 outlets on FM, spoke to Howard about filling a morning vacancy left by Elliott and Woodside. WLUP-FM in Chicago contacted Howard, but he showed no interest in working at a station that had fired Steve Dahl the year before. Larry Berger, program director at New York's WPLJ-FM, a highly rated rock station, went so far as to offer Howard a job, but he did not want to work at night.

In a repeat of Hartford and Detroit, Howard was not burning to leave. He and Alison, who had her own local career as a social worker, liked living in the Washington area. They had a comfortable apartment in a Bethesda high-rise overlooking Spring Hill Lake. Except for a miscarriage that Alison suffered, which led to a row between them after Howard had twisted the misfortune into radio comedy on "DC-101," they were a tight and loving couple, content with each other and their surroundings. "I think Howard was having fun with what he was doing," Chaconas, of the Think Tank, recalled. "I don't think he was so driven that he was looking to take the next step right away."

Howard also was beginning to enjoy the fruits of fame beyond radio. A pair of local entrepreneurs, doing business as Wren Records Limited, approached him to record an album of comedy bits. Instead of opting for generous royalties based on sales, he wanted big money up front (a practice he would follow on a grander scale when his radio show went national) and received what to him was a whopping advance of $35,000. Royalties were to kick in after the producers had recouped the advance and production costs.

"Howeird," as he was identified on the cover (he now wore with honor the nickname he had disliked when Joe Piasek devised it at WRNW), and Fred were listed as the producers. They dominated the album and wrote all the material except for the title song, Harry Cole's "50 Ways to Rank Your Mother," on which the Think Tank provided background voices. Other song parodies, such as "I Shot Ron Reagan" (based on "I Shot the Sheriff," the Bob Marley tune that Eric Clapton had turned into a hit), and skits from the radio show were re-created in the recording studio. The skits included two "Beaver Breaks," titled "Unclean Beaver, Part I" and "Unclean Beaver, Part II," as well as "Family Affarce," a wicked take-off on TV's treacly *Family Affair.* *

"We did a record store appearance when the album came out, and there were lines around the block," Chaconas said. "After a while it got boring, just signing and signing our names, so Howard and I tried to outdo each other writing obscene things."

In addition, Howard and Fred started to package "Beaver Breaks" for syndication to other stations.

Despite the renown, Howard faced continual criticism from the management of "DC-101" in the form of directives to do this and avoid that. He reacted by firing back during his show.

"I remember Howard going out of his way to make Goff his foil," Don Davis, the program director, said. "Here was a guy on the radio bitching about his boss. I always thought Goff was really cool about letting him pull stuff."

Howard took to calling Lebhar "Goof LePhoof" on the air. The design of the station let Howard sit at his microphone and ridicule Lebhar while looking at the boss in his office on the other side of the studio glass.

---

*Rights to the comedy album later changed hands. In November 1994, it was re-released, as *Unclean Beaver*, by Citizen X/Ichiban Records.

Their relationship worsened as contract discussions to keep Howard at "DC-101" sputtered along. Although Howard had the advantage of being able to weigh Lebhar's salary offers against the riches that awaited him at WNBC, Lebhar's apparent ignorance of the New York offer restrained him from going far enough. "The truth of the matter is, if Goff had offered him twenty-five thousand a year more, he probably would have stayed," Southmayd said.

In what may have been a variation of his father's frosty-office strategy, the general manager clouded the air during negotiations. "Goff smoked these foot-long cigars and he would close the door to his office so that it was God-awful, nauseating, to be in there with him," Southmayd added. "He was a street-tough pain in the ass. He'd say, 'Here's what the offer is. Take it or leave it.' Or he'd say, 'Fuck you, get out of here.' He tried to bully people. He tried to bully Howard. It was a poisonous atmosphere." (Asked in 1995 to discuss Howard's time at the station, Lebhar said it was too long ago and that he did not wish to talk about his former morning man.)

When an Indianapolis disc jockey known as Adam Smasher went to Washington early in 1982 to discuss taking an afternoon job on "DC-101," he was put on Howard's show as part of the interview process. Smasher became the prize on that morning's dial-a-date. When he revealed that his real name was Asher Benrubi, and that he was of Greek ancestry, Howard remarked: "Uh-oh, don't anybody in the studio bend over!" It was typical Howard and gave Smasher a sense that it would be liberating for him, too, to work at "DC-101." At the same time, Smasher heard so much Stern slamming of Lebhar that he was stunned. "Howard was going off big time on Goff," he recalled. "I thought, If this guy doesn't get fired, I'll be surprised."

Howard continued to brace himself with daily Transcendental Meditation. "He talked about it, but he did not proselytize," Cole recalled. "That's how he derived his energy—he ascribed it to the meditation."

Added Chaconas: "One day Howard was sitting on a bed in my house. I thought he was in a coma and it freaked me out. I said to him, 'Howard, are you all right?' He opened his eyes for a second and said, 'Yeah, I'm meditating, I'll be done in a minute.' He said it really helped him clear his mind."

The growing tension at "DC-101" may have had a lot to do with Howard's ballooning weight. "He ate junk, greasy food," Chaconas said. "Subs, pizza, doughnuts, cold cuts, sandwiches."

After years of being skinny, he became so self-conscious about his weight that he began to wear sweatpants to mask the added pounds. He also had the cover photo on his comedy album retouched so that the leather-suited "Howeird," his whip brandished over the head of a cowering old woman, did not look so thick in the butt and thighs.

NINE

Howard still had not signed a contract to work at WNBC-AM. As negotiations over fine points in the deal continued in early 1982, his suitors put on an impressive show. When Howard and Southmayd flew to New York, WNBC sent a limousine to pick them up at the airport. They were taken to the RCA building, in Rockefeller Center, for a tour of the WNBC studios and a lunch in the Rainbow Room, whose panoramic view from the sixty-fifth floor showcased the nation's largest city.

Meanwhile, Howard's loyal troops were becoming apprehensive about his future at "DC-101" and were wondering where they would be if he left the station. "No one knew what was going on," Cole recalled. "Howard was keeping very close cards about his plans."

The cards were exposed unexpectedly in March 1982. Newspapers reported that Howard was heading to WNBC after his contract expired at the end of July. Lebhar, whose station had a contractual relationship with NBC Radio's youth-oriented news service (The Source), told *The Washington Post* that he had not spoken to NBC, and he emphasized that Howard was still under contract. Clearly he had been blindsided by the news.

Sherman said the announcement had been withheld to give Howard time to inform Lebhar; the NBC Radio executive said he felt bad that Lebhar had learned about Howard's plans from the press.

Howard's radio partners were crushed by the added revelation that they would not be going with him. Fioravanti, the WNBC general manager, revealed as much during a meeting in Washington. Sherman stated bluntly that NBC was interested in Howard alone: "No insult intended, but I don't know who Fred Norris is," he told the *Post*. "We have had no discussion at NBC about the potential value of Robin Quivers."

There it was. Howard Stern was leaving "DC-101" after all.

Howard's furtive maneuvers and the newfound realization that she was not part of his future made Robin angry because her career had been taking off, she had become a dominant presence on Howard's show—his conscience, foil, and straight woman—and now she was being left behind. She looked for other radio work in Washington but found that she had been typecast. News stations considered her tainted and questioned whether she had the credibility to do hard news. Personality-oriented stations declined to hire Robin because of a misguided perception that she simply was a newsperson.

Lebhar eventually offered Robin a lucrative deal to remain, and she was about to sign, but then she decided to leave instead. At the end of June, she returned to Baltimore, joining WCBM-AM as a reporter.

"I met the program director of WNBC and congratulated him on getting Howard," Douglas remembered. "I also said that the station deserved the award for asshole blunder of the universe, because they hadn't hired Robin, too. However, Robin's rise with Howard had been so vigorous—and so fatiguing—that I don't think she pressed him to bring her along. She needed time off."

Radio personalities usually moved to their next job abruptly and without warning, or they were fired by management and told to exit immediately, without being able to say good-bye to their listeners. Cut and burn.

This was different. Howard had four more months on his contract. Having a "lame duck" for a morning man created an awkward situation at "DC-101." The station now had to fill a huge hole in its schedule and to face advertisers' concerns about making long-term commitments to the most important time period. "Part of the frustration was that the station was beginning to reap the financial rewards of Howard's ratings," said program director Don Davis. In addition, Lebhar and Davis feared that Howard might become even less restrained on the air now that he had the security of a New York job.

"I was pissed off that Howard and Goff were fighting," recalled Douglas, who had helped bring Howard to the station. "I knew it was personal between them." Behind the scenes, Douglas was lining up Howard's successor.

"We really wanted Howard to stay until the end of his contract," Davis added. "We tried to have an uneasy truce so that we could convert his ratings into revenue. In most ways, Howard tried to be professional about the fact that he was leaving. But he said on the air what the general manager's compensation package was [a six-figure sum]. It was too much for me to sit still for. Goff didn't mind being made fun of, but I had a shorter fuse, especially when Howard crossed over into personal territory."

The station also was facing a kind of death watch for Howard's show that threatened to sour the prospects of whoever succeeded him and to drive away listeners after he was gone. As the crucial spring ratings period neared the end, Howard received written instructions from management. He could not mention other radio stations. His superiors still had not learned that Howard was likely to respond to a direct order by resisting it, as though he were a child determined to sneak a macaroon from the cookie jar after his parents had denied him one. Sure enough, Howard lashed out at a pair of stations in the Midwest that he claimed had ripped off two of his bits. After a rocky, albeit profitable, fifteen months of Howard, this infraction appeared to be the final straw.

On June 25, 1982, disc jockey Asher (Adam Smasher) Benrubi happened to be in Washington for a briefing about the afternoon job that he had accepted at "DC-101." Listening to Howard's show, he thought that the morning man sounded angrier than he had seemed during the newcomer's previous visit. As the disc jockey remembers the morning, Howard was calling Lebhar "Goof LeBoof" and complaining that he had been mistreated by the general manager.

When Benrubi arrived at the "DC-101" studios for his 10:00 A.M. meeting with management, he was told to wait—a delay that stretched to ninety minutes as Howard received and made sense of a memo signed by Davis stating that he was suspended. By the time Benrubi met with Davis, the new afternoon talent was asked to take over the morning show for an interim period starting July 5.

A memo given to the station's receptionists said: "If anyone calls on the phone to ask where Stern is or what has happened to him, you are to reply that Howard is no longer on the air at DC-101."

Days later, the station officially confirmed that it had hired Adam Smasher and a new morning host, a graphic storyteller known as the Greaseman. In other words, Howard's success had cleared the way for two more high-profile talents to join a music station.

"I was thrilled to be working for WWDC, and I love my audience," Howard told *The Washington Post*. "I'm sorry I'm not being given a chance to say good-bye to them. I'm really shocked and disappointed."

When the station's attorney made it official that the "suspension" was permanent, Howard took the opportunity to bid farewell in interviews sought by other local radio stations. He spoke by phone to Elliott and Woodside on WRQX and visited Cerphe, a disc jockey on WAVA-FM, which competed with "DC-101."

Lebhar cut his station's ties to NBC's The Source. Fred Norris held on to his job, doing production work and air shifts. Alison went to New York to find a place where she and Howard would reside.

Howard moved in with Steve Chaconas and finished business in Washington, including a farewell extravaganza that a local promoter was planning at the Capital Centre. Howard and his cohorts were to be paid for their participation in various stunts, such as a hot-dog-eating contest in which blindfolded women were to eat franks placed strategically in front of the men's crotches.

However, because Howard no longer was on the air to hype the event, ticket sales were sluggish and the evening was canceled.

Instead WAVA-FM helped put together a raucous send-off for hundreds at Numbers, a nightclub located near "DC-101." Howard entered to the theme from the movie *Rocky* and mooned the crowd.

Like Rocky, Howard was going out in triumph. In the July issue of *Washingtonian*, the magazine's annual best-and-worst edition, he was named the best disc jockey in town and appeared in a cover shot wearing devil's horns.

His final report card, the spring ratings, showed that he had delivered his best numbers in Washington. Claiming a huge eight percent share of the morning listening audience, he had more than tripled the ratings during his brief stay. He was ranked third, behind WMAL-AM's top-rated team of Frank Harden and Jackson Weaver, the long-standing champs, and WKYS-FM's Donnie Simpson.

The ratings, the response, the recognition within the industry—all had come together, forming a solid foundation as Howard prepared for the challenge of New York radio: "I think when I was in Washington I was convinced I had it all figured out."

Doug (the "Greaseman") Tracht, who had been a Top 40 disc jockey on Washington's WRC-AM until 1973, ended a seven-year run on WAPE-AM in Jacksonville, Florida. He was wooed back to the capital to take over Howard's show by a $1 million, five-year contract. His specialty was the vividly told tale; many were dark inventions, and others reflected a macho swagger in "Grease" himself. All of his stories were enlivened by carefully chosen sound effects.

Soon after returning, he took his listeners into the basement of "DC-101," there to behold the artifacts of programs past. In one dusty corner he found Howard Stern's shrunken head in a glass jar.

TEN

To work at WNBC was to be somewhere special. The radio station occupied spacious studios within New York City's spectacular 30 Rockefeller Plaza, known as the RCA Building, the stately skyscraper that towered over the Rockefeller Center complex and the jewel of an ice-skating rink in the middle of it all. In the sixty years that WNBC had been on the air, most of that time from "30 Rock," the station's local and network programming had encompassed a long roster of famous performers, including Arturo Toscanini, who conducted orchestral concerts in the giant Studio 8H (now the home of television's *Saturday Night Live*), the comedy team of Bob and Ray, the chatty duo of Tex McCrary and Jinx Falkenburg, Long John Nebel and the other groundbreaking call-in hosts of the 1960s, and bad boy Don Imus. Daily tours of NBC, which counted the *Today* show and the newly launched *Late Night with David Letterman* among its Rockefeller Center showpieces, also offered visitors a peek at the fifty-thousand-watt radio beacon.

Despite the distinctive history of WNBC and the steady profits it had generated since the outcast Imus had returned from Cleveland in 1979, the New York station and NBC's other radio properties had become afterthoughts in the media empire, which faced alarming problems. As Howard Stern was heading to WNBC in the summer of 1982, NBC television ranked as the embarrassment of broadcasting. The network was earning only a fraction of the profits being hauled in by both ABC and CBS. It had suffered several years of dismal TV ratings, finishing the 1981–82 season without a single prime-time show in the top twenty. As the new chairman, Grant Tinker, strove to rebuild the network, employees, advertisers, and the press groped for evidence that NBC would rise again.

It appeared that Howard was entering a radio environment secure enough to withstand his anarchic skills. WNBC's profit had soared to an estimated $2.5 million in 1981, and the station's main rival, WABC-AM, had silenced its longtime format of hit music on May 10, 1982, and switched to talk programming. The mischievous Stern was viewed by those inside and outside WNBC-AM as a comic who would complement Imus while also serving as an insurance policy in the event that the popular morning man became derailed by the drink and drugs that had accounted for his erratic behavior. (Imus declined to be interviewed for this book, explaining, "I don't have too many memories" of the period because of the heavy drinking.)

Unlike Imus, Howard did not receive the creative license that he expected to find waiting for him—or hoped to earn swiftly. On the contrary, the decision to hire him had been seriously questioned at the highest level of NBC in the months before he even did his first New York broadcast in August.

Causing the concern had been a report on raunch radio presented April 2 by *NBC Magazine*, the TV network's latest attempt to develop a prime-time newsmagazine. The segment featured Stern, Steve Dahl in Chicago, and Dennis Erectus in San Jose, California—and by any measure of journalistic enterprise, then or now, it sounded like a hatchet job:

"What you are about to hear is going to shock and disgust you, because it's vulgar, even obscene," NBC reporter Douglas Kiker began grimly. "A warning: If there are children in the room, you might not want them to watch this report. It's X-rated radio, barnyard radio, and there's more and more of it on the air, because the kids love it."

After a brief glimpse of Howard on the air in Washington ("Hey, man, I hears your pappy is so disgusting that he takes a bubble bath by farting in a mud puddle"), the camera returned to Kiker, this time seated at home with an arm draped around his toddler son, who was sucking on a bottle. Kiker explained that his Washington residence was secured by locks and an alarm system. "What I cannot prevent from entering my home are the sounds coming in over this radio. The idea for this story originated a few weeks ago when I heard my seven-year-old son, this one's older brother, coming down to breakfast saying the same things you just heard this disc jockey say." There was more of Howard, this time singing "50 Ways to Rank Your Mother": "I've heard she's frigid, but she might just be hard to please / But if that's so, why does she douche with antifreeze?"

Kiker then introduced "a group of concerned parents," including a man who said he had persuaded sponsors to pull their ads from Howard's show.

"If somebody doesn't want to listen to my radio program, they should turn the dial and listen to some other jerk," Howard said in the piece. "If people didn't want to listen to me, I wouldn't have the ratings. It's as simple as that."

"Can't something be done to get this filth off the air?" Kiker asked. According to the reporter, the Federal Communications Commission said no, but agency officials declined to admit as much on camera.

"While we were in the process of producing this report, Howard Stern was lured away from his Washington radio station by a New York City station, which offered him a big increase in salary," Kiker continued. "That station, you guessed it, is WNBC-AM, which is owned by NBC." He quoted Fioravanti, the general manager, as saying WNBC "is mindful of its responsibility to present programs in accordance with acceptable public taste." According to Kiker, Fioravanti declined to say as much on camera.

NBC Magazine scored anemic ratings and faded from the TV schedule later in the summer. But Kiker's piece was seen by enough executives in and around Tinker to muddy the welcome mat. Suddenly this guy named Howard Stern was a headache; his antics might tarnish the image of the TV network. "Within weeks of the

Kiker piece, I had several meetings with the NBC brass to talk them out of withdrawing Howard's contract," recalled Robert Sherman, the NBC Radio executive who was bringing him aboard. "The question being asked was: could we get out of the contract? I said that Howard was manageable. The sense I got from him in Washington was that he was willing to be managed." In addition, NBC would have lost around $500,000 to back out of the deal.

The preliminary crisis largely escaped Howard's attention because Sherman intervened—indeed, industry observers believed that the man who was able to return Imus to New York was a manager well suited to a Stern challenge. As Sherman himself put it, "I would have attempted to coax Howard into a bell-shaped curve of acceptability to his audience and to NBC." But Sherman left NBC to join an advertising agency a few weeks after the Kiker piece had aired. (Sherman's partnership with ad man Jerry Della Femina would count WNBC among its clients.) It fell to the new executive vice president of NBC Radio, Bob Mounty, as well as to the management team in place at WNBC, to launch Howard's show.

Mounty recalls that he, too, had to confront second-guessing about signing Howard—from Tinker and Bob Walsh, the NBC executive who oversaw the network's TV stations, sports operations, and radio division. According to Mounty, he pointed out that it would cost a lot of money to pull out of Howard's contract. Mounty also reminded Tinker and Walsh that Imus, considered smutty by some, had become successful because of strong management and programming guidelines. "There was no reason that we couldn't do the same thing with Howard Stern," Mounty argued.

Although Howard finally did join WNBC-AM, broadcasting 4:00 to 8:00 P.M., the expressions of concern on the sixth floor—where Tinker and Walsh had their offices—echoed long after his arrival. The station's general manager and program director policed Howard's show like monitors in a schoolyard. They were so anxious about Howard, so fretful about how Tinker and company would react to the object of Kiker's ire, that they spent more time trying to prevent trouble—that is, restraining their new drive-time disc jockey—than they did trying to establish his show. In a reflection of the mood, the striking red carpeting installed at WNBC when Sherman had been general manager was now a bland beige under Fioravanti.

According to Fioravanti's program director, Kevin Metheny, who clashed heatedly and often with the newcomer, thus earning Howard's nickname "Pig Virus," management concerns so intensified that there arose a desire to have an attorney from NBC's department of standards and practices listen to every word on the program while manning a so-called dump button. In the event that Howard veered into an offensive area, the attorney would have the license to cut the segment and to insert filler material, such as a jingle, to cover the omission. "We struck an agreement with standards and practices: I would man the dump button," Metheny said. "I used it infrequently—maybe a half dozen times—and I can't recollect what those occasions were."

A collage of photographs showing adults and children gathered at dinner tables was hung in the studio with a handwritten admonition to the effect: Howard, this is your audience. Management criticized the length and content of some on-air remarks, as well as Howard's deviations from the station's rigid format, which called for a prescribed number of songs per hour and traffic reports from the N-Copter every twenty minutes. The traffic reporter, Roz Frank, "probably gets more time than I do, if you add it all up," Howard complained one day. "And the stupid music gets more time than I do."

"One of the driving values of Howard's show was not weather and traffic, but we did not know that at the time," Metheny conceded. "It was a learning process for us."

"Howard used to call me, and I continued to go up to New York for these long, tedious meetings with management—which for me was a real pain in the ass," recalled Jeffrey Southmayd, Howard's Washington-based attorney. "Essentially, they were trying to break him. At least with Goff Lebhar, we knew what we could get away with. Now, suddenly, there was censorship. Howard would say to them, 'What did you hire me for if you wanted me to be another kind of person?' They'd say, 'Howard, we want you. We're programmers. We know the best way to help you be successful.'"

Fioravanti also went public with his views—surely a humiliation for Howard. "What we're trying to do is to bring Howard more into line with respect to what we know our audience is," the general manager told *Newsday* two months into the show. "Howard tends to play young. We're trying to bring it more into an adult frame of reference."

Fioravanti revealed that Stern was ordered to take the perceived hostility out of his voice: "We really want him to be a nice scoundrel. We'd like him to make people happy by being happy." Howard responded on the air one afternoon by saying: "I'm feeling real excited today because . . . first of all, I'm being a nice guy on the air. My boss tells me I'm coming off too nasty, so I'm going to be nice to anybody who calls in today." Unlike Imus, who was allowed to riff about adult topics such as sexual positions and regularly played the over-the-top evangelist Billy Sol Hargis, Howard was instructed to stay away from sex and religion. "If it's not funny, people will view it only in the dimension that it's tasteless," Fioravanti said.

A prime example of material deemed tasteless was a segment that Howard did early on of "Virgin Mary Kong," a so-called video game, modeled after Donkey Kong, in which the Virgin Mother was pursued and raped by a denizen of a Jerusalem singles bar. Walsh, a Roman Catholic, fumed at the blasphemy. Howard was suspended for a few days.

Howard ached under the weight of orders and suspicions. He finally had Fred Norris to lean on and to help him come up with comedy—Fred had lingered at "DC-101," then was hired by WNBC-AM at Howard's insistence—but he needed someone to banter with during the four long hours on the air. He needed Robin Quivers.

"We were not in a position to hire Robin without firing someone else, which we were disinclined to do," Metheny said. What's more, there was a belief in higher management that Howard would be easier to control without a sidekick. "He wanted Robin to come with him from the beginning," Sherman remembered. "But being the smartest broadcaster in the world, I thought he needed time to develop—without crutches. 'I want you to work your comedy,' I told him. I thought he would do so if he was alone and scared. Of course, looking back, I can see that was colossal horseshit on my part. It did slow him down to be without Robin."

Weeks into the show, Howard sounded tired and lost. Like a disc jockey built on an assembly line, he "talked up" the records that he played, reciting the time and call letters until the exact moment that the vocals kicked in; between songs he appeared to grope for things to discuss or dragged Fred into meaningless conversations.

One broadcast, for example, found Howard rambling on about a WNBC promotion that involved weight-loss maven Richard Simmons (who years later would become a willing guest, but an unwilling doormat, on Howard's show).

"I like this whole deal we're doing with the Richard Simmons thing," Howard said.

"Yeah," Fred replied.

"You hear we're giving away a cruise with Richard Simmons?"

"Is that right?"

"I like the whole idea, except I hate when, like, Richard Simmons comes on the air here and, like, starts yelling into the microphone: 'Hey! Richard Simmons! Hi, how ya doin'? Let's exercise!' He's like the most annoying of the exercise fanatics around now, ya know? Hey, remember Jack LaLanne, man? Guy used to come on, exercise, no big deal. Jane Fonda. Who else was there? Arnold Schwarzenegger."

Howard repeated his contempt for the spot voiced by Simmons, played it, and mimicked Simmons again. Having talked his bit to the end of an alley, he quickly said, "Let's talk to some people on the phone here."

Toward the end of the broadcast, a commercial ended, a song started to play—and there was no Howard. "Oh," he said finally, as if he had snapped out of a nap or a bad case of boredom. "Hi. Ha-ha. Remember me? Seven forty-nine at W-*Ennn*-B-C. I've run out of things to say. I'll give you the temperature here. It's seventy-four degrees at *Ennnn*-B-C."

In place of Robin, WNBC reporter Neal Seavey did the news during the show and was lured into routines. "And he keeps screwing them up," Howard told the audience. "We'll give him a couple of more chances." Howard also joked with Judy De Angelis, who anchored newscasts on the program off and on.

As Metheny put it, "Neither Seavey nor De Angelis made Howard comfortable. Neither of them seemed to get the joke the way Howard wanted it gotten. It was a lesson for all of us: When you hire someone, hire the entire act."

After what Metheny described as Howard's "relentless pissing and moaning," WNBC brought in Robin from the Baltimore station she had joined in June. She had overcome her annoyance at being shut out of the initial romance between NBC and Howard and rejoined him at the end of October. She read the news twice an hour in a professionally serious manner ("Here in the tristate area, for some homeless men a Harlem schoolhouse has become a haven") and traded lines and laughs. There was a belated sense among station executives that she would counterbalance Howard's wilder impulses—in other words, fill a role similar to that of Charles McCord, the talented newsman and writer on Imus's show.

Publicly, Howard expressed respect for Imus. "Imus does his thing and he's fantastic," he told an interviewer. He said he didn't want "to out-Imus" and was honored to be working on the same team.

At the same time, Howard sought to separate himself from the Imus legend. "I think the reason NBC hired me is that I *am* a different performer from Imus—after all, there are a lot of guys out there copying Imus," he said. Howard chafed at the homage paid by his superiors to the morning man. In 1982, NBC Radio put together a two-hour retrospective of the network's decades of comedy. Johnny Carson, the host of the special, voiced a promotional spot that aired during Howard's show; in the script written for him, Carson emphasized that the program would feature not only Burns and Allen and Fred Allen, but also "Don Imus, better known as top New York City disc jockey Imus in the Morning."

John Donald Imus, a former miner and railroad brakeman, erupted on WNBC-AM in December 1971. He was lionized by *Life* magazine with a five-page spread, which called him "the most outrageous disc jockey anywhere" because of his roof-raising, "say Hallelujah" portrayal of the Right Reverend Dr. Billy Sol Hargis (of the "First Church of the Gooey Death and Discount House of Worship in Del Rio, Texas") and his renderings of the lisping Hy from Hollywood and Crazy Bob, a teller of fractured fairy tales. Imus repeatedly punctuated his show with a duck's "quack-quack." He asked women callers, "Are you naked?" He screamed ratings threats at his WOR competitor, "I'm gonna get you, John Gambling!" A mumbling, grumbling gonzo force, he made the happy voices on WNBC and other New York stations sound sleepy and uninspired.

After years of being the star—on stations in Hartford, Detroit, and Washington—Howard found himself in the position of understudy. Sherman and the other NBC executives saw him as Imus Junior, the heir apparent, if the morning man self-destructed. Meanwhile, they dared not put Stern in the spotlight long focused on Imus, the irascible franchise. A TV campaign launched after Howard's arrival played up Imus's program. As Metheny recalled, "You dance with the one that brung you. Our wisdom at the time was to continue to be known as the Imus radio station and to hope for a cross-pollination with Howard's show. Imus was not of a mind to give Howard much of a leg up—and Howard came to resent him."

Privately, Howard considered Imus a burned-out shell of his former self, an image that stemmed in part from the morning man's boozy shuffle, unpredictable work habits, and abrasive manner. Howard also learned that Imus, who avoided him around the station, belittled his talent. "That's what chapped Howard's ass—that

Imus was saying these things behind his back," Southmayd recalled. "Howard basically wondered, 'What's this guy's problem?'"

Imus says he gave up cocaine in 1983, but he was still no sweetheart. He lorded his high six-figure salary by displaying wads of cash and coolly peeling away the paper bands so that they fluttered shamelessly to the floor. He played the self-absorbed star, sniping at people cruelly and cutting them down with saucy remarks when strangers were in the room. "Ignorant slut" was a favorite description of female staffers. Most times Imus was downright surly. One afternoon, a WNBC salesman thanked him for the extra spin he had put on a client's commercial. "Fuck you—and fuck your client," Imus barked, then continued walking down the hall. Truth was, the I-Man continued to drink on the sly—inching his way toward the crash that would come four years later, when he ended up at the Hazelden Clinic and finally dried out.

Sweetheart or not, Imus pulled in such fine ratings that he was outperforming the station when Howard joined. In the summer of 1982, WNBC claimed a 4.4 percent share of the total listening audience during an average quarter hour—and Imus delivered a heftier 5.2 in his morning time slot. His numbers rose to 5.5 in the fall and 5.6 in the winter, though the station's overall ratings dipped slightly.

Howard, on the other hand, was still trying to establish his comic, sex-crazed personality within the narrow parameters that the station laid down for him (but not for Imus). He had to announce so many time checks and station IDs ("W-*Ennnn*-B-C"), he had to pause so many times for traffic tips from N-Copter reporter Roz Frank and for news updates from Robin, and he had to play so many records that his creative bits and chatter were squeezed into the proceedings with little margin for improvisation. Some of the routines, such as periodic dial-a-dates and weather reports from "Your Holiness"—that is, a booming-voiced "God" played by Fred— were reliable holdovers from Washington. "Beaver Breaks" were back, too, including one in which "Beaver and the Cleavages" went to see Liberace in concert ("Wally says he's wearing an ermine T-shirt and a special pair of Liberace foxfire hot pants").

In the spirit of "50 Ways to Rank Your Mother," Howard squared off with callers in mock-out exchanges, sometimes with an in-studio guest to judge the joust.

"Howard, I hear that your sister's into magic," one contestant said. "Every time she does a trick, she stands on her hind legs and claps." To which Howard remarked: "Hey, man, I hear they're going to put artificial turf into Shea Stadium so your mother won't graze after the game."

Fred put his musical skills to work on warped song parodies. He followed a commercial for a French wine by imitating singer Kenny Rogers, to the melody of "The Gambler": "You've got to know when to drink wine . . . Don't drive your tractor in / To a Greyhound bus."

The effeminate "Out-of-the-Closet Stern" emerged to interview B-list celebrities and to indulge Howard's baby-boomer interest in TV has-beens, such as Butch Patrick, who played son Eddie on *The Munsters*. Howard also put "Out-of-the-Closet" to work in all his flamboyant glory when Bob Hope naively phoned one afternoon to plug another of his prime-time specials.

"First of all, we heard there was some trouble with your guy and now your guy is fine," Stern's "Out-of-the-Closet" vamped. "I didn't know that you were out of the closet as well."

"No, I've got a little hemorrhage in my right eye," Hope replied.

"Oh, your *eye*. Somebody told me your *guy*, and I said, 'Bob Hope, an American institution, is like 'Out-of-the-Closet Stern'? No way!" He added that he loved the USO tours that Hope did because "all those men gathered in one room, to me, would be such a thrill. That to me would be better than going to prison, Mr. Hope."

After the on-air dialogue, an annoyed Hope phoned the station and complained about the "rude woman" who had interviewed him.

For all of the constraints placed on the show—they made Howard's life miserable—he managed to forge a reputation for un-predictability. Nowhere else on the New York radio dial were New

York listeners likely to hear a showbiz legend being put on by a wacky queen. Howard also distinguished himself by being ruthlessly outspoken—some would say honest—about celebrities (how they looked, whether they had silicone injections) and by providing sexual titillation in the form of leering conversations.

As hours of snowfall buried the city one winter afternoon, he asked Robin: "How many inches are you hoping for, Robin?"

"Well, I've been promised twelve."

"Twelve inches, huh? You think you're going to be able to—"

"I could handle even more. I mean, it's the weekend."

As Howard put it, "The premise of the show here is to talk about everything." Case in point: Sexual Innuendo Wednesday. "I know the people want sexual innuendo, and I give it to them better than any disc jockey in America."

One woman, describing herself as twenty-two years old and having a 35-24-35 figure, called to say that she had been sexually harassed by her male boss, but the man was single and she did not object. He asked her to dinner, and later they went to his place.

Nothing happened, she told Howard: "I'm a good girl."

"You're a good girl? What the hell kind of story is this?"

"Yeah, well, I'm not going to get into intimate details."

But as Howard demonstrated time and again, the real reason that sexy-voiced women often called his show was to share their secrets—eventually.

Not taking no for an answer, he pressed on. "Did you kiss?"

"Yeah."

"Did he blow in your ear?"

"Uh-huh."

Howard then wanted to know if she had gone "a little further."

"Maybe," she admitted. "What's really exciting is that you have to keep whoever you want interested by being creative."

She recalled that she had returned the favor by inviting the man to her place, "and we decided to, ah, take a bath. Instead of using water, I used strawberry Jell-O."

"Whoa! That's it. You get tickets to David Brenner. Not only that, you win a trip to tour this studio right here. Now we're on the road."

Robin agreed: "This is the kind of thing we're looking for."

Indeed it was. WNBC's research in 1983 revealed that 81 percent of the station's afternoon audience were in cars. Squandering precious hours as they crawled along the Long Island Expressway or the Henry Hudson Parkway toward Westchester County, these listeners enjoyed in Howard a zany distraction from the vehicular torture. Motorists in particular constituted Howard's best audience. With their eyes on the road, they had to listen—and unlike other music-intensive programs, Howard's was meant to be listened to.

"When I'm doing the show, I think about what the listeners are doing," he told an interviewer. "I picture them usually alone, stuck in traffic after a long hard day of work and wishing they had something to distract them—*me*. I want to shake people up and get 'em happy."

ELEVEN

As Howard built a following, listeners with a keen appreciation of New York's colorful radio roster heard echoes of Bob Grant and Alex Bennett, two of his heroes.

Grant carved out a niche as a well-read, talk-radio wild man with a short fuse. His politics were ardently conservative and insistently law-and-order. Once, a caller told him that Rikers Island prison inmates would be having Cornish hens on Thanksgiving. "Isn't that sweet?" Grant responded. "I'd like to get each little hen and inject it with some strychnine." His patience with those ideological foes or dunderheads who got through to him was often brief. "Get off the phone, you creep!" was his war cry before hanging up.

Grant spent seven years on WMCA, a stint that started in 1970, when Howard was still in high school, and then stayed a shorter period as host of an overnight show on WOR before moving to WABC. Listeners were drawn to his serious discussions with political leaders and newsmakers, as well as to his theatrical brawls at the unlikeliest moments. In 1973, there was a program in which an elderly woman scolded Grant: "You sound like a screaming hysterical woman. So you ought to cut it out and have more dignity." Grant erupted: *"You come down here and I'll knock your nose right down your throat, do you understand that? . . . You little pipsqueak!"*

A decade before Howard's radio employer drew the punitive heat of the Federal Communications Commission for allowing indecent material to air on his show, the agency cracked down on the company that owned WMCA. The FCC found that Grant had violated a rule against personal attacks when he remarked that a New York congressman who had declined to come on his show was a "coward." (The FCC finding was later vacated by a federal appeals court.) Grant practiced pugnacious radio, as provocative as it was outrageous.

Among Grant's listeners in those early years on WMCA was young Howard. Grant recalled being approached at a public appearance by Ben Stern, who introduced Howard and said that his son wanted to go into radio. "I looked at this big, gawky kid and I said to him, 'Just be yourself,'" Grant remembered.

It was the first of several occasions in which Howard would show his respect. Years later, he interviewed Grant for a videotape intended for use at Howard's personal appearances. There also was this exchange when Howard appeared on Larry King's new CNN show in 1985:

King: "Quickly, what broadcast personalities, here or anywhere, do you like?"

Howard: "I've always admired Bob Grant, who's a local talk-show host."

"Anyone else around the country you like?"

"Ah. No. I'll be honest with you, I just don't."

Grant also was an invited guest at one of Stern's birthday broadcasts from Tavern on the Green.

However, as Howard became increasingly popular, he altered his assessment of Grant, at least in public. Boasting to an interviewer about his own impact on New York radio, he said: "The whole nature of the broadcast dial has changed. I hear Bob Grant talking about women and talking about his sponsors and talking about this and that. I mean, this guy—he's learned at my feet." He derided Grant as a former liberal and a skinny old man.

No one was more understanding of the about-face than Grant himself. "I think it's all part of his act," he said in 1995. "I find it amusing, even though a lot of people no doubt believe what he says. He was listening to the radio when, in September 1970, I came along on WMCA and said, 'Get off my phone!' He identified with that, but he says things today that I wouldn't dream of saying, about bodily functions, about women being 'a piece of ass.' It jars me to hear that. Howard was just right for the times. The country degenerated at the right time for him."

Unlike Grant, a neatly groomed conservative, Alex Bennett was a long-haired liberal. He influenced Howard and a number of other young radio broadcasters by bringing a hip, irreverent sensibility to the staid AM dial and to the talk format. He, too, built a following at WMCA, where he vented about the Vietnam War, sex, drugs, and rock music and conversed with anti-Establishment figures such as satirist Paul Krassner, radical lawyer William Kunstler, psychedelic guru Timothy Leary, and David Peel, an anarchic Greenwich Village street musician (who was befriended by John Lennon, wrote a song for Bennett, and later found a place in Howard's orbit of zanies, composing a Stern-for-governor theme in 1994). Bennett broadcast at night until WMCA fired him in 1971, claiming unconvincingly that it had to make room on the schedule for the New York Yankees' games.

The self-described "freak" then spent six years on rock station WPLJ-FM. He continued to demonstrate that talk radio could reach out to young listeners, dabble in comedy, and still focus on issues of the day. Bennett opened his phone lines to "quickies," allowing caller after caller to blurt out a line or two during the few minutes before sign-off. (Howard's version of this was "One Question and One Question Only." The listener could ask Howard any one thing in the final moments of the show, "because it gives me an excuse to hang up on people.")

If Bennett had had a bad day, he told his listeners about it. He described his on-air manner this way: "Why do you have to be so damn serious all the time? Why can't you take a few moments to have a good time?"

Before leaving WPLJ-FM in the late 1970s—Bennett has since returned to radio in his native San Francisco—he popularized a spontaneous, unaffected attitude on the New York airwaves that was recalled when Howard came to town and created a similar atmosphere.

In much the same way that Howard regarded Grant, he remembered Bennett respectfully at first, then downplayed his influence. For example, after Howard joined WNBC, his show contacted Bennett in San Francisco. As Bennett recalled the moments before their on-air exchange, "Howard said to me, 'I want to interview you because I used to listen to you when I was growing up and you were my inspiration.' Later, Howard runs around and starts saying to everybody, 'Hey, everybody's ripping me off. Alex Bennett rips me off.'"

Bennett returned fire during a visit to WMCA in 1989. Bennett described his former fan as "that coward, that thief, that lowlife. . . . He's afraid to look me in the face. This little son of a bitch . . . goes around on the air saying how everybody's stealing from poor little Howard. Hey, Howard, you stole *from me*, okay?"

Besides Bennett's candor, his just-say-it approach to a show, and his periodic displays of emotional vulnerability, there were other elements from his broadcasts that fans continued to recognize as Howard established himself at WNBC. Bennett griped on the air that he had to "get out of this business," saying, "I'm going to quit next year." Howard expressed similar sentiments whenever he argued that the press or people in the industry were giving him a hard time. In addition, the radio form of TV's *The Dating Game* was closely associated with Bennett years before Howard came on the scene and presented dial-a-date. In 1995, Bennett credited Howard with giving a funny idea an ingenious twist—lesbian dial-a-date.

But still irking Bennett was Howard's unwillingness to concede that any predecessor had directly, or indirectly, shaped his controversial style. "All of us in radio borrow or steal from somebody else at one time or another," said Bennett, who identified Jack Paar, Jack Benny, and Don Sherwood, a rebellious San Francisco disc jockey, as his own influences. "It's just that most of us are willing to admit it."

* * *

As Howard concluded his rocky first year at WNBC, he warmed to major changes at home, at the station, and in the New York radio market.

Before making the daily subway commute to the station from his apartment in Queens, he was captivated by his firstborn, Emily. He confessed that he sometimes watched the infant with wonder for hours at a time. After all, he insisted, in his real life he was different from the man on the radio. "I can't be like that twenty-four hours a day," he explained to a reporter from Gannett's suburban newspapers. "I'd burn out. It's just when I'm on the air that I start to froth at the mouth."

Kevin Goldman, his former college classmate, experienced the two sides of Howard during a reunion at WNBC. At lunch in the commissary, Howard talked about old times and said he was thrilled when Goldman, then a reporter with the show-business weekly *Variety*, let on that he was living with a woman. However, when Goldman then innocently asked what Robin was like, Howard became upset, in a chivalrous way, that his friend would make such an inquiry while involved with another woman. When Howard did his show that afternoon, he trashed Goldman.

On the radio, he was definitely "Howeird." He aired a graphic tape of the sounds of squirting water and a woman's wails that he identified as the agony of his wife during labor and the birth of their daughter. Alison had cooperated in making the tape—but Kevin Metheny, the program director, made it clear afterward that Howard had manufactured the bit at WNBC.

Metheny and Howard prepared for a new boss when general manager Domenick Fioravanti accepted a position with MTV. Fioravanti's successor was thirty-three-year-old Randall D. Bongarten, known to all as Randy, who, as vice president/radio at GE Broadcasting Company, had recently completed a sell-off of the firm's radio stations around the country. Before Bongarten officially joined WNBC, he visited the station early in the summer of 1983 in order to meet the staff. Howard used the occasion to complain about some of the problems he had been having with management, but he did so in such a good-natured way that Bongarten came away liking him. This was fortunate for Howard. NBC executives had told Bongarten little about the daring deejay, but they informed the new general manager that he was free to fire Howard. Driving home that night, Bongarten turned on WNBC and heard Howard addressing him by name. Stay out of my way, Howard warned him. Bongarten was amused.

As it turned out, the content of Howard's program was of little immediate concern when Bongarten arrived officially in July 1983. WNBC faced not one, but two new competitors in the Top 40 format. ABC, which had switched WABC from Top 40 to talk in 1982, resurrected the hits format on its FM station, WPLJ, on June 30. On August 2, Malrite Communications Group, the new owner of WVNJ-FM, changed the call letters to WHTZ ("Z-100"), scuttled the station's pitifully rated easy-listening sound, and replaced it with a brash Top 40 format; Scott Shannon quarterbacked the outlet's fast-paced *Morning Zoo*. (Howard later ridiculed him on the air.)

In the ever-evolving radio business, the creation of two Top 40 stations marked a fascinating return to the future. The heyday of Top 40 radio had been the 1950s and 1960s, when big-voiced jocks spun 45 RPM records by Elvis Presley, the Beatles, the Four Seasons, the Supremes, and other artists of mass appeal. But as the cleaner stereo sound of FM radio began to flourish in the late 1960s, and newly positioned FM stations offered young listeners the fresh alternative of rock-album cuts without commercial clutter and over-powering announcers, Top 40 slowly fell out of favor on the AM band, as evidenced by the ratings demise of the once invincible WABC. The conversion of WPLJ and the startup of "Z-100" reintro-duced the brassy, hits-driven format to a new generation of listen-ers. The revived mode of programming drew from a motherlode of crowd-pleasing music by Michael Jackson, Cyndi Lauper, Culture Club, and Madonna—artists who also were able to add more women to the Top 40 audience than the male-oriented, album-rock format. Although New York radio traditionally has been slow to follow programming trends, the two switches to Top 40 in the summer of 1983 signaled to stations around the country that the format was back from the grave.

In the Big Apple, this also meant that Bongarten had a big problem—WPLJ and "Z-100" were crowding a field that WNBC had owned by default since WABC had gone talk the year before. On closer examination, WNBC's position also seemed less competitive because it was a Top 40 station at war with itself, trying to showcase the comic side of Imus and Stern while insisting that they play a requisite number of hits per hour. As Bongarten saw it, the parameters that Fioravanti and Metheny had laid down restrained Howard's natural style.

"WNBC was an AM station when FM was coming on strong," Bongarten explained. "You didn't lightly throw away any assets you had. You tried to save them and get them back where they needed to be. The two greatest assets were Imus and Howard. I felt Howard was very talented. Because I didn't believe in the viability of the Top 40 position anyway, I thought we should let the personality aspect come to the fore. So I reduced most of the structures imposed on Howard's show."

Howard applauded Bongarten's leadership, because the new general manager exhibited an interest in his show and expressed confidence that it would achieve better ratings in time. "I think the big difference from before was that Howard knew I was going to support him to the best of my ability, and that was the first time he had ever had that in New York," Bongarten recalled. In addition, he found Howard easy to work with.

One afternoon Howard started to go on about why Jewish women use their mouths only to eat Chinese food. Howard was being explicit; he phoned his wife—and Bongarten's wife—to bring them into the discussion. Bongarten sensed that the bit was too risqué for the station. He called the on-air studio and ordered Howard to back off. Howard complied, but not before he cleverly turned the episode into a whine about whether Bongarten was right to censor him.

Howard further warmed to Bongarten because the general manager seemed a good sport even when the show slammed him.

Howard once aired the winning entry in a song-parody contest, a take-off on Van Halen's "Jump" called "Hump," as in "Randy is a hump." Bongarten was among those who laughed at the ridicule.

In order to maximize Howard's viability in the WNBC lineup, he scheduled him more prominently in afternoon drive—from 3:00 to 7:00 P.M., instead of from 4:00 to 8:00 P.M.

Before Bongarten arrived at WNBC, the station's advertisements identified *Imus in the Morning* as the cornerstone. An exception was devised by Della Femina, Travisano, and Sherman—the ad agency whose principals included Jerry Della Femina and former NBC Radio executive Robert Sherman. Separate subway placards showing that Imus *and* Howard bookended the broadcast day were created by artist Jack Davis, whose work included the zany illustrations of character Billy Sol Hargis on Imus's 1973 comedy album, *One Sacred Chicken to Go.*

Sandwiched between the headings "Morning Sickness" and "Imus in the Morning," a devilish-looking I-Man, dynamite plunger at his feet, fronted a raucous crowd that consisted of "Billy Sol," "Crazy Bob," newsman Charles McCord, and many others. Davis's other eye-catching billboard, proclaiming "Night Schtick," depicted Howard in a Boston University letter sweater with a telephone at his ear as his towering body broke through the top of a phone booth. Besides Robin, copter reporter Roz Frank, and "Earth Dog" Fred Norris (who crouched on all fours, with a dog tag around his neck and a meat bone in his "paws"), the busy advertisement also portrayed Howard in the guises of "Out-of-the-Closet Stern" (a coat rack on his shoulder) and a nerdy Beaver Cleaver.

When Bongarten took charge, he wanted to offer further evidence both to the industry and the listeners that Howard was just as important to the station as Imus. He wanted to dispel the widely held view that Howard was being groomed by WNBC as "Imus Junior" and to promote the two men as costars. "There could only be one position for the radio station: We needed them to be together," Bongarten recalled in 1995. "It just had to be."

In November 1983, Bongarten retained Penchina, Selkowitz Inc., a young and creative advertising agency, to design a TV campaign featuring Imus *and* Howard. The firm produced a humorous message and commercial that were vividly remembered in radio circles more than a decade later—no small feat, considering the difficulty that the agency would have in bringing Imus and Stern together on camera.

The agency's research showed that WNBC listeners had in common a giddy anticipation of what the two disc jockeys would do next on the air. "The real reason that a lot of people listened to Howard in the beginning was that they wanted to be listening when he was yanked off the air," Steve Penchina, the chairman and creative director, recalled. "People were waiting for it to happen." It also became clear during the research that Howard was perceived as such a bad boy that his audience included many closet listeners. Women who noted on the pages of their Arbitron ratings diaries that they had tuned in his show denied that they were fans when contacted by the ad agency. "We concluded that the women were lying to us," Penchina added. "They were closet listeners who sat and listened to this raunchy guy—loyally, like every day. They were part of his core audience."

These observations helped the agency to articulate what people were experiencing: "If we weren't so bad, we wouldn't be so good." To convey this new WNBC message on camera would be the hard part.

This was the first time that Stern and Imus would appear together. It was a big problem for Imus. Before the scheduled shoot, Bongarten had to negotiate all the details with Imus's agent, Michael Lynne. Like a Hollywood star teamed with a rising newcomer, Imus was especially concerned about how much time he would be seen in the commercial, compared to Howard. "The whole issue of Imus's having to share the spotlight was sensitive," Arthur Selkowitz, the agency's president, remembered. "And then, on the day of the shoot, we were all on pins and needles as to whether Imus would even show up."

He showed up all right. He arrived at the West Side production studio about two hours late, then announced that he was not going to cooperate after all. He walked out and drove around the city with his girlfriend, leaving a camera crew and the ad agency principals to await instructions. Howard also sat around wondering what would happen next. Bongarten was on the hook for about $150,000 in production costs.

Bongarten talked some more with Imus's agent. Finally, in a brilliant move, Bongarten told Lynne that they would produce the commercial without Imus if necessary. "Frankly, I don't know what we would have been able to do without Imus," Penchina said. "I had written the spot for the two of them."

However, Bongarten's threat apparently worked. Imus returned to the studio, facing the prospect that Stern might have the TV spotlight all to himself, and decided to go along. The two disc jockeys—Imus in a leather jacket, Howard in a sports shirt—took their assigned positions on opposite sides of the suited Bongarten, who began the commercial: "Because of certain indiscreet remarks by Don Imus and Howard Stern, WNBC apologizes to the following," and he proceeded to name everyone from the National Organization for Women to the New York Jets. Bongarten stopped at one point in the litany and displayed his diplomatic skills by turning his head right to give an accusing stare at Imus, the first of the two jocks to be singled out. He then continued: "Nassau Community College, the Gay Men's Choir . . . my wife." Bongarten turned left to stare down Howard. The tag line was voiced by Imus (of course): "Sixty-six, W-*Ennn*-B-C. If we weren't so bad, we wouldn't be so good." And still more from Bongarten: "Queen Elizabeth, Mayor Koch . . . "

Imus wore a stone face through the first of about thirty takes, until director George Gomes, who was used to dealing with fussy celebrities, obtained a looser performance. As Bongarten now read the list of the offended, Imus yawned on camera, fidgeted with distractions, and grabbed the list of names that the general manager was reading and tore it in half. As Imus played the shaggy-haired, imperious renegade, the more youthful Howard looked here, there, and down at the table, like a wise guy being scolded by his stuffy high school principal, namely, Bongarten.

The TV commercial was so popular that it made Howard instantly recognizable in public. No more commuting to work by subway. As a security precaution, Bongarten arranged for Howard to be driven in a luxury car (but not a limousine). In addition, the theme ("If we weren't so bad, we wouldn't be so good") was repeated on outdoor billboards featuring Imus and Stern.

When Penchina, Selkowitz later wanted to freshen the radio station's pitch, the agency decided to avoid another studio session rather than repeat the tense episode with Imus. Stern and Imus were photographed separately and their pictures placed side by side on a wall poster. In the second TV spot, the poster was seen being defaced by a series of passersby representing the panoply of New York life: an old woman, a miniskirted white woman, a black woman, a nun, an old man, a Hasidic man, a Boy Scout.

As they converged on the poster, a voice-over narrator said: "WNBC Radio's Don Imus and Howard Stern may have stepped on the toes of a few people with their outrageous antics. Maybe some of the things they said were a little indiscreet. But lucky for us, our listeners are the kind of people who can *really* take a joke." By the time the group parted, Stern had been marked up to look like a devil with horns and Imus resembled a circus clown with an arrow through his head. A dog looked up at the marred poster and barked.

In a competition sponsored by Tri-State Chevrolet Dealers, contestants picked up copies of the poster at Chevy showrooms, then retouched them with creative abandon. The winner turned the poster into a three-dimensional assembly: Howard, wearing a plaid dress, was aiming an aerosol can of "instant fart spray" at Imus, who had a cigarette dangling from his mouth, was attired in little boy's overalls, and clutched a decapitated toy soldier in one hand and its head in the other.

The ads and promotional tie-ins bolstered WNBC's image as the home of *two* outrageous personalities. An added intention was to lure listeners so that each man's success would rub off on the other. Facing mounting competition from New York's FM music outlets, Bongarten believed that Imus and Stern needed each other. At the same time, Bongarten was aware that WNBC had become a three-headed monster, satisfying separate appetites for Imus, Stern, and the mix of hit tunes and oldies that the station played. WNBC saw substantial recycling of its audience as many of Imus's listeners also tuned in Howard and many in Howard's afternoon audience returned in the morning for Imus.

As 1984 unfolded, Howard turned his ratings in an upward direction and held that course for the rest of his stint at WNBC. Something *was* happening. He went from a 3.8 share of the total afternoon listening audience in the spring, to a 4.2 in the summer, to a 4.6 in the autumn survey, which sponsors and ad agencies studied closely. In addition, he showed a more impressive—and more marketable—share of men eighteen to thirty-four years old.

"Now look who has the ratings! Look who has the ratings now, you dog-mouth devil!" he bellowed on the air at Fioravanti, the by now former general manager, whacking his snare drum and cymbal for emphasis. "Look who has the ratings now—because you're gone and I didn't listen to you. *I'm a hero! Yeeessss! . . . I'm the greatest radio personality that ever lived!*"

Despite Howard's success, his outspokenness still caused concern within NBC. When CBS's *60 Minutes* sought to interview Howard for a piece on outrageous radio hosts that was to air following the network's 1984 Super Bowl broadcast, Bongarten denied him permission to take part. The decision to keep Howard away from *60 Minutes* on one of the biggest TV nights of the year had been made in NBC Radio management above Bongarten. Although the highly rated Sunday newsmagazine used part of an interview Howard previously had given New York's WCBS-TV, the restraining order infuriated him. "I've worked my whole career to get that kind of recognition," he complained.

As Imus's ratings wobbled during this same period, the morning man saw that the upstart Howard wasn't such a punk after all and probably was good for business. In a striking about-face, Imus began to visit Howard's show and phoned in, so as not to miss out on the action.

"You like my jacket, Howard?" Imus asked one afternoon in early 1985 as Howard was protesting the switch to a new studio by watching *The Newlywed Game* on a TV monitor during his show.

"Imus, I'm watching TV, leave me alone," Howard replied. "Look at how ugly that guy is. Not you, Imus. I mean the guy on TV. Sorry."

"Don't you want to talk about my jacket, Howard?" Imus pressed. Lettering on the jacket read "Friend of Dennis Stein," one of Elizabeth Taylor's boyfriends.

"Oh, get outta here," Howard said. "You wear all that trendy crap, don't you?"

When Imus insisted that the new studio they occupied was better than the previous one, Howard cut him off, screaming, "You know, you are an idiot! I'm sick of you! I hope you get drunk and fall in a phone booth and urinate on yourself."

"Well, I hope you trip over your nose," Imus countered.

After Imus explained that he was hanging around the studio so late in his day in order to arrange for the use of a limousine, Howard said. "Boy, Imus has got some big problems, huh?"

Finally, in mock solidarity, Imus announced that he, too, did not wish to work in the new studio after all.

"He's a good man, that Imus," Howard remarked after he left.

"Yeah, he's coming around," Robin threw in.

"After I yell at him for twenty minutes."

Much of the time, Howard's show was less offensive than just plain silly. On one of his periodic spoofs of *The Match Game*, which had returned to television, Howard played the role of emcee "Gene Rayburn, Jr." (just as he had played Rayburn in phone pranks as a youngster). His "panelists" included a WNBC cleaning woman and various supporting players in the roles of Ann Landers, Pat (Mr. Haney) Buttram, Lou (*The Incredible Hulk*) Ferrigno, and Richard (*Family Feud*) Dawson. Asked to fill in the blank in "Woody Wood—," a female contestant correctly said, "Pecker," and five pan-

elists matched her answer. "Vice President George—" was completed by a male caller who said, "Bush," but only four panelists
came through with the match.

"Four bushes, and the girl had five peckers, so I guess she
wins," Howard said to the man.

To which he responded, "I don't get much bush."

Turning to Judy De Angelis, who was anchoring the newscasts
that day in place of Robin, he referred to her as "Sweet Cakes" and
said, "In honor of Valentine's Day, Judy's going to read the news
without any panties on. You guys think about that."

The men closest to Howard's show functioned much like his Think
Tank at "DC-101." Besides Fred Norris, the versatile writer and
master of voices, the group came to include Al Rosenberg and
Jackie Martling.

Al Rosenberg originally worked as an assistant vice president
in an investment banking firm on Wall Street. He specialized in selling municipal bonds and being the office clown, amusing colleagues
with his frequent impersonations of "Earl C. Watkins," a schemer
who pitched coin-operated pacemakers and portable tollbooths.
Eventually Rosenberg phoned Imus, who invited him on his show
and liked the Watkins character and other bits so much that the
banker comic was brought back morning after morning—and getting paid for the visits. A booking at The Improv, the New York
comedy club, followed in 1981. Rosenberg was thirty-six years old.
The New York Times reviewed his stand-up act and raved.

The critical reception prompted Rosenberg to give up the
security of his day job and throw in with WNBC. He first worked
with Imus but also was allowed to write and do voices on the Stern
show when Howard joined the station and needed assistance.
Rosenberg, who had a family of four children to support in the New
Jersey suburbs, barely earned a living from his contract-player arrangement with WNBC, but he was determined to root himself in
show business. To save on travel and to be able to contribute to
shows scheduled at opposite ends of the day, he sometimes lived

out of a suitcase and slept in the disc jockeys' lounge. Rosenberg liked the creative process on Howard's show; the host listened to the ideas presented to him and displayed a kinship with those who were on his team. (Involvement with Howard propelled Rosenberg in 1989 into a cohosting job with Bob Fitzsimmons on the morning show on New York's WNEW-AM, where he was able to put his voices and glib observations to wider use.)

John C. Martling, known as "Jackie the Joke Man," grew up on Long Island—like Howard, he was from Nassau County—and rock-and-rolled his way to a degree in mechanical engineering at Michigan State University. After graduating in 1971, he kicked around Long Island as the lead performer in the Off Hour Rockers, a novelty band that dished out jokes and original songs. Following the breakup of the group, Jackie tried stand-up comedy. He got hooked on Long Island's developing comedy scene, which included such busy venues as Richard M. Dixon's White House Inn, in Massapequa, and oddball acts like the Identical Triplets. The trio consisted of two white guys—Bob Nelson and Rob Bartlett (who later joined Imus's show)—and Eddie Murphy, who came from Roosevelt and would go on to join the cast of *Saturday Night Live*. Jackie became so tight with six other local comics that they took to calling themselves "the Magnificent Seven."

But unlike comedians who concentrate solely on lining up their next club date, Jackie helped market himself by churning out joke books, party albums, and videotapes to showcase his often perverse comedic skills. Along with his partner (and later his wife), Nancy Sirianni, he established a phone line to dispense X-rated jokes and information about his upcoming appearances by rigging an array of answering machines in his parents' attic. Collectively, this busy cottage industry of products and services reflected Jackie's boundless ability to hustle his act and his bottomless well of material about sex and raunch.

In Jackie's *Just Another Dirty Joke Book*, the first of several paperbacks that he wrote for Pinnacle Books, he gives this definition of a lady: "Someone who doesn't drink, doesn't smoke, and only curses when it slips out." From *The Only Joke Book You'll Ever Need*: "Did you hear about the college kids that had a nice date? They played Scrabble, and he licked her." And so on.

"I went to school to be an engineer, but I always collected jokes," Jackie recalled. "I've always been the guy at the bar annoying people with jokes. It's a weird obsession."

To see Jackie perform in a smoky club packed with beer-tilting fans was to catch a throwback to the vaudeville era. A veritable comedy machine, laughing maniacally with the audience at his grossest bits, he fired off joke after rhyme after ditty, for nearly two nonstop hours. In an era that had long since come to favor personal and ironic observations, like those dispensed by David Brenner and Jay Leno, Jews, Catholics, Italians, Irish, Poles, gays, and the elderly all came in for blunt swipes during Jackie's marathons at the mike. Just one example: "You hear about the Polack who jerked off in a restaurant? The sign said, 'First come, first served.'"

Although blissfully out-of-date as a performer, Jackie probably would have continued to play the club circuit and to appear on TV comedy shows. However, as part of his marketing campaign, he sent copies of his self-produced comedy albums to about four hundred agents, performers, and others who might book his act or take an interest in his career. Howard, who was then beginning to rise in the ratings at WNBC, was among the few to respond.

Howard first used Jackie in "Stump the Comedian" and "The Match Game"—periodic exposure that gave him the opportunity to plug his club appearances. The Joke Man later contributed to Howard's radio follies by writing gags on a part-time basis and filling a full-time writing slot. Jackie, born in 1948, was six years older than Howard, but they were contemporaries when it came to comic maturity.

"We hit it off," Jackie said. "I fit into the puzzle."

Rounding out Howard's team was Gary Dell'Abate. He, too, hailed from Long Island. He went to Adelphi University, not far from his home in Nassau County, and pursued a desire to work in radio while still a college student by interning in lowly positions at local stations. After graduation, he passed months in dreary jobs until he managed to talk his way into an entry-level slot at WNBC as part of the station's traffic-reporting team.

Other backstage assignments at WNBC followed before he learned in the fall of 1984 that Lee Davis, whom Howard called "Boy Lee," was giving up the producer's post on the Stern show. The job essentially called for a glorified go-fer, as evidenced by the salary of less than $200 a week, but Gary insisted to whoever would listen that he badly wanted the position. Perseverance paid off. He became "Boy Gary," tending to clerical duties and striving to keep Howard's day uncomplicated so that the disc jockey could focus his energy on developing material for the show. Dell'Abate built a network of contacts as he went about the frustrating business of trying to book guests on a program whose reputation for buzzsaw interviews conspired against him.

Dell'Abate experienced firsthand abuse. Soon after going to work for Howard, the disc jockey heckled him as a lazy oaf, saying that his producer "has nothing to bitch about. He has nothing to do, anyway." Although Dell'Abate's features and dark hair prompted people on the street to mistake him for John Oates, of the rock duo Hall and Oates, Howard often drew attention to his producer's prominent teeth and thick diction. "When people meet me," Dell'Abate explained to a reporter, "they're surprised that I'm not ugly and my caps aren't huge."

It was all coming together for Howard.

His ratings were rising, he had put together a creative team, and he had in Randy Bongarten a sympathetic boss who had loosened the restraints and elevated him through advertising to an equal level with Don Imus.

What he did not foresee was that Bongarten's skill would earn the general manager a higher position outside the radio station. In the summer of 1984, a year after Bongarten's arrival at WNBC, he was named president of NBC Radio, a promotion that put him in charge of all the NBC-owned stations and the NBC Radio Network. He now had less time to spend worrying about—and looking after—Howard. That responsibility fell to John P. Hayes, Jr., whom Bongarten brought from NBC-owned KYUU-FM in San Francisco to succeed him at WNBC as general manager. Howard went out of his way to mock Hayes even before he had reached New York, but Hayes seemed eager to get started just the same. "The strength of WNBC is its personalities," Hayes said in an interview with the *Daily News*. "I plan to build on that strength to enhance our personality image. Imus and Stern are without peer in New York or anywhere else."

Hayes went so far as to say he was prepared "to be made a fool of." When asked about Howard's show specifically, he said: "I like controversy, I like to cross over the line of good taste, decency, to offend one group or another. That's okay. We all tell jokes, have prejudices, and a tendency to cross over lines, and radio people should, too. Their job is to relate to the audience, and the best way to do that is to be a person yourself." Hayes said he considered Howard "very democratic in his prejudices," and he dismissed the notion that his pokes at various ethnic groups inflamed tensions, as the Anti-Defamation League of B'nai B'rith and other critics had charged. In a skit called "Hill Street Jews," policemen with Yiddish accents ripped down a Nativity display. He called Hempstead, Long Island, "Hempstead, Africa" because of the community's expanding black population.

"Humor is . . . a good way to douse the flames," Hayes added. "I fully expect Stern, and Imus, too, to take shots at me. I'm not a sensitive person. You develop a thick skin in radio."

Hayes's public attitude toward Howard was magnanimous, but his arrival at WNBC on October 1, 1984, marked the beginning of the end of Howard's stay.

TWELVE

Both on the surface and in temperament, Howard and his new boss had little in common.

Unlike Howard, an overweight guy known for saying dirty things on the radio, Hayes was a trim, crisply groomed executive and executive's son known for running a tight radio ship. His father, John Patrick Hayes, had worked for National Gypsum Company since 1947 and was now chairman of the board and chief executive officer. As described by a WNBC colleague, young John's prep-school tales and bearing made him seem "pink and green up to his eyeballs."

Despite Hayes's gracious remarks to the *Daily News*, after taking over as general manager he showed little appreciation for Howard's off-color antics and seditious comments.

"Half the management in this company are cheating on their wives," Howard alleged in an interview with *People*. "I see what's going on. And they have the nerve to tell me to lay off the sexual stuff, when their whole lives are filled with lies and cheats."

Bongarten often had been able to steer Howard away from especially offensive subjects by resisting the heavy-handed approach—by trying not to act like a whip. Bongarten liked Howard personally and had made a point of seeking him out at the station. He presented himself to Howard as a cheerleader. He urged Howard to back off from time to time while reassuring the disc jockey that he wanted him to succeed. For example, Bongarten convinced

Howard that he should not belch on the air (for a while, that is) by explaining that it turned off female listeners. It was Bongarten's belief that Howard resented authority so bitterly that to confront him head-on increased the likelihood that he would defiantly go further and further with his material. "Once you tell me I can't do something on the air, I feel compelled to do it," Howard admitted.

Hayes, like Bongarten, told Howard that he was too inventive to have to use so much smutty material. Howard's daffy charisma, not the sexual stuff, was the main reason people tuned in. But Hayes had a harder time communicating this message. He sometimes stayed away from Howard, or left it to Dale Parsons, who became program director in January 1985, to rein him in. The disc jockey responded with racier programs, if not to test Hayes, then certainly to irritate him. He goaded the general manager in the same way that he had needled Goff Lebhar during the final months at "DC-101."

Howard's goal was to become more disgusting. At a 1985 Super Bowl party that Howard staged at a Long Island hotel, he audiotaped the male guests as they relieved themselves in a bathroom. The next day he aired the tapes, commenting on who had been able to urinate for the longest time. Parsons told him afterward that the bit was out of line; Howard wanted to know if the program director was mouthing an order dictated from an executive at NBC Radio.

"I was trying to take the program to the next level and expand the audience," Parsons said. "Howard was one of the most creative, funny people I know, but I thought he was going for the easy, cheap laugh. I wanted him to attract more women, because his show was top-heavy with men. I told him that if a bunch of guys are sitting around, and they all crack up laughing because one of them farted, any woman in the room would get up and leave. He understood that, but I don't know if he ever realized that he didn't have to go for the cheap laugh."

Howard often scored simply by offering iconoclastic commentary on the day's news. When New Yorkers were debating whether Bernhard Goetz had been justified in 1984 when he shot four teenagers who allegedly had confronted him in the subway, Howard argued that the so-called subway vigilante should be given the Congressional Medal of Honor. "I used to ride the subway," he told an interviewer, "so I know what it's like." Furthermore, he added, "I think rapists should be castrated. It's an inexcusable act."

When a pregnant woman was shot during a baseball game at Yankee Stadium, Howard saw a grisly connection to ballpark promotions such as Jacket Day and Cap Day, remarking that the incident had taken place on "Bullet Day."

After a group of Columbia University students staged a protest against apartheid in South Africa, drawing impassioned support from the Reverend Jesse Jackson, Howard remarked: "Doesn't he realize that those white kids [at Columbia] don't allow black people to live in their neighborhood? . . . There's not even one of those kids who would even bunk up with a black person for a night . . . in the same dorm, let alone the same room."

The difference between WNBC and "DC-101" had to do with corporate culture. Yes, Howard was confronting Hayes from a position of strength in the ratings. "I will do anything to get ratings, because once you start to slip, they'll throw you out on your butt," he said. "Management doesn't give a hoot about you. They're all a bunch of whores and slobs."

But Howard failed to recognize two things.

The first was that the bawdier he became on the air simply to tick off Hayes, the more nervous attention he generated on a level well above the general manager. Parsons received calls from Bob Mounty, who had succeeded Sherman as executive vice president of NBC Radio, as well as from NBC chairman Grant Tinker, in response to outrageous bits presented on Howard's show. "Everyone in that building was aware of Howard," Parsons recalled.

The second thing that Stern did not recognize was that the ratings of WNBC, let alone the much improved numbers of his own program, mattered hardly at all within the larger broadcasting empire of NBC. The network's fortunes mainly were tied to the performance of its prime-time television shows. The radio division was an afterthought, its problems of little consequence to Tinker and the other TV-oriented executives with whom he surrounded himself on the sixth floor of the RCA Building—unless, that is, a radio problem became an annoyance or a distraction to Tinker himself.

As it was, WNBC finished 1984 with a profit of around $4 million—an impressive sum that reflected the drawing and selling power of Imus and Stern. Early in 1985, Bongarten boasted that Howard was number one among a segment of the audience targeted by many leading advertisers—listeners twenty-five to fifty-four years of age. In this prime demographic, Howard led his nearest competitor, WLTW, the soft-sounding pop station known as "Lite-FM," by almost 40 percent.

Reaching nearly one million listeners a week, Howard also was the most popular afternoon personality among men eighteen to forty-nine and men twenty-five to fifty-four. His solid standing among men and his willingness to meet with sponsors enabled WNBC's salespeople to bypass the resistance that many Madison Avenue advertising agencies and national advertisers showed toward the content of his program and to draw commercials from local retailers, financial services, and liquor distributors. In meeting after meeting with sponsors, Howard demonstrated, as one WNBC salesperson put it, "that he could talk about replacement windows as if he did all the time, even if he knew nothing at all." In marked contrast with Imus, who resisted contact with clients, Howard impressed advertisers with the earnest way that he inquired about their products. He discussed with the sponsors how he should go about pitching their commercials, and he thanked them for coming in to meet with him.

To the perverse delight of some of these visitors, he went on the air and turned them into minor celebrities, claiming this one had a stain in the crotch of his pants and that one was a terrible dresser. Reading copy for a men's clothing store, he said of the proprietor, "Just look for Mr. Lubin's bad toupee." He distinguished the spots for a woman's skin cream by howling, "Shave that thang!" He introduced listeners to the versatility of plastic by raving at length about the home furnishings and gifts created by a local manufacturer. He worked especially hard for the Beanstalk restaurant, located near the WNBC studios, delivering mouthwatering descriptions of the dishes that he and Robin had eaten there and adding remarks such as "You don't walk out of there with a bloated, disgusting feeling. It's a well-prepared meal, you feel satisfied, you feel healthy, and the food tastes good." As a result of repeated endorsements, he packed the place.

WNBC was able to command the highest rates in afternoon drive—$600 a minute—because clients found that it paid to advertise on Howard's show.

As head of NBC's radio division, Bongarten responded to Howard's mounting success and value to the station by ripping up his contract early in 1985 and working out a new arrangement. Howard had joined WNBC in 1982 under an agreement that reportedly was to pay him a total of $1 million over five years. Most of the riches were built into its final years.

The new deal was for three years and immediately raised Howard's annual salary to around $400,000. For a while, at least, he stopped griping about being underpaid, admitting, "I'm sitting pretty."

Now that the Imus and Stern shows anchored the broadcast day—the howling Wolfman Jack was installed in the fall of 1984 on the overnight shift—WNBC sought to broaden its image as the outlet for offbeat personalities by bringing in a fourth. The veteran comedian Soupy Sales, who had entertained Howard and other kids in the mid-1960s as the popular host of a pie-slinging TV show on New York's WNEW-TV, returned to his radio roots when he took over WNBC's midday slot on April 22, 1985. Between Imus and Stern, the lovable, old-fashioned Soupy tapped a bottomless well of jokes, silly songs, and even sillier puns, reaching for adult listeners whom he had tickled when they were youngsters.

Soupy's arrival gave WNBC a quartet of bulging egos who eyed one another warily. There was so little chemistry among the four that the station's public relations department became exasperated trying to photograph them all together. When one star was a few

minutes late for a scheduled shoot, another left in a huff. This child-
ishness went on for three days before the men were all in place together, careful not to brush up against one another as the photo was
taken.

In the closing moments of Imus's show, which ended at 10:00
A.M., Soupy often stopped by to fire off a few jokes in a bid to carry
over the audience. It sounded as if he and Imus enjoyed the get-
togethers. But it was different with Howard. Although he had loved
Soupy's TV show two decades earlier, and interviewed Soupy on
"DC-101" when the veteran entertainer was promoting a comedy
album, they came to operate on opposite sides of a divide at WNBC.
"It wasn't a team effort at all, which it should have been," Soupy recalled in 1995. "I think Howard was just immature at the time. He
was very jealous of everybody and resented everybody."

Howard resented that Soupy was treated by management like a
star and allowed to hire two cast members, Ray D'Ariano and Paul
Dvir, who also played the piano that was newly installed in the
studio at Soupy's request. After all, Howard had had to beg the station to hire Robin, and now, three years later, he still felt that he was
being denied proper respect. As a result, Howard wanted to retaliate
against Hayes and others in management for real or imagined
slights, but he wound up taking out his anger on the innocent bene-
ficiary of their confidence, Soupy Sales.

After Soupy joined, broadcasting five hours a day, Howard invited him on his own show to schmooze. Howard teased the comedian, suggesting that a man Soupy's age (fifty-nine at the time)
should cut back to four hours. He asked Soupy why he spent so
much time preparing material when he could simply wing it. He
questioned Soupy's need for a staff that included not only D'Ariano
and Dvir, but also a producer, Lee Davis (who, as "Boy Lee," had
held the same position on Howard's show).

For a long time, Soupy played along with Howard. Soupy had a
reputation as one of the nicest guys in show business, especially
with younger comics who were opening acts on his many club
dates. But Howard's remarks became increasingly nasty; after five

hours on the air, Soupy tired of having then to fence with Howard. He stopped dropping in on Howard's show.

"It was like Howard was competing with Soupy for ground, when all that Howard really wanted was respect from NBC," Dvir recalled. "The treatment he gave Soupy, calling him old and tired, had to do with NBC angering him. It had nothing to do with Soupy."

Yet the taunts continued after Soupy no longer came around. Soupy updated a bit from his children's television show of the early 1960s, giving a rundown of the day's lunch menu; on WNBC he presented "Let's Have Lunch with Soupy." Pretending to be in the crowded NBC commissary, Soupy described the lunches that were sent up by the Beanstalk, apparently as part of the restaurant's advertising contract with WNBC. This, too, irked Howard, who did not receive a free lunch.

Howard complained that Soupy and his crew would leave the remains of lunch lying around the studio. One day, a spill of salad dressing on the floor prompted Howard to threaten on air that he would start cutting wires in Soupy's piano unless the mess was cleaned up. He protested to Soupy directly on the phone, but Soupy made it clear that cleanup was not his job. At this point, as Howard claimed that afternoon and since, he started to cut wires—four in all. Indeed, to anyone hearing the episode on the radio, it sounded as if Howard really was slicing the wires, especially when he said he was tapping an affected key and producing nothing more than a *thunk*.

Despite Howard's boasts that he had damaged the piano, it never happened. He declined to admit it publicly, but he had stuffed paper under the hammers to produce the muffled notes that sounded so convincing to his listeners. Once the paper was removed, the piano worked perfectly.

Another time Howard irritated Soupy by relocating the piano to the program director's office in order to clear room in the studio for the members of Menudo, the young Latino singing group. He also accused Soupy of stealing personnel when a young intern assigned to work for Howard started to review movies on Soupy's midday program.

"People liked listening to the goings-on between Howard and Soupy," Dvir remembered. "But working there was like being in a swamp with an octopus—you felt as if you couldn't swim." The atmosphere unsettled Dvir because, off the air, Howard went out of his way to befriend him and insisted that he should not take seriously anything directed at him during the program. "Howard was a sweet guy," Dvir said. "At a company picnic, he made a point of introducing his wife to me. But when I flipped on his show, I used to cringe."

According to Soupy, Howard "was just fucking nuts. He was constantly out of his head . . . a temperamental type of performer. He was a madman."

A few years later, after both men had left WNBC, they crossed paths at the New Jersey studios of WWOR-TV. According to Soupy, Howard was friendly and told him, "I don't even know what I was so upset about back at WNBC." However, Soupy added, Howard later described the encounter in an insulting manner, saying on the radio that the comedian had looked old and frail. "He was the same prick he always was. He insulted me on the radio show. It was a lack of class, but everyone knew that Howard had no class."

Days after Soupy recalled the incident, in 1995, the comedian appeared on a TV telethon, prompting Howard to comment later: "Soupy Sales, now 137 years old . . . Soupy Sales, Civil War veteran." He would not let go.

In the spring of 1985, Howard soared to a 5.7 share (percent) of the listening audience during an average quarter hour. This was the highest rating earned at WNBC since Imus had pulled a 6.6 share four years earlier. Howard's show was such a magnet that it dramatically outperformed *Imus in the Morning* (3.9 share) and the station as a whole (3.0).

Howard had such clout that he played few records and did almost, but not quite, an all-talk broadcast. After nine years in radio, he had come within reach of a format that could be described as "All Howard, All the Time." Robin's newscasts were interspersed with editorial comments from the star of the show. Various bits, such as Howard's contacting Elvis Presley in the Great Beyond, ran much longer than management had allowed in the past.

Day after day, Howard pressed harder and harder against the boundaries of taste. "I see nothing wrong with filth and bad taste," he said during an appearance in Connecticut. "It's made me a very wealthy man."

One afternoon Fred Norris put on his best accent to play Danish socialite Claus von Bulow, who was being retried on charges of attempting to kill his wife, the heiress Sunny von Bulow, then hospitalized in a coma.

"Does she still put out?" Howard asked "Claus."

"As much as she used to, yes. As a matter of fact, she's a little easier now than she used to be." He added: "I just unhook some of the wires and roll her over."

An episode of the periodic "Lifestyles of the Radio Famous" wickedly spoofed Paco, a Puerto Rican disc jockey who recently had been released by WKTU-FM ("Disco 92") and returned to Spanish-language WJIT. Calling himself "Howard Leach" and imitating TV host Robin Leach's nasal voice, Stern explained that Paco lived in New York's barrio, on the seventh floor of a walk-up, "just above Our Lady of Agonies Abortion Clinic. Our amigo Paco shares his apartment with his mother, fourteen sisters, six brothers, his uncle Fredo, and two darkies." The bathroom was shared by all the residents of the seventh floor, Howard added, "and half of Honduras."

After the general manager of a New Jersey radio station editorialized on the air against Howard, Stern said of his attacker: "Due to the length of his genitalia, he probably hasn't been able to satisfy his wife." The episode reminded Donna Fiducia, who had succeeded Roz Frank as WNBC's traffic reporter, that the New Jersey man had once aired a commercial on his station that had to do with a vendor's "big plastic balls."

"You stay up at night thinking about King Kong?" Howard asked Fiducia.

"I knew I shouldn't have brought it up," she said.

"No, evidently you're very fascinated with the thought of big balls. . . . I just hope, Robin, that John Hayes was listening to this and he understands that Donna is into blue material. . . . I just think saying the words 'plastic balls' on the air . . . is pretty dangerous."

It also was becoming dangerous for Howard to talk dirty on NBC's flagship radio station. This was clear to Parsons, the program director, after Howard announced plans to present bestiality dial-a-date, in which he intended to fix up a man and a woman who had had sex with animals.

Bongarten ordered Howard directly not to do the bit. In addition, Hayes instructed Parsons to stop Howard from going through with it. As Parsons remembers the conversation, Hayes said, "Tell him whatever you want, but tell him he has to back off for his own good."

During a commercial break, Parsons asked to speak with Howard outside the studio.

"I wish you wouldn't do this," Parsons said.

"How come?" Howard replied.

"Because you just have to."

"Okay," Howard said. And back off he did. No bestiality dial-a-date. Parsons sensed that Howard knew something was up, even if the disc jockey failed to appreciate how much of a renegade he had become.

Bongarten conveyed his own warning during the summer of 1985. Having received signals from NBC superiors that they regarded Howard as a blight on the company, Bongarten cautioned Howard that he was presenting strong material. Apparently Howard did not see the full ramifications of what he was being told. Instead he girded himself against the second-guessing from on high.

Ted Bonnitt, who had worked with Howard at WRNW in Westchester, called him at WNBC. "They've got a gun to my head," Howard said. "It isn't much fun right now." Howard then asked Bonnitt what he thought of the show. Bonnitt, trying to tease him, responded: "I think you're a sick son of a bitch."

Howard was in no mood for teasing. He said he had to go and hung up.

As described by Howard, the final chapter in his war with NBC grew to the level of myth. It was the myth of the inventive radio personality clashing with the stuffed shirts of a mighty network—until an unseen someone, perhaps never to be identified, abruptly intervened and banished him from the premises forever. It was a perfect myth for Howard, because it allowed his ultimate victory in New York radio to taste so much sweeter and to seem like the most gratifying revenge.

However, research for this book shows that Howard's final struggle at WNBC reflected nothing more noble than a clerical oversight, public relations concerns, and his own exaggerated response to Soupy Sales. Revenge would still be Howard's, but mainly as a result of silliness that now marked his last days at WNBC.

It was NBC's honorable practice to make sure that all complaints from listeners and viewers were answered by the appropriate executive. Parsons, for example, recalls that he frequently phoned people who had addressed angry letters about Howard to WNBC, to NBC chairman Tinker, and to Thornton Bradshaw, the chairman of RCA, which owned the company. Often the complainants simply wanted to vent their ire about Howard and were satisfied that Parsons called them. Parsons told unappeased letter writers that he was sorry to lose them as listeners.

Unfortunately for Howard, one such complainant did not receive a prompt response. He was a man from New Jersey who explained in a letter to Bradshaw that he had stumbled onto Howard's broadcast one afternoon while driving with youngsters in his car. Although there are varying recollections about what Howard supposedly said on the broadcast that day, two elements may have been most troubling to the letter writer. Howard had criticized the well-publicized campaign, led by Chrysler chairman Lee Iacocca, to raise millions of dollars in order to refurbish the Statue of Liberty. He joked that the funds might be used to equip the statue in New

York Harbor with a giant Tampon or to acquire the many gallons of copper that Miss Liberty needed to douche. Another Stern remark—something to do with cementing a woman's breasts to the floor—is also remembered as being cited in the New Jersey man's letter.

The letter to Bradshaw was forwarded to Hayes for a reply—but it languished, Parsons said, because the WNBC general manager was away and a temporary secretary did not reroute it for prompt consideration. "Originally, all the guy wanted was someone to listen to him, so he could vent a little," Parsons recalled. "But when his letter wasn't responded to right away, he felt ignored, I assume, and he went off the deep end. He wrote back to Bradshaw, this time saying he was going to address the matter of Howard Stern in his own way. He said he was going to bring the issue before an RCA stockholders' meeting. Of course, no one wanted that."

This second letter came to the attention of Bud Rukeyser, NBC's director of corporate communications and Tinker's closest adviser on public relations matters. In 1995, Rukeyser said he had no recollection that the letter writer had threatened to make a public protest. Rukeyser remembered that the letter and a subsequent phone conversation revealed the correspondent to be "a concerned father, a solid citizen, not the least bit hateful or anything."

As a result of the man's persistence, high-level conversations about getting rid of Howard were begun at NBC.

"It was not as though this was the first time that Howard Stern had come to our attention," Rukeyser said. "Frankly, radio did not take up a lot of our time, but everyone always felt vaguely uncomfortable with the idea that Howard Stern was broadcasting on *our* station. That letter from the man in Jersey made some of us think again as to why we were keeping Stern around."

At a meeting of Tinker's Chairman's Council—which consisted of Tinker, Rukeyser, and division heads such as Bob Walsh, who had questioned the decision to hire Howard three years earlier—the issue of WNBC's late-afternoon disc jockey was discussed. Bongarten, who reported to Walsh, was unable to attend the session and learned about it afterward. Without mentioning the specifics of the meeting, Bongarten warned Howard to be cautious, even though it was probably too late by then to save him.

Bongarten tried to arrange a meeting with Tinker in hopes of arguing that Howard was essential to the continued success of WNBC. He wanted to make the case that problems with Howard were the fault of management, including himself. Bongarten told Walsh that there were better answers than firing Howard—why not sell WNBC while it still had value? Bongarten, a radio man outnumbered by TV executives, appeared to be alone in seeing that the fortunes of WNBC would collapse if Howard departed. Bongarten wanted time to correct the Howard problem.

Tinker declined the request for a discussion, but Bongarten asked Walsh to talk with Tinker again. Walsh returned with the news that Tinker had made up his mind: Howard had to go. Walsh told Bongarten to fire Howard when he wanted to. It did not have to be that day.

Because NBC had put up with Howard for nearly three years, Bongarten chose to wait. For two months he maintained one of the best kept secrets in a business that has few.

Tinker writes in his autobiography, *Tinker in Television*, that he tuned in Howard's show for the first time after hearing about the New Jersey man's complaint and that he was appalled by what he heard. When Walsh explained that Howard was "the difference between profit and loss" at WNBC, Tinker responded: "If that's the only way to make money, we shouldn't be in business." With the concurrence of Walsh, Tinker adds, Howard was fired. Tinker claims that he hadn't listened to Howard sooner because he had been so preoccupied with television matters.

Tinker may not have listened, but what about the WNBC and the NBC Radio executives who remembered hearing from the chairman during the previous three years with regard to Howard's show? Their recollections raise an intriguing question: Why did Tinker finally order Howard's dismissal? Why after three years?

"I can tell you precisely: Grant Tinker knew about this from me, and Grant made a decision to do something about it," Rukeyser, who collaborated on Tinker's book, insisted in an interview. "Grant used to come in from California on Monday nights and go back on Thursdays. Stern was being aired only in New York at the time, but Grant was busy running around and did not listen to him. The watershed moment was this guy's letter—a letter from a perfectly reasonable guy."

After three years of Howard Stern, Tinker may have come to believe that the disc jockey had become a personal liability and had to go.

Hayes told Parsons to make sure that Howard arrived at the station early on September 27, 1985. When Parsons asked why, Hayes said that there was going to be a meeting. Parsons drew the right conclusion.

However, September 27 loomed as a frightful day in New York. Hurricane Gloria threatened to strike the city around midday. Most people stayed home from work on that Friday rather than brave the fierce elements that were sweeping up the East Coast. When the storm hit, drenching waters and strong winds combined to turn weekday Manhattan into a ghost town. The RCA Building was all but empty, except for the buzzing newsrooms of NBC and New York's WNBC-TV, which was providing continuous coverage of the storm.

On the second floor, a different storm was about to break.

Although Long Island, where Howard lived, was being severely whacked by the hurricane and would suffer power outages for days, he made it to work, as did his team, and the show did go on. Parsons got in as well, but not Hayes and Bongarten, who remained in their homes in the Connecticut suburbs. With the planned meeting called off because of the storm, Hayes phoned Parsons and told him to reschedule Howard's early arrival for the following Monday. "We have to let him go," Hayes admitted. Parsons pressed for a reason, and Hayes replied, "I can't tell you." Parsons would remain outside the small group of managers privy to what had precipitated Howard's exit.

Howard spent much of the stormy afternoon complaining bitterly on the air that Soupy Sales was going national, as the host of a syndicated radio show. Howard did not know that Soupy himself had leaked the news so that it would make Howard flip out. Soupy had instructed his piano player, Paul Dvir, to plant the information in Howard's camp; Dvir tipped off a WNBC engineer, who predictably alerted Howard.

Howard, who had been angling to develop his own national radio show, threatened to quit if the news about Soupy was true (which it was). He did not know that his threat to bail out was about to be rendered moot. He ranted and accused on the air—and suggested that he might not return on Monday sooner than have to endure the humiliation of Soupy's success.

Over the weekend, Howard injured himself while jogging and ended up on crutches. It was a pitiful-looking giant—slow, crippled, and unaware of his fate—who hobbled into WNBC at the start of the new week. Arriving early as requested, he was met by Hayes, who directed him to see Bongarten on the sixth floor. As he followed instructions, Hayes sat down with Robin and told her that she and Howard were out.

In previous weeks Howard had talked to Bongarten about doing his own network program, so when Bongarten somberly informed Howard that he was "canceling the show," Howard naively assumed that he meant the network venture. No, Bongarten corrected him, *The Howard Stern Show* on WNBC was being discontinued.

Howard calmly asked why. Bongarten explained that the show was heading in a direction inconsistent with the long-term interests of NBC. Technically speaking, this was true. At the same time, Bongarten felt bad, because Howard looked so weak on crutches and because the firing seemed like a blunder.

Howard took the bullet, struggled up from his seat, and headed to his office downstairs.

Robin had already returned to the office and was fuming. She flung a pile of publicity photos. She volunteered no explanation.

Only when Howard limped in did the Stern gang learn that he and Robin had been fired. Howard appeared unusually composed, as if relieved finally to have shed a great weight from his shoulders. After all his hateful remarks about the station and the people who ran it, he showed no sign of bitterness.

Hours later, when a colleague phoned to wish him well, he sounded like a kid: partly contrite, but mainly wondering why it had happened, how it could possibly have happened.

WNBC had to address serious damage and provide damage control.

Learning that Howard had been axed, the sales department pulled $300,000 in commercials committed to his show. It was clear that the station would never be paid for them if Howard was unavailable to read the copy. That morning, the Beanstalk had agreed to nearly $30,000 in spots. More lost business.

Hayes left detailed instructions with receptionists and secretaries as to how they should respond to calls. They were to say that Howard's show was discontinued because of "conceptual differences" between him and the station. Listeners were invited to express their views about the decision in writing to Hayes, who did not intend to accept calls on the matter. In a highly unusual move, Hayes recorded a brief announcement about the cancellation and aired it periodically throughout Stern's time slot, which was filled by disc jockey Janet Bates, known as "Janet from Another Planet." "Your comments are welcome," he said.

When radio stations fire a popular air personality, they usually fill the vacated slot without explanation and carry on as if nothing had changed. Sometimes listeners who phone the station are told that the ousted personality merely is on vacation. To level with fans is rare; stations most often try to ride out a transition with the knowledge that audience anger subsides before long.

This time, however, Hayes's invitation to comment, coupled with Howard's enormous popularity, generated so much mail that the station had to hire a secretary to deal with it. Most of the correspondence was in support of Howard. In a response to Roger

Hatfield, a New Jersey resident who had written to complain about the cancellation, Hayes stated: "There is no doubt that Howard Stern is a talented performer. There were conceptual differences between NBC Radio management and Howard Stern, however, as to the program." Hayes did not elaborate on what the "conceptual differences" were. He added: "We think there was no alternative but to have taken this action. We appreciate your support of the Howard Stern program while it was broadcast on WNBC."

If Howard had been fired on Friday, as originally planned, the news would have had less impact because Saturday newspapers have a smaller circulation. Because Hurricane Gloria bumped Howard's dismissal to Monday, the New York media now spent the week highlighting the story.

"We had a running difference of opinion on what the program should be, and I think that led us to a point, over a long period of time, where we decided that his show was no longer appropriate for WNBC," Hayes said.

Bongarten also left Tinker out of the story, explaining to the *Daily News:* "We just didn't agree with him on how the program ought to be done." He conceded that content had been part of the problem. To another reporter, Bongarten said: "I made the decision [to fire Howard]."

"As far as I know, I've been given no reason," Howard stated in an interview with *Newsday.* "The only thing I'm guilty of is getting the highest ratings the station ever had. The only thing I can think of is that somebody upstairs didn't agree with what I was doing. It was one of those things where they don't even give you a reason." Howard insisted that there were no conceptual differences: "Everyone knew where we were going."

All four of the New York dailies reported the story. The extent of the coverage appeared to surprise Tinker. Holding the Tuesday papers, the chairman entered Bongarten's office and asked his radio president how long it would take to "replace" Howard.

"We're going to put somebody on in there," Bongarten said, "but we're not going to 'replace' Howard."

"Oh," Tinker murmured—and walked out.

Tinker's name never became part of the story. The industry buzz was that RCA chairman Thornton Bradshaw held the smoking gun in Howard's dismissal. "I can honestly say I never heard Stern on the air," Bradshaw said a few days afterward. "I had heard *about* him, of course. That was a station decision."

The firing did not surprise Imus. The morning man maintained that Howard never would have sustained his ratings—a contrary view that probably intensified Howard's animosity toward his now former colleague. "You can't be negative every single day and make it," Imus said. "It works for a while. It did for me, but then I had to change my act. Instead of being dirty, I had to be funny."

Howard proclaimed his innocence in a stream of print and television interviews. He did not slink away and hide. "Robin and I are looking for work," he said on New York's WCBS-TV. "Please give me a job. . . . There's a huge audience for what I'm doing. I'm a damned good entertainer. I do want to work in New York."

At a press conference, his remarks reflected none of the hatred for WNBC that he later would express. He was hard-pressed to contain his disappointment that the station had let him go. Casting humor aside, he uncharacteristically revealed himself to be vulnerable—not the hardened rebel of the airwaves. "I have a reputation for nobody knowing how I feel," he said. "I am genuinely upset over this, mostly because I didn't know it was coming." He added: "It came out of the blue. Had I known it was in the works, I could have sat down with management and worked things out." He said that he had routinely complied with directives from his superiors, including the mundane requirement to air traffic reports as scheduled.

Although Hayes declared repeatedly that the firing was irrevocable, Howard went so far as to say publicly that he would like to talk with WNBC about a reconciliation. After all the warfare at WNBC, was Howard begging for a second chance?

He was hurt, because he sincerely wanted to work at WNBC. The station represented the big time, and he knew it. For all the difficulties that WNBC faced amid the exodus of listeners to FM radio, Howard recognized that only a few other stations had such a history and brand-name identity.

Howard was pleasantly overwhelmed by the surge of interest in his situation among the media and by the expressions of support from his fans. It wasn't as if he had fallen into a void; WNBC was obligated to pay him the final two years on his contract, around $400,000 a year, even if he chose to stay home and vegetate rather than to hook on elsewhere.

But Howard was too competitive, too shrewd in the ways of radio, to welcome his jobless status. Where was he going to work next? And how soon? New York wasn't Washington, where "DC-101" axed him when he was preparing to leave for a better gig. This time he had nothing lined up, no immediate prospect of holding on to his audience. This unsettled him, given the public's all-too-fickle attention span. To a friend who called him at home, he whined that he probably would never get another radio job in New York.

It would become Howard's custom to grant interviews when he had a pay-per-view special, a videotape, or a book to sell. Now, in search of a new job, he started to sell himself. As the novelty of the firing became last week's news, he kept his name and face before the public by appearing on Larry King's new interview show on CNN, by writing a humorous essay about his hiatus from radio for the *Daily News*, and by appearing on the TV program *Comedy Tonight*, where he bound host Bill Boggs in handcuffs and a leather S&M mask. He considered dates on the comedy club circuit, eventually agreeing to appear in November at Club Bene in New Jersey and the Candlewood Playhouse in Connecticut. At a Jersey show he dialed a phone-sex service and plugged the call into the club's sound system, treating his audience to a jolt of dirty talk free from FCC scrutiny. After three years of talking to New York-area listeners from a glassed-in studio, he was surprised to look out at paying customers and see that they included not only rowdy young men, but also well-dressed couples in their thirties and people his parents' age. After all the strife and turmoil, he realized that "real folks" enjoyed what he did.

Just as it had been unusual for WNBC to announce Howard's departure and to welcome comment on the decision, it was strange that he had been let go before the station found a successor to fill his time slot. Al Rosenberg and Fred Norris, who had not been fired, took over Howard's show on their own, and Gary Dell'Abate continued to serve as producer. Howard understood their need to stay on and collect a paycheck, especially Rosenberg, who had a family to support.

Hayes conceded that the station had yet to decide on its next move, but he predicted that Howard's permanent successor in afternoon drive would be "very high-profile." Parsons was ordered to ignore any candidate who was like Howard. This edict made the talent search difficult; as part of Parsons's contract with WNBC, he had earned bonus money whenever Howard improved his ratings among listeners twenty-five to fifty-four, and now the program director had to go out and find someone he was sure would be far less successful.

Parsons combed comedy clubs around the country. He dropped in unannounced and at prearranged auditions. He caught Elayne Boosler's act and called her. He also contacted Jay Leno, but the club-hopping comedian did not want to be tied down five days a week. George Carlin declined the job for the same reason.

Months into the search, the station settled on veteran disc jockey Joey Reynolds, whose string of radio jobs had taken him most recently to WKBW, in upstate Buffalo. His on-air troupe included Brett Butler, who did voices and wrote material (and later starred in the TV sitcom *Grace under Fire*).

Reynolds displayed manic energy on the air and loved to involve listeners in his show. But the ratings at WNBC began to sink. Without Howard's antics during the afternoon, the station was no longer top-of-the-mind. The bottom line suffered. In 1986, WNBC would show a loss of about $1.5 million, compared with the $4 million profit posted in 1984.

Howard would revel in the decline of his former employer and take much of the credit for the downturn. Resurfacing on radio weeks later, he repeatedly blamed NBC for boneheaded management, citing the decision to fire him. When Tinker's autobiography was published in 1994, Howard attacked the by now former NBC chairman on the air. Tinker's matter-of-fact description of Howard's dismissal, making it seem like the easiest decision in the world, could not go unaddressed after Howard had spent so much time through the years limning the image of NBC's great corporate power massed against him.

"Howard would like to believe that there was some earth-shattering reason that he was fired—but there really wasn't," Rukeyser said. "It was the least sexy reason in the world."

But the mystique of Howard's WNBC years would help him, probably more than if he had stayed and prospered at the station. To hear Howard tell the story time and again, WNBC was like his Bosnia, where he had to fight every day. The station's misfortunes in his absence became a yardstick by which he measured his own importance and ratings value. He would have the last laugh—being fired turned out to be the best thing that could have happened to him. The ouster defined who he was. It led him to an employer that had none of the scruples of NBC and a great desire to help make Howard Stern the king of radio.

THIRTEEN

Only one person in Howard's camp was not fretting over the dismissal from WNBC—his agent, Don Buchwald.

Buchwald had signed Howard as a client in 1984, succeeding Washington attorney Jeffrey Southmayd, who professed a lack of expertise in assessing some of the business offers that were coming in and was delighted to be free of his periodic trips to New York.

Buchwald had started in the entertainment business as an assistant to Harry Abrams, a principal in Abrams-Rubaloff & Associates Inc., a New York talent agency that counted WABC's Dan Ingram and other top disc jockeys among its clients. "He was an errand boy for Harry, the kind of guy who was easy to throw lines at and tease," one old-time radio executive recalled. "I would never have predicted Don's own extraordinary success. I didn't think he was tough enough."

However, Ingram and other agency clients grew fond of Buchwald, who was personable, smart, and tougher than he had let on. As a result, when Abrams and his partner in Hollywood, Noel Rubaloff, had a disagreement that threatened to disrupt their business, Buchwald was in a position to benefit.

"We were having lunch at the Friars Club when Don asked me what I would do if the agency broke up," Ingram remembered. "I told him, 'I don't know about the others, but I'm going with you.'

Don said, 'Do you mean that?' I did—and I've been with him since the day he started his own agency."

Don Buchwald & Associates Inc. was opened in New York in 1976, the year before Abrams and Rubaloff ended their partnership. Besides signing Ingram and other radio personalities who had been in the Abrams-Rubaloff fold, Buchwald actively recruited clients. Radio was at the low end of the entertainment industry, so most of the top show-business agents ignored the medium and its talent. In addition, many New York radio broadcasters were comfortable enough in their jobs that they declined representation sooner than part with an agent's fee.

Buchwald, on the other hand, recognized that radio broadcasters formed a lucrative market. They usually signed contracts that ran for three years or more, thereby guaranteeing him a 10 percent fee over the length of a deal based on only one negotiation. In addition, Buchwald specialized in a related field, supplying talent for commercial voice-overs and thereby generating bigger revenues for his clients and himself. In New York, the center of the advertising industry, the production of TV and radio commercials created a constant demand for voices. A man or woman booked to narrate a commercial that went into wide distribution stood to reap an attractive sum in fees and residuals. "Don was the top guy," said Ted Brown, a client who was the morning man for many years on WNEW-AM and the voice heard on dozens of national campaigns. "If you wanted to get the most out of the station you worked for, and you wanted to do commercials, too, you went to Don."

As Buchwald saw it, his primary role was to build a client's career over the long haul. He showed a special interest in personalities who demonstrated to him that they had staying power. One of them was Howard Stern. Buchwald thought he was an original who, the agent later said, "would be able to sustain for Johnny Carson-type years with perhaps even broader success."

"Don believed in him from the minute he heard him," a friend and client of the agent remembered. "He saw the Howard Stern thing taking off early on, while I told him that his longevity would probably be a minute and a half."

Buchwald advised Howard on matters large and small. He had negotiated with Bongarten the three-year contract that Howard signed with WNBC early in 1985. He suggested that the lazily dressed disc jockey buy neater clothes to wear at the growing number of business meetings he had to attend.

Howard listened to Buchwald.

It was one of the smartest things he ever did.

The day after Howard was fired, Buchwald took a call from Mel Karmazin, then executive vice president of Infinity Broadcasting Corp. Infinity was a struggling player in New York radio, but the two men had a relationship that dated to the 1970s, when Karmazin ran rock station WNEW-FM and the legendary WNEW-AM, a longtime outlet for Frank Sinatra's music and disc jockeys William B. Williams, Ted Brown, and Jonathan Schwartz. Now, in October 1985, Karmazin wanted to talk about hiring Howard Stern.

That Howard was regarded as a pariah by many in the radio industry did not bother Karmazin, a blunt bottom-liner who courted no one's favor and saw both a strategic and a public relations advantage in signing a renegade. Six years earlier, when weatherman Bob Harris was fired by *The New York Times* and WCBS-TV for misrepresenting his academic credentials, Karmazin swiftly put him on WNEW-AM. He argued that Harris was the best forecaster in New York and ran print ads that said "He may be off a degree, but . . . " Karmazin's similar interest in Howard would become even more important to the disc jockey's career than Buchwald's shrewd representation.

Karmazin had a problem and needed a solution. The glory days of Infinity's costly FM station, WKTU in New York, were long gone. Under the previous ownership of SJR Communications Inc., the outlet had junked a mellow-rock format on July 24, 1978, and switched to a souped-up disco sound ("Disco 92") that immediately hooked a huge segment of the urban audience. The format made history in its first full report card, soaring to number one in the market with an 11.3 percent share during the fall of 1978 from a previous 1.4. It was the highest rating ever achieved by an FM station in New York, booting WABC, the Top 40 powerhouse, from the lead position for the first time in more than a decade.

Recording artists such as Donna Summer and Chic provided WKTU's musical pulse, and a multiethnic array of disc jockeys, such as Paco ("This is the hour of *love*. Come to Paco"), called the tunes. WKTU burned so hot that by the time SJR Communications sold the station to Infinity, in 1981, the price of $15.5 million was a record sum for a single radio outlet. As Infinity closed on its purchase, part of a $32 million package that also included New York's WJIT-AM and Philadelphia's WYSP-FM, the principals in the company, Michael A. Wiener and Gerald Carrus, wanted to expand their business instead of holding the outlets in order to sell them at a higher price later. To operate the Infinity stations, they lured Karmazin away from WNEW in November to serve in a dual role as general manager of WKTU and president of Infinity's radio division with a three-year deal that initially paid him $125,000 annually. "You can't have three people run a company," Karmazin recalled. "Wiener and Carrus were gracious—and they turned out to be very smart, because not many people would give up operating control of their company."

On the highly competitive New York dial, Infinity in 1984 responded to the revived popularity of Top 40 in the postdisco era by adding mainstream pop to WKTU's dance-oriented format. The resulting hodgepodge did not stem WKTU's downward slide in the ratings as the true Top 40 outlets, WHTZ ("Z-100") and WPLJ ("Power 95"), dominated the market. In addition to Infinity's ratings woes, the company encountered a gnawing perception among advertisers that WKTU's largely urban audience was undesirable. What to do?

In the spring of 1985, when Howard was at the peak of his ratings at WNBC, Infinity commissioned a study of New York–area men who were sixteen to thirty-four years old and described themselves as fans of rock music. The study, prepared by FMR Associates Inc., of Tucson, Arizona, found a strong potential for a new rock-and-roll radio station, largely because WNEW-FM ("Where Rock Lives"), the favorite outlet among the surveyed group, enjoyed a weakening level of listener loyalty after eighteen years on the air. Its so-called default appeal stemmed from a widely held belief among men that it was the only station of its kind available. According to FMR Associates, a new rock station that favored more of the older, classic rock tunes could expect to draw about half of its audience from WNEW-FM.

Infinity reacted quickly to the encouraging survey, which it received in June 1985. On July 13, the company dropped the WKTU call letters and all that they represented, renaming the station WXRK and nicknaming it "K-Rock." Like WNEW-FM, "K-Rock" offered an album-rock format, but it leaned more toward the tried and familiar. It played entire sides of famous albums during the evening hours.

Howard, still at WNBC, was amused. He made fun of WKTU as its ratings slipped. When the WKTU disc jockey Rosko (Mercer), a black man, was fired by Infinity for insubordination—he alleged on the air that Karmazin had been "motivated racially" to change the format—Howard invited the jock to his own program to dish dirt. Infinity was "an embarrassment, let's face it," Howard told Rosko. WKTU once was "worth eleven or twelve million dollars a year in [commercial] billings, and they blew the whole thing, man. I think that's pretty awesome." Howard went on to tell his listeners that Rosko had had the bad luck to be "linked up with the likes of Infinity Broadcasting, which has zero money."

If Karmazin even heard these insults, it was a measure of his competitive instincts that he did not let them stand in the way of business. For now, three months later, Karmazin wanted Howard to help shore up Infinity's big investment in "K-Rock." As Karmazin later recalled, "Howard was a very popular radio disc jockey on an existing radio station and with a very large following of advertisers, and that was what we were aware of." In particular, Karmazin was struck by Howard's large following among men eighteen to thirty-

Howard Stern in his 1972 gradu-
ation photo at South Side Senior
High School, Rockville Centre,
New York.

(Courtesy of Seth Poppel Yearbook Archives)

Stern, in 1980, when he was the morning man on
WWWW-FM in Detroit, on his knees begging TV view-
ers to tune into his show.   (Courtesy of WXYZ-TV)

Stern, in 1977, on the air at WRNW-FM in Briarcliff Manor, New York. "To see
him back then was like seeing a Beavis and Butt-head nerd kind of guy," a colleague remembers. "He had thick glasses and was much heavier. His short hair
was like Brillo."   (Fred Conrad/NYT Pictures)

A comedy album, the first product in a long line of merchandise, was released during Stern's stint at Washington's WWDC-FM (1981-1982). In 1994, the recording was rereleased as "Unclean Beaver."
(Courtesy of Citizen X Records)

Stern received $1,000 in 1984 to appear as a wacky newscaster, whom he named Ben Wah, in an independent film, *Ryder, P.I.* "I'm proud to be in it," he told his listeners when the detective spoof was released in 1986.
(Courtesy of YGB Distribution Inc.)

Randall D. Bongarten (center), general manager of New York's WNBC-AM, "apologizes" in a TV commercial to a long list of those ridiculed on the air by his morning man Don Imus, yawning at left, and Stern, the afternoon-drive host. The commercial was significant because it marked the first time that Stern received star billing alongside the influential Imus. (Courtesy of Advertising Agency: Penchina, Selkowitz, Inc.)

Photos of Stern and Imus later were paired on billboards for WNBC that repeated the station's slogan, "If we weren't so bad, we wouldn't be so good."
(Courtesy of Advertising Agency: Penchina, Selkowitz, Inc.)

Stern and his on-air crew in a 1990 team photo. From left, in front: Gary Dell'Abate, Fred Norris, and Jackie Martling; Stern is flanked by Robin Quivers and Stuttering John Melendez. (DMI)

Above: Robin Quivers was teamed with Stern on Washington's WWDC-FM in 1981. Except for a brief separation in 1982, they have worked together ever since. (Noah K. Murray/*Asbury Park Press*)

Inset: Robin Quivers after she joined the Air Force in 1975 as a second lieutenant. A nurse at the time, she was assigned to the United States Air Force Medical Center at Wright-Patterson Air Force Base near Dayton, Ohio. (National Personnel Records Center)

Stern wore prison stripes at a 1987 rally in New York's Dag Hammarskjold Plaza held to protest the Federal Communications Commission's ruling that his show had aired "indecent material." Addressing a crowd of about 3,000 supporters and those listening on the radio, he asked, "Is it spelled FCC or KGB?"
(AP/Wide World Photos)

Above: Stern, who played with puppets as a youngster, does so again in 1984 with his first child, Emily, then seventeen months old, and his wife, Alison. After Emily was born, he sometimes watched her with wonder for hours at a time, explaining, "It's just when I'm on the air that I start to froth at the mouth." (Ken Regan/Camera 5)

Right: Howard and Alison Stern. (Ari Mintz/*Newsday*)

Right: In one of their rare public outings, Howard (conspicuously without shades) and Alison meet Joan Rivers backstage in 1994 after seeing the comedienne in her Broadway show, *Sally Marr…and Her Escorts*. Rivers presented the couple with a cake marking their sixteenth wedding anniversary. (Aubrey Reuben)

Below: At a New York party in 1993 celebrating publication of his first book, *Private Parts*, Stern was joined by two of his fellow Long Island residents, Mary Jo and Joey Buttafuoco, the couple made famous by the Amy Fisher scandal.
(Robert Clark for the *Chicago Tribune*)

Howard and his parents, Ben and Ray Stern, in their bedroom on Long Island. "My father yelled at me, yes, but I see that he cared about me," Howard said. "With my mother, it's a true, unconditional, unselfish love, and when you have that kind of love, things do go right in your life."

(Ari Mintz/*Newsday*)

Dressed like a beauty queen in floor-length gown, fake diamond tiara, and long gloves, Stern arrives at a Fifth Avenue bookstore in 1995 for the first signing of his new hardcover, *Miss America*. Thousands of fans lined up for six blocks waiting for his autograph.

(AP/Wide World Photos)

Stern in 1992 with his closest adviser and deal-maker—the man he calls "superagent"—Don Buchwald. (DMI)

Mel A. Karmazin, now the president of Infinity Broadcasting Corp., salvaged and propelled Stern's career in 1985 by hiring the fired broadcaster for New York's WXRK-FM and giving him broad license to be outrageous on the air. (Chuck Pulin)

Stern claims victory after winning the Libertarian Party's 1994 nomination for governor of New York at the group's convention in Albany. He promised to restore the death penalty, quicken traffic flow, and ensure that road construction took place only at night. (Tim Roske)

Above Left: Is Howard at home? The neglected house in Plainview, Long Island, as it appeared in 1994. Stern claimed the dwelling as his voting address in order to avoid listing his real residence on filing papers for governor. (Paul D. Colford)

Above Right: John S. Hagelin, the 1992 presidential candidate of the Natural Law Party, advocated a greater use of Transcendental Meditation and wanted all candidates to undergo an electroencephalogram to determine their stability in a crisis. Howard and Alison, who also practice TM, each contributed $250 to Hagelin's campaign, even though Howard said on the air that he backed Bill Clinton. (Courtesy of John S. Hagelin)

After dropping out of the race for governor, Stern backed George Pataki, who went on to defeat Mario Cuomo in the 1994 election. Stern's support on the air earned him one of the best seats on the dais when Pataki was sworn in (above). Speaking to Mrs. Pataki on the radio, Stern said, "You're a very sexy woman."
(Dan Goodrich/*Newsday*)

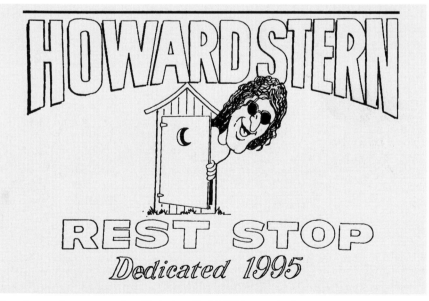

Stern's on-air support for Christine Todd Whitman in her victorious 1993 campaign for governor of New Jersey was recognized two years later when she named a highway rest stop after him in the rural community of Springfield Township. An aluminum plaque depicted Stern at an outhouse door. "I've always dreamt of a rest stop that I would drive by with my family and people could relieve themselves while they see my name," Stern said. (AP/Wide World Photos)

A Rogues' Gallery
of Influences

Bob Grant, now on WABC, joined the New York radio dial in 1970. Stern listened to him first on WMCA, where the acerbic talk-show host presented staunch conservative views and often berated his callers. Stern later said in an interview that he "always admired" Grant.
(Courtesy of WABC-AM)

Alex Bennett brought a hip, irreverent sensibility to the talk format when Stern listened to him on New York's WMCA and WPLJ in the 1960s and 1970s. Although Bennett influenced Stern's radio style and was saluted by the disc jockey on WNBC, Stern later claimed that Bennett was copying him.
(Courtesy of Alex Bennett)

Steve Dahl, the Chicago radio legend. While working in Hartford during the late 1970s, Stern listened to tapes of Dahl's wild broadcasts on Chicago's WLUP-FM. They later competed on the Detroit and Chicago dials. Each accused the other of stealing their act.
(Courtesy of WMVP Radio)

Joe Piasek, known as "Joe from Chicago" when he worked with Stern as an innovative disc jockey and program director of WRNW-FM in the mid-1970s. Piasek, who nicknamed Howard "Howeird," inspired the timid Stern to loosen his approach on the air and to take the first steps toward developing his crazed radio persona.
("Joe from Chicago" Archives WPIX-FM New York, circa 1978)

The King of All Media, 1993.

(Ari Mintz/*Newsday*)

four years old, the same audience that the new "K-Rock" was trying to reach as a result of the confidence-building consultant's survey.

Karmazin had seen the future, and it was in quality demographics, not quantity of listeners: a select audience, not mass appeal. Why fuss around trying to nurture and develop a sound that would appeal to your target audience when you could simply hire the guy who already had that audience? Why wait for a rookie pitcher to mature when you could sign a free agent with a blazing fastball?

Although Karmazin had reason to believe that he was the only serious suitor for Howard's services—rock station WAPP-FM also approached Howard—the executive was unable to cut a deal quickly. Buchwald extended the discussions as Karmazin considered the financial impact of hiring Howard and his crew.

At the time, "K-Rock" was paying its morning man, Jay Thomas, $260,000 a year. Dan Ingram, whose stint in afternoon drive had stretched only from January until the format switch in July, had been hired at the rate of $300,000 a year. These were the station's top salaries (both men were clients of Buchwald), but they paled alongside Howard's WNBC deal, which was still earning him around $400,000 a year and had two more years that his former employer was obligated to pay.

In an astute move, Buchwald gave Karmazin written testimonials from advertisers who had bought time on Howard's WNBC program. They emphasized that Howard had been good for their businesses and that they were prepared to advertise with him again. Impressed with the evidence, Karmazin overcame his caution about spending a lot of money to sign Stern. In addition, Karmazin came to believe that sooner or later he would be able to take full advantage of Howard's drawing power by moving him to mornings in place of Thomas.

Eager to get back on the air, Howard agreed to a contract that initially was to pay him what he described as a "hefty six-figure amount"—most likely $500,000—and escalating amounts in successive years. Like Buchwald, he was beginning to see that being fired by WNBC was the best thing for his career.

The station's records show that Robin Quivers, incorporated as R.O.Q. Inc. (Robin Ophelia Quivers) and being represented by Buchwald, signed for $100,000 the first year and $150,000 the next. Fred (Earth Dog Fred) Norris, who had lingered with Al Rosenberg in the afternoon slot at WNBC, followed Howard to "K-Rock" for $85,000 in the first year and $105,000 for the second.

Not until Howard was on the air for a few days did he persuade his new employers that he again had to have Gary Dell'Abate, his WNBC producer, to help organize the show. They relented. "Boy Gary," who had hung on at WNBC in misery, finally made the switch, at a salary of $27,000.

WNBC agreed to let Howard out of his contract so that he could join "K-Rock." He was sure to present strong competition, but WNBC wanted to save the money it otherwise would have to pay him. In addition, Bongarten, who had been reluctant to fire him, did not wish to stymie his career. (The two remained friends.)

On November 6, 1985, "K-Rock" announced at a press conference in the Beanstalk restaurant, on Avenue of the Americas near WNBC, that Howard would take over the 2:00–6:00 P.M. slot starting November 18. "Howard can do whatever he wants," Tom Chiusano, the station's vice president and general manager, declared. "You don't hire a great sculptor and tell him to paint."

Howard, dressed in black suede pants and a black suede jacket, promised that his first day back "will be really unique—it will be a Roman orgy." He stated that AM radio was dead and could not be revived: "I'm thrilled to be on FM radio in New York. 'K-Rock' is the right format, has the best music, the best sound, is the best station, and I hope I don't get fired."

Chiusano characterized Howard as "the final building block in 'K-Rock's' foundation." Others at the station were less certain. "I remember at first, no one could believe that Howard had been hired," recalled disc jockey Meg Griffin, who had worked with him at WRNW in Westchester and now would be doing the program before his. "I remember feeling a certain amount of respect for Mel Karmazin, seeing that he did not let his ego get in the way of good business, but I was confused. What did the arrival of Howard mean for the future of music at the station?"

"The music on 'K-Rock' really agrees with us, and I'm looking forward to mixing up some records with what we do," Howard said. "I think that will be real strong."

In the beginning, at least, Howard played four or five songs an hour by Stevie Nicks, Tom Petty, Aerosmith, and the others on the station's playlist. He kept the rock in "K-Rock," dismissing as "junk" the pop music he'd had to play for three years at WNBC. Moreover, Howard shared with his listeners the surprise that "K-Rock" management was not weighing him down with rules and warnings. On his first afternoon back on the air after a seven-week absence, he complained about his lack of office space and the inferior quality of the studio equipment, which he had to operate himself, in lieu of the engineers who had worked on his broadcast at WNBC. That said, he offered a warm review of his new environment—from the "pert breasts" of his female program director, Pat Evans, to Chiusano's encouraging pep talk.

He also attacked WNBC. Revealing a continued ignorance that Tinker had ordered the firing, he cited a published theory blaming an "RCA board member," who was said to have belatedly discovered his show during a limousine ride. Then, addressing his former employer, he said in a sinister tone: "I will devote my night and my day to the destruction of your radio station."

As for Tinker, on learning that Howard had landed at "K-Rock," he asked an associate to make him a tape of the new show. The chairman later returned the cassette with a note stating that he believed no one would ever listen to that stuff.

FOURTEEN

The presence of Howard Stern on "K-Rock" represented aggres-
sive programming and Infinity Broadcasting's determination to stiff
out any protests. Not that the posture was new to the company.

Jay Thomas worked on New York's WXLO-FM before going to
Hollywood in 1979 to join Robin Williams and the cast of TV's *Mork
& Mindy*—he played Remo DaVinci, the deli owner. After Infinity
took over WKTU in 1981, Karmazin hired Thomas as the morning
man. He presented characters such as Dr. Chu Hung Lo, a sex thera-
pist, and Buck Ramos, a Latino from space, all the while maintaining
that he had no desire to offend listeners with risqué material. However, Thomas's occasionally blunt comments angered blacks and
Hispanics, who constituted a sizable portion of the station's audience. When Eartha Kitt released "Where Is My Man?" in 1983,
Thomas said that the black, felinelike singer was one of the ugliest
women he had ever seen. "Where is her man?" he said. "Honey,
you're as ugly as the pope." His remark drew the editorial wrath of
the *Amsterdam News*, New York's black-oriented newspaper.

Thomas continued to work mornings after WKTU became
WXRK ("K-Rock") in 1985 and Howard added his own politically in-
correct commentary to afternoon drive. Two weeks into his stint,
Howard told a caller to his show that WKTU had been a popular sta-
tion, "but the only thing they had listening to them was blacks and
Puerto Ricans."

"That isn't bad," Robin said.

"No, that isn't bad, but you just go try to sell advertising time when you got blacks and Puerto Ricans listening." Howard assumed a caricature: "Excuse me, man, but would you like to buy some Afro-Sheen?" He added: "They were smart to get rid of that disco format. . . . even when they were a big station, how much money could you make selling Afro-Sheen?"

It was well documented in the radio industry that highly rated black-oriented stations routinely trailed less popular white-oriented outlets in advertising revenue. Stations with a large minority audience have greater difficulty attracting commercial dollars commensurate with their ratings. Howard's awareness of this fact, conveyed in a crude manner, was singled out by the black disc jockey Rosko as he pressed complaints against Infinity, alleging racial discrimination and breach of contract in connection with his being fired from the old WKTU in 1985. When Rosko was rebuffed by the New York State Division of Human Rights and the Equal Employment Opportunity Commission, he then sued Infinity in U.S. District Court.* Asked by Rosko's attorney for a response to Howard's Afro-Sheen remark, Karmazin conceded that "it may be racially offensive to some people, yes." Asked if the comment would cause him to reassess the employment of Stern, Karmazin said: "No, I don't believe so . . . because this is a country where people are entitled to First Amendment rights and those opinions reflect his opinion." He maintained that Howard's comment did not reflect upon management of the radio station. "It reflects Howard Stern's opinion." As far as Karmazin was concerned, "Howard, in our belief, is not a racist."

---

*Karmazin and Infinity vigorously defended themselves against Rosko's suit for years. However, after the case was cleared for trial, the parties in 1991 agreed to an out-of-court settlement. But the matter did not end there. The once-confidential settlement—Infinity had paid Rosko $137,500 for his legal fees—was described in a 1993 breach-of-contract suit filed in New York State Supreme Court against Rosko by Infinity. This time, Infinity alleged that the disc jockey had violated the terms of their 1991 agreement when he charged in a 1993 complaint to the New York City Commission on Human Rights that his former employer had refused to hire him (back) "because of his race and color." By December 1995, Rosko's complaint had been dismissed and Infinity's suit was still pending.

In depositions and other forums, Karmazin would continue to defend Howard, and he would do so on a grander and costlier scale when the disc jockey's program caused the Federal Communications Commission to levy escalating fines for indecency against Infinity.

The indecency charges would reflect the increasing frankness and frat-house antics on Howard's show. Soon after he started on "K-Rock," he translated his special interest in sex between women into a game of dial-a-date that featured three members of the rock group Bon Jovi. Female callers to his show competed for a chance to date Jon Bon Jovi, Richie Sambora, and Dave Bryan by agreeing that they would have sex with another woman and then answering questions posed by Howard and the musicians.

One caller said she would go to bed with another woman if Jon Bon Jovi watched. She was asked to reveal her measurements, when she'd last had sex, and whether she shaved "that thang." She stated: "All I can say is that if he wants a nice-looking redhead with a nice ass who could knock his socks off, I'm it."

Another woman, following instructions, said she had taken her pants off and was sitting atop her stereo speaker with the volume turned up high. At this point Howard and his guests made vibrator noises while urging the woman to moo like a cow. Which, of course, she did.

What homebound commuter, hearing this lunacy on his car radio, would not stay tuned, at least for a while, simply out of curiosity?

That was the idea!

As radio theater, specifically as radio theater designed to draw young male listeners (and the advertisers that wanted to reach them), this dial-a-date revealed Howard's effective strategy of leading his audience along. He teased listeners with sexual come-ons over an extended period of time in his show, thereby carrying along an audience through successive quarter hours (the units of time measured by the Arbitron ratings service). His following, though large in number, would send his ratings skyward mainly because fans spent *more time* listening to his show than, for example, audiences spent tuned to all-news radio.

One female contestant, when asked to moan as though she were having sex, complained: "Why do you want to do this to me?"

"Because we want to get ratings," Howard said.

Howard was warming up on "K-Rock" while Jay Thomas was cooling off as he neared his fourth anniversary as Infinity's morning man. Howard was testing the limits of what he could get away with as Thomas was feeling management's squeeze on his own comedic license. Behind the scenes, "K-Rock" was talking with Steve Dahl about joining the station as morning man, a move that would have put the Chicago radio star in the New York spotlight alongside Howard. However, contractual wrinkles prevented Dahl from pursuing the discussions, and he left Chicago's WLS-AM/FM to rejoin WLUP-FM.

Although "K-Rock" had no successor standing by, Thomas became history on January 6, 1986. Chiusano, the station's general manager, said that "it just wasn't working." He noted that Thomas's ratings paled alongside the numbers "K-Rock" was pulling during the rest of the day. It was an unpardonable offense: the morning hours are radio prime time, and a morning show is expected to set the station's pace.

Thomas received a large severance check and publicly thanked Karmazin for being generous. Nevertheless, it bugged Thomas to be leaving because of a different set of rules. "It's impossible to know what they want," he told a reporter. "On the same day that Howard Stern did his lesbian dial-a-date, I was told I couldn't say my 'If you don't believe it, stuff it' bit." Thomas complained that management "shut me up" by limiting his mike time to eighteen seconds—and only if he had "a really good bit."

It was a peculiar charge, especially considering that Thomas, who did stand-up comedy, had established himself as a funny jock known to take time with his material. But radio is a cruel business. Infinity saw a bigger opportunity in morning drive, though Chiusano declined to forecast the station's next move. Sure, Howard would be a great morning man, Chiusano said, but he was not offering to take the job.

Thomas joked about his situation in a phone conversation on the air with Howard during the afternoon show. Their joviality betrayed no hint of the hostility that would develop between them after Thomas returned to Los Angeles and achieved great success on radio and in TV sitcoms. Their relationship would resemble Howard's involvement with Soupy Sales: initial camaraderie followed by nasty squabbling. (In a radio exchange five years later, he told Thomas, who was the morning man on Los Angeles' KPWR-FM and had roles on the sitcoms *Cheers* and *Murphy Brown*, that he was "a bargain-basement Soupy Sales. . . . You're only good at reading other people's lines." Thomas replied: "You're an evil, evil individual. . . . You lie constantly.")

A month passed with Jimmy Fink, a rock veteran and an early addition to "K-Rock," doing the morning show. Meanwhile, Howard discussed on his own program whether he should switch to mornings. It would mean having to retire in early evening and drag himself out of bed in the chilly darkness before dawn. Finally, the competitive bug got to him. Although he had been able to sleep, eat, and socialize when most people did during his three and a half years hosting an afternoon show—that is, live a normal life—he recognized that the real action was in morning radio. Besides, a return to dawn patrol would allow him to go up against Imus on WNBC and prove once and for all that his former employer had been stupid to treat him as the I-Man's understudy. Revenge would be sweet.

The word went out that Howard would become the new "K-Rock" morning man starting February 17, 1986. Fifteen years after Imus had come to New York radio and changed the dial forever with his bellicose style, the stage was set for an even more radical overhaul that over time would help to loosen on-air behavior around the nation.

As part of the transition to the more competitive morning hours, Howard received permission to hire a writer as the fifth player on his team. He reached back to his Washington days and chose Steve Chaconas, the former member of the "Think Tank" on "DC-101," who had remained a friend. At the time, the twenty-nine-year-old was working in the hospital supplies business.

Chaconas planned to commute from Washington instead of re-locating. He boarded a train in the capital on Sunday nights, slept en route, awakened in the bowels of New York's Penn Station around 4:00 A.M., and headed to the "K-Rock" studios to prepare for the 6:00 A.M. sign-on. During the week, he lived with Fred, then flew home for the weekend.

One of Chaconas's contributions was a game of "Filipino Family Feud," presented when Corazon Aquino became president of the Philippines in early 1986, succeeding the ousted Ferdinand Marcos. Asked by host "Richard Dawson" for the best way to defeat a political opponent, "Corazon" said that one should clearly define a campaign platform. Chaconas originally wrote the skit so that "Marcos" was to say that you should gun down your enemies on the tarmac, a reference to the 1983 assassination of Corazon Aquino's husband, Benigno, at an airport in the Philippines. Howard re-worked the punch line so that "Marcos's" answer was that the candidate should wrap piano wire around the opponent's private parts.

Howard demonstrated that, as host of the morning show, he bore the responsibility for its success or failure. "If someone came in and complained about getting a parking ticket or something, Howard would cut him off," Chaconas said. "He'd say, 'Let's stay on target. We have a show to do.' He was like the quarterback of a foot-ball team."

Soon the quarterback seemed to conclude that Chaconas's fractured existence between New York and Washington prevented the writer from giving his best performance. "As a writer on the show, you had to be part of everything, see everything, and try to find material in current events," Chaconas said. "It was hard for me to adjust. Howard wanted me to be on the air more. He basically wanted me to replace Al Rosenberg, but we never clearly defined my role. Besides that, I wasn't happy commuting, even though I might have gotten used to it."

A few weeks into Chaconas's stint, he was finished. "Howard told me it wasn't working out," he said. "He was good to me—and I was happy that the word came from him directly."

Chaconas went to work for Infinity Broadcasting again, as program director and anchor of Washington's WPGC-AM, a business-news station. After its format changed in 1995, he joined another Washington-area station, WBZS-AM, which added business programming.

Listeners who have tuned in Howard's New York show since the beginning now think of Chaconas in the same way that the Beatles fans remember drummer Pete Best, the original "Fifth Beatle," who was jettisoned to make way for Ringo Starr. In Howard's autobiographical *Private Parts*, published in 1993, he mentions Chaconas only in passing (misspelling his name)—in connection with the "Think Tank." However, the reference was noticed by some of Chaconas's Washington colleagues, who suddenly viewed him as one who had worked with the Master. To Chaconas, it was all very amusing. He stayed in touch with Howard, saying, "I only have fond memories of him."

Chaconas's departure cleared the way for Jackie Martling, who had remained a contributor since the WNBC days, to join the show as a writer. He had earned little more than carfare when he visited Howard's show at WNBC, using the exposure to promote his club dates and merchandise. After being added to the "K-Rock" payroll in August as Off Hour Rockers Inc., the name of his business, he earned nearly $35,000 for the balance of 1986 and $78,000 in 1987. The sums were significantly less than those paid to Robin and Fred. Indeed, as the years passed, Jackie would gripe to station management about his compensation, pointing out that he had become an indispensable member of the Stern gang and deserved more.

Seated opposite Howard in the Madison Avenue studio, Jackie would go through a thick stack of writing paper each morning as he scribbled one-liners, puns, and other nonsense on sheet after sheet and passed them over to his boss. By Howard's own estimate, he used 95 percent of Jackie's material. Listeners often could hear Howard crumpling one of Jackie's pages and tossing it away. After more than four hours of this, the floor would be carpeted with paper, requiring an immediate cleanup before the disc jockey scheduled after Howard could begin his or her show in the same studio. "That was a travesty as far as the trees were concerned, to see Jackie's one-sheets lying all over the floor," said disc jockey Meg Griffin, who worked at "K-Rock" and often had to endure Howard's verbal abuse.

As Jackie became the quick-thinking joke machine who constantly added to Howard's cornucopia of nutty material, Robin still functioned as his sounding board and news reader, and Fred continued to pepper the show with sound effects, prepared sketches, and song parodies. It was a measure of Fred's shyness as a person and modesty as a performer—a true sidekick—that he remained content to give *The Howard Stern Show* the fruits of his own creative genius. It was Fred who stepped in with memorable mischief as fans of the Rolling Stones and rock stations eagerly awaited the release in 1986 of the band's new record, "Harlem Shuffle"—a Stones video was to introduce the song during the Grammy Awards telecast. In advance of the premiere, Fred took a copy of Bob and Earl's original 1963 version of the rhythm-and-blues tune and recorded a rendition with a band in the way that he expected the Stones would perform it. The finished product, aired as an "exclusive" during Howard's show on the day before the Grammys, sounded so much like Mick Jagger and company that competing stations complained to Columbia Records that "K-Rock" had been given first crack at the release. The record company begged Howard to reveal his scam—and he did, eventually. Score one for Howard and the gang.

Besides Fred, Jackie, Robin, and Boy Gary, a fifth person inter-
acted with Howard—in the unenviable role of doormat. Susan
Berkley was a reporter for Shadow Traffic, the radio service that
monitored road and transit conditions and provided periodic commuter reports on stations throughout the New York area. "At the
time, I was the program director at Shadow, so I basically put myself
on Howard's show," she recalled. "I was a fan of the show, but I was
shocked at first when I went on with him."

It seemed that nothing was off limits. As Berkley sat and talked
with Howard from Shadow's Union, New Jersey, studios, he called
her "Susan Berserkowitz" and asked—on the air, of course—about
her sex life, her menstrual cycle, and other female matters. The segments were among the lewdest that would be heard on Howard's
show. Jackie dashed off litanies of insults that Howard rapid-fired
at Berkley, such as, "Hey, Susan, may you French-kiss a thousand
toothless grandmothers."

Berkley's experience with the daily onslaught revealed that
Howard's outrageousness was designed mainly for shock value—in
the same way that a youngster might use a four-letter word to get a
rise out of people. "I called him up after the show at one point and
said I didn't want to be on anymore, and he said to me, 'It's all a
joke. Don't take it personal,'" Berkley recalled. "The first time I went
to the station to meet him, I looked the guy in the face and I saw the
sweetest man in the world. He made me feel as though I were an
integral part of the show."

By calming Berkley, and convincing her that his intentions
were purely showbiz, he was able to develop the playful tension
between them into a kind of serial drama. How far would he go to
humiliate her? How would she react to his sexist attacks? Howard
knew better than anyone that it made for good radio theater, just
like dial-a-date. He was the master at this sort of thing.

What's more, by tweaking Berkley time and again, he took control of the traffic breaks and prevented them from slowing down the
program. "They call it a traffic break because it breaks us down, it

breaks us from our comedy flow," he once said. Berkley recalled: "I tried to do my job, but I rarely got the chance to give a traffic report." Instead, their exchanges "had an interesting effect," she said. "People cheered me on. Some could relate to what I had to put up with on the air. They basically liked the interplay."

When listeners were invited to request photographs of Berkley, hundreds did so. Howard also used her during his personal appearances, including a date at Club Bene, in South Amboy, New Jersey. Her baton twirling was part of the night's entertainment. Crude as many of Howard's comments were, she became satisfied that he was "all an act." She left Shadow Traffic and the show in the fall of 1987 to open her own business, saying Howard was "actually the sweetest person off the air."

Others were less comfortable with Howard's assaults. "Off the air, Howard came across as a sweet, laid-back family man," former "K-Rock" disc jockey Stephen Capen remembered. "But on the air, he used to come at me like a piranha." For example, Capen was seeking a reconciliation with his ex-wife, who had worked with Howard years earlier. During on-air conversations with Capen, Howard expressed a sexual desire for the woman and asked him how she was in bed. The ease that existed between Howard and Berkley was absent here. "Howard never made sure that I knew it was all fun and games," Capen said. The bawdy remarks so unsettled the ex-wife that Capen asked Chiusano to have Howard back off. Howard complied.

"My God, this is a real movie!" Howard said when he saw the opening minutes of *Ryder, P.I.* in a film editing room. "My agent's going to kill me."

In the fall of 1984, Howard was paid $1,000 to appear in the detective spoof. He showed up at a Long Island production studio and in about ninety minutes completed his wacky portrayal of a TV news anchorman, whom he wanted to name "E. Rection" but ultimately agreed to call "Ben Wah" (as in ben wah balls, the sexual device). Now, in the spring of 1986, as *Ryder, P.I.* was nearing release in theaters, he saw that it was not a low-budget student film like the one he'd made at Boston University.

Karl Hosch, the producer and codirector, had raised a six-figure sum, mainly from friends and relatives, to make the movie. To avoid using a lot of costly film, he took what was then the novel step of shooting the action on videotape and transferring the finished footage to 35-millimeter film for theater projection. He drew on his close ties to New York and Long Island comedy circles to cast the story with stand-ups such as Bob Nelson, Max Alexander, Jackie Martling (in a voice-over), and Dave Hawthorne (as the pudgy and incompetent sleuth Sky Ryder). Hawthorne, who had appeared on Howard's WNBC show, helped to arrange the broadcaster's cameo appearance as Ben Wah.

"It's a funny movie," Howard told his listeners. "I'm proud to be in it."

At the time of its release in 1986, Howard was successful enough to be wary of association with just any old project, especially one from a journeyman period of his career. He asked Hosch, who lived near him in Nassau County, to refrain from publicizing the Stern connection to *Ryder, P.I.* unless it was a hit.

"It was a mistake on my part to go along with that request," Hosch recalled. The Stern connection could have gone a long way to help the independent film survive and prosper among the more heavily financed releases backed by major Hollywood studios. Still, it looked as though *Ryder, P.I.* was going to buck the odds and break through. A favorable screening for representatives of the major theater chains resulted in the film being booked on thirty-one screens in the New York area, an impressively wide release for an independent, let alone one that the filmmaker was distributing himself. By Hosch's estimate, he spent $60,000 in print advertising and commercials on Howard's show to trumpet the theatrical release. *Variety* gave a rave review, calling the movie "an amusing little feature. . . . Fans willing to take a goof on a low-budget pic will enjoy it." (The paper's assessment of Howard was less kind, saying he was "unimpressive" [sic] as the anchorman.)

However, a bad review in *Newsday*, the Long Island daily, and a lack of funds for more ads prompted theater owners to drop *Ryder* after a week.*

WNBC's demise was reflected in ratings that showed a mass defection of listeners. Nearly 80 percent of the station's afternoon-drive audience had left since Howard had been fired, prompting him on May 1, 1986, to stage a mock funeral for his former employer. Wrapped in a black coat, he drove in an open limousine to NBC's Rockefeller Center headquarters and held a wooden box as he addressed a gathering of fans: "Before I spread these ashes at WNBC, I want to wish ten plagues on NBC—locusts, boils, and low ratings among them. Good-bye, NBC!"†

Howard and his crew would offer more street theater in New York and other cities as the morning show became a force in the industry. In the meantime, the boast that Howard had nearly tripled the size of the morning audience at "K-Rock" during his first few months failed to impress Imus. "He said he was going to beat me in the morning, and he didn't," Imus noted after the winter ratings came out. "We had a 4.0 share at NBC. They had a 3.4 share. Case closed." For the time being.

The first casualties of Howard's growing success would be counted a few months later, when WNEW-FM, the album-rock leader and direct competitor of "K-Rock," discontinued its own talkative wake-up show, cohosted by Richard Neer and Mark McEwen

---

Ryder P.I. was released on videocassette in 1988, but distribution to rental and retail outlets was spotty. Howard, now a big star, objected to the use of his picture as Ben Wah on the video box. The film's short-lived commercial life enhanced cult interest. Copies of the video were being sold and swapped by Howard's fans. In 1995, Karl Hosch, based in Port Washington, New York, reclaimed the rights to "Ryder" from the video distributor and was exploring the possibilities of rereleasing the movie in theaters and on video.

†The actual death of WNBC-AM came in 1988. The station was among five sold by NBC to Emmis Broadcasting Corp., which silenced WNBC on October 7, 1988, and immediately used its 660 AM dial position as the new home for WFAN, the company's one-year-old all-sports outlet. Don Imus remained at 660 AM as WFAN's new morning man.

(now a cohost of TV's *CBS This Morning*). It had fallen to thirteenth place in the summer ratings while Stern had raced his "K-Rock" morning program into the top five. McEwen conceded that everyone was "taking a beating" from Howard; WNEW-FM, for one, didn't know what to do about it.

Such concessions made Howard cluck. One of his tactical moves as a morning man was to zero in on rivals and ruthlessly belittle their talent. A favorite target was the legendary disc jockey Scott Muni, who joined WNEW-FM shortly after the station had switched to an album-rock format in 1967. He was celebrated as "the Professor," because he was older than his colleagues and knew many of the rock greats and their music. The end of Neer and McEwen's show inspired Howard to mimic Muni's gravel-edged voice, as if he were oh-so-seriously speaking with the singer Julian Lennon. He poked fun at Muni's age by introducing the hiss of a respirator and the beep of a heart monitor. It was an outrageous conceit—cruel, too, given the love-and-peace theme that ran through a lot of album-rock music. In private, Muni professed to ignore the taunts, but he drew the line at Howard's irreverence toward the late John Lennon. (Imus also was inspired to add a "Scott Muni" character after the I-Man switched to New York's WFAN in 1988.)

As Howard's show added affiliates, he became famous for mocking and attacking his new competitors as if he was wielding a truncheon. The first of nearly two dozen out-of-town markets (as of December 1995) exposed to his competitive wrath was Philadelphia, which Howard had chosen to enter on a dare.

In September 1985, the city's Infinity-owned station, WYSP-FM, had switched to a hard-rock format featuring disc jockeys such as Animal, Scruff, and Killer, but struggled to reach a large audience. Looking to jump-start the operation, the twenty-four-year-old program director, Andy Bloom, seized on the idea of simulcasting Howard's show out of New York. The precedent for this tactic had occurred in the early 1980s, when Steve Dahl's Chicago-based program on WLUP-FM also was carried by WABX in Detroit (pitting Dahl against Howard, on WWWW-FM, for a time) and WQFM in

Milwaukee. The raucous Dahl gave his two affiliates jolts of attention despite modest ratings.

Bloom and his general manager, Ken Stevens, who previously had run WQFM, were introduced to Howard during a meeting in Karmazin's New York office. Bloom courageously—perhaps foolishly—said that the disc jockey reminded him of Steve Dahl. Howard became irritated at the very idea, arguing that Dahl had ripped off the Stern act. Bloom countered by suggesting that maybe Howard could do what Dahl had failed to do—be a ratings success in two cities at once. Howard paused, as if fascinated by the possibility.

Months would pass as Karmazin considered the ramifications of extending his Stern franchise to WYSP, and Howard, advised by agent Buchwald, came to recognize that syndication offered him an opportunity to become more popular than anyone in New York radio.

On August 18, 1986, WYSP-FM started carrying his show. This time, Howard turned his mockery against a newly perceived foe, the top-rated John DeBella, of Philadelphia's WMMR-FM. In the City of Brotherly Love, hatred would fuel their rivalry. Howard declared that DeBella was ugly and his *Morning Zoo* lame. DeBella said that he welcomed the free publicity that Howard was giving him. (This dismissive posture would haunt DeBella: Howard became number one in Philadelphia in 1990. The defeated DeBella, out of a job three years later, had to go on the Stern show in 1994 and ask the king's "permission" to accept another radio position—on WYSP.)

Howard acted as if he was putting himself in fighting trim for expansionist wars in other radio markets. His fat days were behind him. No more wolfing submarine sandwiches and cheesecake as he had before, when he asked that the picture on his comedy album be retouched in order to thin his bottom and thighs. He had ballooned in early 1984 to around 235 pounds—a bloated, six-foot-five mess at war with WNBC. During the next two and a half years, he began to knock off about fifty pounds by sticking to a diet high in baked potatoes, brown rice, boiled chicken, and turkey. He ran on a track near his split-level home in the affluent Long Island community of Manhasset Hills, and he spent four afternoons a week building up his body with weights and exercise under a trainer's supervision at a gymnasium in nearby Port Washington.

He regained some of the weight before easing back below 200. The lasting difference was in his attitude. He once eyed Chaconas and Fred as they ate steak-and-cheese sandwiches and said to them, "You're both going to die."

FIFTEEN

The Federal Communications Commission began to police *The Howard Stern Show* without warning. Until the end of 1986, as raunchy as the program often was, it was protected by the First Amendment to the Constitution ("Congress shall make no law . . . abridging the freedom of speech") as interpreted by the FCC.

Nevertheless, the FCC received complaints about Stern as early as 1981, when he was broadcasting in Washington. A woman in Clifton, Virginia, protested that he "asked every female that called the station one morning how often they truly reached an orgasm. . . . I urge you to listen to him one morning and take appropriate action." In response, Stephen F. Sewell, the assistant chief in the FCC's Complaints and Compliance Division, wrote the woman: "As you may be aware, the First Amendment to the Constitution and the Communications Act of 1934, as amended, prohibits [sic] Commission censorship of broadcast material. Every broadcaster, based upon his studies of how best to serve his community, has wide discretion in the selection and presentation of programming. The Commission does not substitute its judgment for that of station licensees in the selection of broadcast material."

Also in 1981, a woman in Centreville, Virginia, told the FCC of riding in her car with three grade-school students: "I was treated to the moans and groans of Mr. Ed (a horse) having intercourse with his owner's wife. . . . I object to this trash being broadcast over public radio." She described Howard's program as being obscene and asked whether the FCC was monitoring or regulating what is broadcast on the radio. Again, Sewell replied, this time saying that "the Commission cannot take further action on your complaint as presented." The FCC official again quoted the Communications Act of 1934, as amended: the law does not give the FCC "the power of censorship . . . and no regulation or condition shall be promulgated or fixed by the Commission which shall interfere with the right of free speech by means of radio communications."

In a 1982 exchange with Senator John W. Warner, of Virginia, Laurence E. Harris, chief of the FCC's Broadcast Bureau, noted that members of his staff had been listening to Howard on "DC-101" and to tapes of his show in response to inquiries from the Washington area. "From what has been heard by our staff and the additional information provided by persons who have telephoned or sent letters to the Commission about Howard Stern broadcasts, there appeared to be no basis for action concerning material that had been aired in his programs under any law, rule, or policy that this agency administers," Harris explained to Warner, who had forwarded complaints about the radio show from two members of a Falls Church, Virginia, Parent-Teacher Association. Harris added: "Although the C ᵢmmission is authorized by the Communications Act to license broadcast stations and to regulate their operations in some respects, under the prohibition on censorship in the Communications Act and the freedom of speech guarantees in both the Act and our Constitution's First Amendment, neither this nor any other governmental agency can, with limited statutory exceptions, direct broadcasters in the selection and presentation of programming."

The FCC routinely encouraged those complaining about Howard's show to direct their concerns to the radio station, because, to quote one letter from the agency, such "commentary can be effective in influencing broadcaster's [sic] programming decisions."

When Howard joined WNBC in 1982, the FCC continued to articulate a hands-off policy. But the mail kept coming.

A Long Island man vented in a 1985 letter to Senator Daniel Patrick Moynihan, of New York: "It is, in my opinion, one of the most degrading and repulsive radio programs I have ever heard. . . . He went into the deepest details about bloody toilet tissue being found in the [rest] room. . . . I think you will agree that it [is] something more dangerous than it might at first appear. . . . Is there nothing in the law that would prevent this pollution of the air waves?"

In a response to Moynihan, James C. McKinney, chief of the FCC's Mass Media Bureau, wrote: "As deplorable and offensive as certain remarks may be, they are not subject to review and action by this agency."

In 1985, a Bergenfield, New Jersey, woman told of "a very lengthy discourse on the manner he [Howard] uses to relieve himself at the men's urinal in the studio restroom" and "after that, he started to discuss the size of his penis and of the others who were in the restroom with him." Writing to Bill Bradley, one of her United States senators, she asked about the FCC: "What is their function? Are they not there to protect us from such a cancer as this man?"

Answering this woman's query, McKinney explained: "Our role in overseeing program content is . . . very limited. . . . The First Amendment protects the right of broadcasters to air statements which may be offensive, and a free society requires governmental forbearance in those instances."

It was in the fall of 1985, several months after McKinney wrote that letter, that Infinity Broadcasting was considering Howard for the afternoon job on "K-Rock." According to company president Mel Karmazin, he met with McKinney in Washington to learn what the rules were on the matter of indecency. As Karmazin later recalled the meeting, McKinney said "that it's very simple: 'All you need to do is to not say the seven dirty words.' And he gave us what those seven dirty words were. And we entered into a contract with Howard for his doing a radio program, and in the list of things that were prohibited Howard could not say the seven dirty words. We added a number of other things that we didn't want on the radio either, but Howard would not say those seven dirty words." (Interviewed in 1995, McKinney said that he could not recall meeting with Karmazin—but if he had, he added, he would have presented a more complex definition of indecency than Karmazin described.)

The "seven dirty words"—shit, piss, fuck, cunt, cocksucker, motherfucker, and tit—had assumed a level of extreme seriousness in the radio industry as a result of the landmark court case that produced the prevailing definition of broadcast indecency. In 1978, the United States Supreme Court had upheld the FCC's right to ban the broadcast of words that the commission deemed "patently offensive" during hours when children were in the audience. The case stemmed from an October 30, 1973, broadcast by New York station WBAI-FM of George Carlin's "Filthy Words." In the twelve-minute monologue from the comedian's 1973 album, *Occupation: Foole*, he identifies and defangs the seven words that should not be said on the public airwaves, using them in various broad caricatures and in myriad idioms. At one point, Carlin rattles on: "The shit is gonna hit the fan. Built like a brick shithouse. He's up shit creek. Hot shit, holy shit, tough shit, eat shit. Shit-eating grin, uh, whoever thought of that was ill. . . . He had a shit fit, wow! All the animals: bullshit, horseshit, cow shit, rat shit, bat shit."

A New York man who heard the WBAI broadcast, in the company of his young son, complained to the FCC. Its subsequent order forbidding the airing of indecent language was reversed by a federal appeals court, then affirmed in 1978 by the Supreme Court. The majority opinion cited the broadcast media's "uniquely pervasive presence" in the lives of all Americans, the interests of adults who don't wish to be assaulted by offensive language, and society's right to protect children from "inappropriate speech." In a dissent, Associate Justice William J. Brennan charged the majority with "a depressing inability to appreciate that in our land of cultural pluralism, there are many who think, act and talk differently from members of this Court, and who do not share their fragile sensibilities."

The High Court's 1978 decision upheld the FCC's reprimand of WBAI and the commission's definition of indecency as "language that describes, in terms patently offensive as measured by contemporary community standards for the broadcast medium, sexual or excretory activities and organs, at times of the day when there is a reasonable risk that children may be in the audience." The FCC had concluded that certain words in the Carlin monologue depicted sexual and excretory activities in a patently offensive manner. (Indecency was not to be confused with obscenity, which the FCC defined as containing an element of prurient appeal.)

FCC chairman Charles D. Ferris said in 1978 that he did not consider the Supreme Court decision a mandate for the commission to become involved in programming content. But National Association of Broadcasters president Vincent T. Wasilewski warned in 1978 that the NAB "fears that the FCC will not stop with the seven dirty words."

Wasilewski was right.

During Howard's stay at "DC-101" and at WNBC, as well as during his first year at "K-Rock," the FCC's citation against the seven dirty words stood as a simple guide to broadcasters. It was a guide that Karmazin ordered Howard to follow.

The playing field was altered when Philadelphia's WYSP-FM added Howard's program in August 1986. According to McKinney, more people in the Philadelphia area complained to the FCC about Howard's show in its first three months on WYSP than New Yorkers had in three years. After studying a few dozen letters and tape-recorded segments of the program sent to the FCC, McKinney singled out three complaints from residents of Philadelphia. Two of them had been forwarded to the commission by the Reverend Donald E. Wildmon, a United Methodist minister and the executive director of the National Federation for Decency, based in Tupelo, Mississippi. The third arrived directly from a Philadelphia woman, Mary V. Keeley, the mother of a fifteen-year-old Stern fan. She had expressed her grievance to WYSP; after receiving a form letter in reply, she contacted Morality in Media, a watchdog organization in New York that seeks enforcement of obscenity laws. The group directed her to the FCC.

In a letter sent to Howard's employer, Infinity Broadcasting, in November 1986, McKinney essentially launched an investigation into Howard's show. He gave Infinity thirty days to respond to the three listeners' complaints, which alleged that Howard's program was indecent or obscene under Philadelphia's community standards (the broadcasting of questionable material on "K-Rock" in New York was not at issue). The listeners said they had been offended by Howard's comments about masturbation and Robin Quivers's anatomy. Remarks that Howard had made about the much publicized "Preppie Murder Case" of 1985—a young woman was slain in New York's Central Park, supposedly after a rough-sex encounter—especially irked McKinney himself. "It was the routine by Stern about the Central Park murder that sent me over the edge," he told a reporter.

In a forty-four-page reply to McKinney, Karmazin conceded that Howard's programs "are comedic in nature, [but] they are undeniably provocative and controversial, thereby inescapably offensive to some persons of delicate sensibility." However, Karmazin pointed out, the FCC's staff "consistently and repeatedly ruled that Mr. Stern's use of the type of sexually-oriented language now complained of is protected speech." Karmazin added: "The Staff on numerous occasions has recognized the important and legally dispositive distinction between the concentrated stream of 'patently offensive' vulgarities found indecent in connection with the George Carlin monologue . . . and Mr. Stern's incidental use of sexually-oriented language, sexual innuendo and double entendre during his four-hour weekday program. There has been no complaint that Mr. Stern uses the patently offensive language contained in the Carlin monologue." Furthermore, Karmazin said: "The predilections of a handful of complainants, the most vocal of whom is a Tupelo, Mississippi resident on an apparent crusade to impose his personal standards of decency on the rest of his countrymen, cannot establish a local standard for a major metropolitan area such as Philadelphia. The complaints of the very few must be balanced against Mr. Stern's demonstrated, sustained appeal among a significant segment of the listening audience, as well as expressions of support for Mr. Stern from members of the public and other influential local media, all of which help to illustrate acceptance of his program under local community standards."

Karmazin's response noted that Howard had lifted WYSP's morning ranking among men eighteen and older from eleventh place to third in only two months. His response included letters praising Howard and others supporting WYSP for carrying his show, as well as the text of an editorial broadcast on WCAU, one of Philadelphia's leading TV stations. WCAU general manager Stephen J. Cohen had editorialized: "We think the FCC is wrong to investigate Stern on the basis of a handful of complaints. Stern may be distasteful to some or funny as can be to others. But he should be able to broadcast his brand of entertainment unfettered by federal control. . . . The FCC should spend its time on other matters and leave this Stern gang alone, to pass or fail on its merits and not the outrage of a few listeners."

In urging the FCC to dismiss the complaints against Howard's show, Karmazin argued that the broadcaster's sexually oriented, "satiric provocation cannot fairly be equated with obscenity or indecency." He maintained that Infinity sought to operate within the guidelines governing protected speech as the company "has understood them to exist up to this time." However, Karmazin noted that he had detected "the possibility of a shift in the Commission's approach to these matters," in which case "Infinity will of course comply with any fresh guidance which the Commission provides."

On April 16, 1987, the FCC fired the loudest broadside heard in the broadcasting industry since the Supreme Court decision nine years earlier. The commission, rejecting Karmazin's arguments, found that Howard's show had aired "indecent material" on WYSP several times. The decision, approved by the commissioners in a 5–0 vote, stated: "The commission found that the broadcasts in a number of instances did not merely consist of an occasional off-color reference or expletive, but consisted of a dwelling on sexual and excretory matters in a way that was patently offensive as measured by contemporary community standards for the broadcast medium."

The wording of the decision clearly echoed the FCC's earlier definition of indecency, language upheld by the Supreme Court, and heralded a crackdown on broadcasters that promised to go beyond the "seven dirty words" criteria. The FCC imposed no punishment for the Stern violations, explaining that there may have been uncertainty as to the reach of the George Carlin case, but the agency said it would issue letters of warning to Infinity. In effect, the FCC was putting Infinity on notice that the material in question would be actionable under the indecency standard that the commission now believed it had clarified.

FCC chairman Mark S. Fowler, an appointee of President Reagan who was presiding over his last commissioners' meeting, later said he believed that the panel had "acted carefully" when it agreed to enlarge the reach of its indecency enforcement. Commissioner Dennis R. Patrick, another Reagan appointee, who was to succeed Fowler as chairman, signaled his resolve to follow through: "What we are doing today is to correct an altogether too narrow interpretation of indecency." The commission "cannot and will not flinch in enforcing the standard."

But what standard? That's what Karmazin wanted to know. He explained to reporters that Howard would not change his format until the FCC translated its definition of indecency into usable directives for all broadcasters. "If the definition is changed, we will conform to the new guidelines," he promised.

Gray rules had replaced black-and-white rules, making Karmazin's situation far more complicated than it was when he hired Howard. A disclaimer, added at the start of each program, announced that Stern was intended "for adult audiences, and some adults may find portions of the show offensive. Parental guidance is suggested, and adults with delicate sensitivities are advised to seek alternative programming." As Karmazin would recall, "The FCC . . . changed the definition of indecency. They said that you cannot discuss sex or excretory matters in a patently offensive manner. We then called them up and said, 'Folks, we got this definition and it says "patently offensive." Could you give us some more guidance? Because we don't want to break the rules, but we want to understand what you mean by "patently offensive" because you're saying that we can discuss masturbation and we can discuss lesbianism and we can discuss sex, but we just can't do it in a "patently offensive" manner.'"

Karmazin was to face a long wait for "more guidance" from the FCC—he would still be waiting at the end of 1995 when his dispute with the FCC would end—while the commission dramatically intensified its scrutiny of Howard's show. The three major television networks, National Public Radio, and other broadcast media also called on the FCC to provide a precise definition of indecency and to explain its enforcement procedures.

Howard bragged that the FCC's action was the greatest boost for his career and would help his ratings. He also claimed victory. "I'm thrilled," he said. "I never thought we did anything obscene. I never thought we did anything disgusting. I never thought we did anything rude." He argued that the FCC's decision was not a slap against him personally, but its way of putting the radio industry on notice. "They can't touch me because I didn't do anything wrong—unless this is Russia."

The Stern excerpts transcribed by the FCC included exchanges between "Bob" and "Ray," the sound-enhanced macho men portrayed by Howard and Robin. In one segment, Howard (apparently in the role of "Bob") said: "God, my testicles are like down to the floor. Boy, Susan [Berkley], you could really have a party with these." At which "Ray" added: "Use them like boccie balls."

In a discussion about lesbians, Howard stated: "I mean to go around porking other girls with vibrating rubber products, and they want the whole world to come to a standstill."

In an interesting contrast, the FCC also found that two California stations had aired indecent broadcasts. The nonprofit KPFK-FM, in Los Angeles, had presented excerpts from the play *Jerker*, a series of sexually explicit conversations between two men. It was written by Robert Chesley, who said the work was born of the AIDS crisis. The FCC found the selections from *Jerker* to be stronger fare, possibly even obscene, and referred them to the Justice Department. One man in Chesley's play says: "I don't think I've ever had such a gentle sensitive fuck before or after. Well, he must have gone at it for twenty minutes at the very least, just sliding his cock back and forth inside my ass."

Howard said that even he found the use of "the F word" on the air to be offensive.

The Justice Department declined to prosecute.

McKinney had been with the FCC in various enforcement capacities for twenty-four years. Two months after the Stern ruling, when he joined President Reagan's White House staff, he stated that the growth of "off-color programming" around the country had been a source of concern at the commission. Elaborating in 1995, he maintained that the FCC had not undergone a "sea change" in its attitude toward Howard's show but responded to his "more drastic" material. "He ratcheted up the nature of his program," McKinney said. "I do recall clearly that Howard Stern's actions on the air changed—they had become more severe than years before. The commission didn't change, Howard Stern changed. He became more shocking. The lawyers [at the FCC] acted on it."

While independent voices denounced the FCC's action in April 1987 as censorship, and figures in the broadcast industry argued that the ruling would infringe on First Amendment freedom, an inference that could be drawn was that the FCC seriously considered listener complaints that met a requisite level of evidence. It was not FCC policy to order radio stations to turn over tapes of shows cited by complainants, lest such action have a chilling effect on the broadcasters. However, judging from the evidence that went into the 1987 decision, printed transcripts of allegedly indecent broadcasts were welcomed by the FCC when submitted by listeners. The submission of tape recordings was better. Other determined critics of Howard's style would come along to challenge him before the FCC with similar mementos in hand.

And so the shock jock occupied center stage in a debate over free speech and the public airwaves. He was a willing, if controversial, focal point in such a serious discussion. "I am the last bastion of the First Amendment," he declared with theatrical bravado. Indeed, Howard may have become a mouthpiece for listeners who harbored anger at gays, women, foreigners, and others whom he routinely ridiculed. At the same time, as critic Richard Goldstein begrudgingly observed in the *Village Voice*, "There's no more pungent test of free speech than nasty speech, or more tellingly, unpopular speech."

Eight days after the FCC's ruling, Howard drew about three thousand supporters to a morning rally in Dag Hammarskjold Plaza, near the United Nations' headquarters in New York. Dressed in a black-and-white-striped prisoner's uniform, he beseeched the crowd: "Is it spelled FCC or KGB?"

The rally was aired live on "K-Rock" and WYSP-FM, but this did not stop actor Al Lewis, a friend of the show known for playing Grandpa on TV's *The Munsters*, from yelling "Fuck the FCC!" before Howard could pull the microphone away from him. (The FCC said it would not hold the stations accountable for the expletive.)

Howard told the multitude that he didn't think he was in the wrong—"because words never hurt anyone, man. And we're just having fun, man."

SIXTEEN

On April 16, 1987, the day that the FCC thrust Howard into the role of poster boy for shock radio, he huddled in a closed-door meeting at New York's WNYW-TV, plotting his first major foray in television. WNYW was the flagship station of media mogul Rupert Murdoch's Fox Broadcasting Network. When Fox began to woo Howard in the fall of 1986, it was widely believed in TV circles that the fledgling, so-called fourth network wanted him for a program that would follow its newly launched *Late Show Starring Joan Rivers*—in effect, to be a David Letterman to her Johnny Carson. Fox planned to test Howard's new show on WNYW over five nights during the spring of 1987 and then decide whether to put the venture on the network in the fall. But Rivers, who by now was attracting only half the audience that Fox had promised advertisers, was about to be removed as host of the *Late Show*, and the fate of her time slot remained uncertain. When this news got out, there was industry talk that Fox was considering Howard as Rivers's replacement in the 11:00 P.M. hour.

This was heady stuff for Howard—the prospect of a career beyond early-morning radio. He aimed to please during a get-acquainted lunch with Fox and WNYW executives at the swank Hotel Plaza Athénée on Manhattan's Upper East Side. "He could not have been more cordial and delightful," recalled Paul Noble, who was WNYW's executive producer.

Sure, Howard *was* popular. A year into his run as Infinity's morning man, he had dropped almost all of the rock music that by dictum once punctuated his show, and he was rising in the ratings at a much faster pace than he had at WNBC. Numbers compiled by Arbitron showed that he was drawing almost eight hundred thousand New York–area listeners a week. He ranked fourth overall in the morning—behind the city's two all-news stations and WHTZ's raucous *Morning Zoo*. Infinity's bottom line benefited from his appeal to the male audience, which the company had sought to reach when it launched "K-Rock" in July 1985. His was the top-rated morning show among men eighteen and older, as well as among men eighteen to thirty-four years old (the station's targeted audience). The ratings revealed that he was number one among adults eighteen to thirty-four and adults twenty-five to fifty-four (a demographic of great interest to many leading advertisers).

But there also were signs that Howard's day as a national TV star was still in the distance. As popular as his radio program was, it was being heard in only two markets, New York and Philadelphia, and a foray into national syndication had ended in failure. A three-hour weekend version of his show—it typically featured a celebrity guest and was once described by Howard as "a Johnny Carson show for the warped"—had about forty-five affiliate stations around the country when Fox was eyeing him in the fall of 1986. In February 1987, the distributor, DIR Broadcasting, canceled the syndicated program. The company blamed the decision on the show's shortage of national advertising. Whatever reservations there may have been about buying time on Howard's show, the paltry number of stations (forty-five) was not worth the attention of leading sponsors. On top of the cancellation, Howard's developing relationship with Fox unexpectedly was set against a backdrop of notoriety stemming from the FCC warning.

Was Howard Stern too controversial for national television?

Joan Rivers did her final show on May 15 as Howard formalized his romance with Fox by taping five hour-long pilots at a cost to the network of around $400,000. Although the shows were designed to air once a week over five weeks, viewed together the programs were to

give Fox an impression as to how Howard would wear over five con-
secutive weeknights. He had announced the Fox deal to his radio listeners with self-promotional fanfare so that he was more than
committed to ensuring that the pilots drew a huge audience. "They
just fired Joan Rivers, and I figure I'm the most likely candidate to
take her place," he said during the second taping.

But network television did not operate as swiftly and impul-
sively as his morning radio show. By early June, Fox had not scheduled airdates, and Howard had to suffer the humiliation of reading in
the newspapers that the pilots were being tested before focus groups
in California—as if his talent was a new detergent being secretly test-
marketed in the sticks before reaching stores across America. He
started to question the smarts of Fox executives, wondering aloud—
on the air, of course—why they had to audition his stuff when the
network's only full night of programming (on Sunday) was awful.

By July, Howard and those who worked on the pilots still had
heard nothing about airdates. Worse yet, Fox Broadcasting president
Jamie Kellner and other network brass were issuing "No comment"
in response to queries from the press, saying that it was company
policy to refrain from discussing shows in development. This seemed
to say volumes. Although there was no formal announcement, by
mid-July it was more than clear that Fox had shelved the pilots. In the
parlance of Hollywood, Fox was canceling its option to carry the
shows.

But why? What could have been so bad about five hours with a
cult hero?

In 1995, Steve Schwartz, the line producer on the pilots, said
that he was still unsure as to why Fox set them aside. "I thought they
were pretty good," he said. "They were very funny, and Howard had
good guests."

Paul Noble, the former WNYW executive producer, said that he,
too, was never told why they didn't air. "By today's standards, they
were absolutely tame." But Noble added: "They were not the kind of
thing that a local New York television station was prepared to get involved with at that time. It was more like off-the-wall radio."

"We were very excited about the pilots, we liked them," recalled Garth Ancier, the network's first programming chief. "But I think there was a feeling by management of the company that we were not strong enough to endure questions about our broadcast standards that might ensue if we aired them."

Who held the smoking gun? Sources who were high up at WNYW and the Fox network in 1987 say they have no doubt about who made the decision to give up on Howard—Murdoch himself and Barry Diller, chairman of Fox Inc., the parent corporation.

"It was all Barry Diller and Rupert Murdoch, period," said Charles Hirschhorn. As Fox's vice president for programming, he had supervised production of the pilots.

Although Howard did not see the big picture at the time, his controversial reputation, underscored by the FCC's widely reported April 16 decision, struck Murdoch as much too heavy baggage at a time when the media baron was facing larger and more worrisome corporate problems. Not only did Murdoch consider Stern an unnecessary risk to Fox in a fragile period of the network's development, he also feared that putting naughty Howard on television would taint his determined effort to keep the *New York Post*. When Murdoch bought WNYW and six other TV stations from Metromedia in 1985 for more than $2 billion, he became subject to a federal law that barred him from owning a TV station and a newspaper in the same city. In New York, the home of WNYW, this meant that Murdoch had to sell off the raffish *Post*, an especially painful requirement because the tabloid gave him an editorial voice and coveted social entrée in the world's media capital. He rejected Howard's pilots while lobbying to extend—permanently—a temporary waiver of the so-called cross-ownership rule.*

---

*Months later, on December 15, 1987, Murdoch lost his battle to retain the *New York Post* when the U.S. Senate passed an appropriations bill containing a rider championed by Senator Edward M. Kennedy. The rider prevented the FCC from repealing the cross-ownership rule or extending any waivers, such as the one held by Murdoch. He sold the *Post* in 1988, only to reacquire it in 1993, when he won a waiver of the cross-ownership and was free to operate the tabloid along with New York's WNYW-TV.

In hindsight, the Fox finale resembled Howard's ouster from WNBC two years earlier—when Howard's popularity was over-shadowed by the priorities of a massive broadcasting company. However, in 1987, the Fox situation was a mystery to Howard, and the mystery gnawed at him. He poured out his rage on the air through the summer. By August, the tight-lipped executives at Fox had tired of his rants and slipped a devastating assessment of the pilots to Ben Kubasik, the TV columnist of *New York Newsday*. Kubasik's sources, who asked not to be identified, told him "the shows were poorly produced, in poor taste—despite guests Joe Piscopo and Jackie Mason—and unmarketable, meaning ad agencies would not buy commercials on them." One "top Fox executive" was quoted by Kubasik as saying: "The truth is, they were boring."

Howard Stern, *boring?*

It's easy to see why Fox powers would have said so, if only to mask the larger corporate issues behind their decision. However, a viewing in 1995 of four of these hours revealed painfully slow and often witless shows, even by Howard's creatively low-budget standards. Only one pilot demonstrates that he could turn out the kind of inspired skits that would help make his syndicated TV program so popular starting three years later.

In the first pilot, leather-clad Howard appears to be working hard at looking nonchalant while a perky Robin, wearing a blue leather outfit as snug as sausage casing, assumes the Vanna White role of pointing and smiling. As Howard slouches in a gilt-bordered throne and Robin sits in a chair, they address the studio audience for much of the first half hour about who may—and who may not—be among their first guests. Howard explains that Fox executives are watching the taping on monitors elsewhere in the building and says, "Screw it, man, if this doesn't work, I'll just stay on the radio."

Howard's bandleader is his friend Leslie West, the guitar-bending star of the 1970s rock group Mountain. His still mountain-ous frame is loosely sheathed in a canary yellow paisley jacket that would make the flamboyant Doc Severinsen look underdressed. A big man in dazzling duds, West inadvertently steals attention whenever he appears within reach of the camera—which is much of the time. West and another of Howard's portly pals, Steve ("the Legend") Rossi, who wears a white dinner jacket and serves as the announcer and band singer, are positioned directly behind Howard and Robin—not off to the side. At one point they break into a half-hearted version of "Mississippi Queen," the Mountain classic.

Without introduction, comedian David Brenner walks on. He exchanges hugs and kisses, asks Howard to appear in the imminent final taping of his own syndicated show, *Night Life*, and gives Howard three silly gifts (which Howard tosses aside as soon as Brenner leaves). After a commercial break, the action shifts to familiar talk-show territory—a desk, where Howard and Robin sit on chairs straight out of an accountant's office, and a chair to their right for the guests. The first to come on is Joe Piscopo, formerly of *Saturday Night Live* and now famous (to Howard) because he left his wife for a younger woman. The two men shed their jackets to compare muscles, then Piscopo does a Frank Sinatra impersonation, singing "Witchcraft."

The sex quotient is filled by four enticingly dressed women who bump and jiggle as they vie for berths in Howard's dance troupe (to be modeled, Robin says, on the June Taylor Dancers of the old *Jackie Gleason Show*). Next, Howard's obsession with the TV programs of his youth finds release in a guest panel: commercial oddity Mason Reese, Billy Gray (from *Father Knows Best*), and Al Lewis (of *The Munsters* and "Fuck the FCC!" fame). Gray wins the award for having the hardest-luck story: he had been jailed after a drug bust.

Cut to Robin announcing that Jerry Hall, Mick Jagger's girlfriend, will not be appearing on the show after all. "Oh, hell with her," Howard says. "She's dumb and she's from Texas."

Cut to a visit from a "mystery guest," who turns out to be Cindy Adams, a gossip columnist on the Murdoch-owned *New York Post*. She has written nasty things about Howard, so they joust for a few moments.

The hour ends.

It is notable for the relative absence of Fred Norris and Jackie Martling. They appear only in an opening homage to Laurel and Hardy, lugging what is supposed to be a boxed Howard up many exhausting flights of stairs. It also is notable for the painfully awkward attempt to squeeze Howard into a format that looks a little like *Saturday Night Live* and feels a little like *Late Night with David Letterman* but ends up fitting the host like a straitjacket. Unlike the syndicated TV show that Howard would put on the air in 1990, a low-budget comedy hour that reveled in—indeed, celebrated—its cheap look and props, often to hilarious ends, the introductory pilot looks unintentionally tacky. Worse yet, while trying to appear hip and happening, the pilot resembles any number of mainstream talk shows that Howard ridicules most mornings on the radio.

In the second pilot, Howard appears more at ease, more casual, dressed this time in a bomber jacket. "We're trying to make this show more relaxed," he says from his throne. "It's so damn uptight." He brings on Robin, who emerges, hands tented in prayer, and bows to him in the same obsequious manner that Ed McMahon greets Johnny Carson. An *eerie* similarity, considering that Howard has nothing but contempt for Carson.

In this and the third pilot, via a monitor, Howard and Robin watch boisterous fans outside the WNYW studios. According to Howard, he's studying the crowd to decide whom he will admit to the studio taping, in the same way that Studio 54, the New York disco, used to carefully screen would-be patrons at the front door. As the camera pans the gathering outside, Howard singles out a few people for insults—"You look like a homosexual in waiting," he tells one man—and allows even fewer to enter the studio.

After a break, he argues with his executive producer, Peter Calabrese, demanding to know why the action must shift to the desk. "I feel like a Johnny Carson clone," the star says. Instead he heads into the audience to have fun with two interracial couples. "We met at work," a black man tells Howard, who replies, "Where do you work, McDonald's?"

Comedian Bob Goldthwait is the hour's only guest. He appears via satellite hookup: "You couldn't flip for the airplane ride?" he teases Howard. Goldthwait cannot see what's happening in the Fox studio, and he complains in his shrill, tongue-swallowing voice that the audio connection is poor. It makes for an endless and disjointed few minutes during which Howard aimlessly draws eyeglasses and other features on Goldthwait's image on the monitor. There's even less of a payoff when Howard introduces a woman for whom he once lusted at summer camp; she's pregnant, has almost nothing to say, and is seated with her husband, who is unamused. An obvious question is whether anyone checked these two for a pulse ahead of time.

Enter Gary Dell'Abate, Howard's faithful aide, to list the stars who declined invitations to appear: Yoko Ono, Bianca Jagger, Sydney Biddle Barrows, Dick Cavett, Charo, Dr. Ruth Westheimer, and Arnold Schwarzenegger. (After Howard became more popular, Cavett, Westheimer, and Schwarzenegger did visit his radio show.)

No Jackie. No Fred. Robin, who has even less to do than Ed McMahon, spends much of the hour making sure that Howard cuts away to commercials and finally says, "It's time to wrap it up, Howard."

Fox executives who stayed awake until the third pilot saw Howard arrive on the set like Letterman: passing the band while playing a few notes of air guitar. He settles into his throne, but his microphone dies, and it takes a bit of time to fix. "I really want this TV show to work," he says without a hint of irony. "I really don't want radio to be my only job."

To the monitor view of clamoring fans outside, then back to a line that he also used on the first pilot: a woman says, "I'm Polish," and Howard remarks, "So let's go bowling."

He grants admission to two men and two women from outside who first agree to take off their clothes in the studio. But it doesn't turn out that way. One man removes only his shirt, the other only his jacket; Howard dismisses both. "You know, it's really hard to do sex on television," he complains. The two women, discreetly covered, step into a "shower"—a curtained kiddie pool. In a bid for titil-lation, the women's exposed calves are shown as water is poured on them.

The comedian Jackie Mason is asked about an ages-old Las Vegas incident involving Frank Sinatra and whether he ever had "had" two or three women at the same time. He says no. After a commercial, Howard quotes Mason's view that the show will be a hit, because "it would be more outrageous than anything on televi-sion." Hardly. Mason, by now looking anguished, sits through more gyrating women seeking a place in Howard's dance troupe. After an-other break, Mason is gone, and no explanation is given. Did he flee during the commercial?

Enter Frank Zappa—another drop-in via satellite transmission. *The Howard Stern Show* is looking more like *Nightline* with each hour. Zappa looks sullen and acts thoroughly bored. Howard re-peatedly studies papers on his desk, as if searching for a question that might elicit a shred of fun. Zappa remains monosyllabic. Howard is lost: "So what's up, man, you're going to be doing some music or something?" Finally, they trade opinions about the origins of AIDS.

End of hour number three.

The fourth pilot, devoted to all things Elvis, showcases the inventive Howard. He later would rework pieces of this hour on his syndi-cated show.

He comes on stage looking like the King. His locks are slicked back, his collar high. The fit of a gold jumpsuit is broken up by a grotesquely bulging abdomen. To the tune of "Blue Suede Shoes," he sings, "Well, you can do anything / But stay away from my food," at which point he takes gluttonous bites of doughnuts, pizza, sand-wiches, and other fatty treats offered by the audience. Still in cos-tume, but as Howard for a moment, he contacts Elvis in the hereafter. The King is hard-pressed to remember his widow's and daughter's names.

Howard also interviews Sammy Shore, a comedian who used to open for Elvis in Vegas and once prayed with him, and actress Yvonne (Batgirl) Craig, who dated Elvis and recalls that his pet monkey used to drink liquor. "Did Elvis ever say he wanted to see you wrestle in your underwear?" Howard asks her. Much of the hour focuses on Elvis impersonators. Their dubious musical talents and physical dissimilarities to the King leave them wide open to Howard's caustic remarks. To one, a car salesman, he asks, "Don't your kids sorta get embarrassed?"

Lifeless and contrived as the pilots basically were, they might have entertained viewers in New York and Philadelphia who enjoyed Howard's radio show. It is questionable whether people who were not in on the joke, who were unfamiliar with Howard's crazed radio persona, would have had much patience for Fox's clumsy attempt to make him a talk-show host. Shelving the pilots before they suffered a ratings death may have been the best thing that ever happened to Howard's career.

Not that he saw it that way, at least at the time. "The idiots at Fox don't understand what I do," Howard complained. He charged that the heat from the FCC generated by his radio show scared Fox away from him. "That's when the wimps at Fox really wimped out," he said. "But it was a learning experience. It taught me the only way to do television is to do it your way."

He responded to the insult by hooking up with Showcase Talent Productions for a special on cable TV—*Howard Stern's Negligee and Underpants Party*—that would be available to viewers who had addressable converter boxes as part of their cable hookup. He wanted to prove that he had the clout to draw a TV audience. "I'm in charge," he boasted. "Totally. The FCC has no say. This is *The Howard Stern Show*, only on television."

He promoted the special in long radio monologues and arranged a round of print interviews—his custom whenever he had something to hawk.

Subscribers who tuned in on February 27, 1988, saw the studio audience, at Howard's cue, strip to their underwear. There was a lesbian dial-a-date. Leslie West played "Mississippi Queen." Comedians Richard Belzer, Judy Tenuta, and Emo Phillips judged a talent contest. The appearance of Jessica Hahn highlighted the special. The former church secretary, who had become tabloid fodder in 1987 after being involved in a sensational sex scandal with televangelist Jim Bakker, had developed a friendship with Howard. She wore a nightgown and played "Guess Who's the Jew" with "Kurt Waldheim" (Fred Norris in Nazi regalia).

Predictably, TV critics were appalled by much of the two and a half hours, especially the sight of a man in underpants who doused his crotch with lighter fluid, struck a match, then shed his skivvies in terror as the flames rose. Howard professed not to care what the critics thought; his view was that people should be free to pay for whatever they wanted to see.

Pay they did. An estimated sixty-thousand homes in the New York area each paid $19.95 to receive the special. Participating cable systems pocketed half of the $1.2 million gross, while Showcase and Howard were to split the remaining half. On top of Howard's estimated $300,000 payday—far, far richer than any one-night stand on Fox—he retained the videocassette rights and hawked copies at $24.95.

The windfall opened Howard's eyes to the beauty of pay-per-view. Realizing that his hard-core fans would buy just about anything he wanted to sell, he would earn millions of dollars in the years ahead simply by returning to this television gold mine.

SEVENTEEN

As Howard sought to demonstrate that he had a future in tele-
vision, another outrageous radio broadcaster was far ahead of him
in making the transition. Morton Downey, Jr., son of the late Irish
tenor, had practiced an in-your-face style of conservative politics on
radio stations around the country until Quantum Media Inc.
launched him as a TV host on New York's WWOR-TV in the fall of
1987. A chain-smoking thug who bullied guests, bashed liberals, and
stirred studio audiences into fanatical whoops of support, Downey
proved so popular so quickly in New York that MCA Television put
his nightly show into national syndication the following spring,
attracting affiliates in eight of the country's top ten markets.

Downey's "talk show" was to intellectual discourse what mud
wrestling was to Olympic sports. His abrasive act was a throwback
to Alan Burke and Joe Pyne, two equally contentious right-wingers
whose antics on TV had been popular briefly in the 1960s. His on-air
brawls and screaming excesses frequently put him on page one of
the New York tabloids, on *Donahue*, on *Nightline*, and in other
forums. He was the conservative brute of the Reagan era.

Impressed by Downey's ability to incite, Karmazin and Chiu-
sano wanted him to moonlight on "K-Rock." Karmazin had brought
Howard to the station because he drew male listeners, and now
Downey's similar popularity among the so-called male, rock-and-roll
demographics acted on the Infinity executive like a siren's song.
Karmazin saw another opportunity to acquire a franchise who al-

ready appealed to a large number of men; he wouldn't have to develop a talent over several years.

At great risk to Howard's calm and self-importance, Karmazin
and Chiusano set out to sign Downey while telling their morning
star little, if anything, about the discussions. So smitten was
Karmazin that he tried to eliminate other bidders for Downey's
radio services. They included Emmis Broadcasting Corp., which
had launched a novel all-sports station, New York's WFAN-AM, on
July 1, 1987, but was having difficulty building an audience, and
Westwood One, a major syndicator with hundreds of affiliates.
Karmazin first proposed an initial payment of $250,000, with the in-
tention of putting Downey on "K-Rock" and Infinity's other radio
stations immediately. Additional earnings for Downey were to come
from the syndication of *The Best of Downey* rebroadcasts to other
stations. Downey rejected the offer, so Karmazin sweetened the pot
to $500,000 for *one* afternoon hour a day on "K-Rock," plus bonuses
that would raise the annual sum to more than $1 million as affiliates
came aboard: a tempting package for little effort.

Downey, basking in the spotlight from his TV show and from
lucrative personal appearances, was in no hurry to cut a deal for
radio chores. As it turned out, he waited too long. The interest of
Infinity and the other radio groups extended beyond the summer of
1988 as he held out for a million-dollar contract to cover just a New
York show. However, during the months of back-and-forth, the loud-
mouth became tiresome. Besides his abuse of TV guests, there was
an incident in San Francisco: he claimed that a group of neo-Nazis
had attacked him and inscribed the swastika found on his face.
Authorities clearly did not believe him. It looked like a pathetic publicity stunt—in 1992, he finally admitted as much.

Downey's TV popularity ebbed. Advertisers balked because
of his unpredictable behavior. Affiliates did not renew the show.
Infinity's interest cooled, too. In July 1989, only fourteen months
after going national, Downey's TV program was canceled and he
slipped into trivia twilight.

Had Downey signed with Karmazin, or with any of the other suitors, his presence on the New York dial would have had a galvanizing effect. It immediately would have overshadowed Howard. Downey might have remained strong on radio after the loss of his TV program. Stern was still years away from having his own radio show syndicated widely beyond New York and Philadelphia, and he was years away from doing a TV show that would get on the air (and not be pay-per-view).

But Howard *was* growing in popularity, reaching more than eight hundred thousand listeners a week. He continued to rank among the top five draws in New York morning radio, commanding a hefty 6.8 share (percent) of the listening audience in the summer of 1987 and a 6.4 in the summer of 1988. The solid rise in Howard's appeal among key segments of the audience, especially men, prompted Karmazin to think larger than the New York–Philadelphia universe to which the broadcast was still confined. "I think Howard could be a national radio performer," Karmazin stated. "There's no reason he couldn't do a live network program." Toward this end, Infinity gave Howard a third radio market on October 3, 1988. The company-owned WJFK-FM (formerly WBMW-FM), licensed to the northern Virginia community of Manassas, brought his program to the Washington area. He introduced the new call letters by airing the sound of gunshots, then calling WJFK "your assassination station."

WJFK marked Howard's return to the Washington dial for the first time since "DC-101" had fired him six years earlier. Infinity agreed to pay him an additional $300,000 a year in the belief that he would overwhelm the market in morning drive and single-handedly lift the ratings of the entire station. Howard expected nothing less. He predicted a romp in Washington and the swift destruction of his former employer and its morning host, Doug ("the Greaseman") Tracht. He craved revenge.

But Howard's second Washington campaign would prove more challenging than the first. He was slow to rebuild an audience during his first years back on the Washington dial, prompting the station to seek reinforcements at other times of the broadcast day. In an unexpected twist, WJFK-FM planned to put one of Howard's idols, Alex Bennett, in afternoon drive. Program director Ed Levine, who used to enjoy Benentt's lively, left-leaning talk on New York's WMCA and WPLJ during the 1960s and 1970s, regarded him as "the first Howard" and figured that Bennett could add weight to WJFK-FM that the morning man was failing to provide. Instead the station hired two of Howard's morning rivals, the WAVA-FM team of Don Geronimo and Mike O'Meara, and moved them into the afternoon slot. As a midday bridge, G. Gordon Liddy later was signed because of Karmazin's enthusiasm for the former Watergate burglar's hard-guy radio style. In a major development in 1992, the Greaseman was bought out of Howard's way when Karmazin, ever hungry for franchise talents, signed the "DC-101" morning man to a five-year deal that placed the ribald storyteller during the evening hours on WJFK-FM (as well as on Infinity's New York and Philadelphia stations).

Some listeners challenged Howard's on-air remarks.

The Anti-Defamation League of B'nai B'rith voiced concerns to "K-Rock" about what they considered anti-Semitic comments. In one instance Howard had said: "The Jews killed Jesus." Another time he went on about "the Jew bankers." The league accused Stern of bigotry, dismissing the argument that he was satirizing bigotry by being so outspoken. The Gay & Lesbian Alliance Against Defamation (GLAAD) also refused to accept the idea that Howard was practicing satire. Members of GLAAD twice had met with the management of New York's WABC-AM to denounce talk-show host Bob Grant's anti-gay views and his use of the word "fag." Now GLAAD complained to "K-Rock" that Howard was guilty of defaming the gay community under the guise of satire.

An older woman, unaffiliated with any organized group, discovered Howard's show on a winter morning in 1988 and remained riveted—in outrage. She then acted on her ire in a way that would bug Howard and Karmazin over the next few years and again underscore the grayness of FCC policy governing the airwaves.

Howard's "Christmas party" broadcast of December 16 set off the tumult. A typical cast of guest players was on hand—flamboyant homosexuals and female exhibitionists among them. A man was said to be playing "Jingle Bells" on the piano with his penis. Women stripteased, after which Howard noted, "The big black lesbian is out of her mind with lust." A gay choir known as Fruits of the Loom offered its own take on "Walking in a Winter Wonderland." The song referred to amyl nitrate and included this refrain:

> *Take my manhood*
> *Then lick my butt good*
> *Christmas at the Mine Shaft NYC.*

Stern and company hooted and hollered with each "performance." But fifty miles away, in a Red Bank, New Jersey, senior citizen complex, Anne M. Stommel was seething. In the months that followed, the retired technical writer with Vassar College polish peppered her congressman, her U.S. senators, and public figures from First Lady Barbara Bush on down with protests and inquiries. She enclosed transcribed excerpts from the "Christmas party" and asked what legal procedures she could explore to purge such programming from the airwaves. Her lament was one in a vast ocean of citizen complaints generated by various broadcasts around the country. There had been forty thousand complaints in the past two years alone, resulting in only one hundred or so bona fide cases investigated by the Federal Communications Commission.

In May 1989, five months after the Christmas broadcast, FCC chairman Dennis R. Patrick told Stommel's congressman, Frank Pallone, Jr., that "the excerpts provided by Ms. Stommel are insufficient to permit us to review the material in context." The FCC was not about to demand a recording of the broadcast in question from "K-Rock." The request would have had a chilling effect. However, Patrick added, "If your constituent would like to forward the tapes from which the excerpts appended to her letter were taken . . . we would be happy to give them our consideration."

Tapes? Stommel had tapes. Why hadn't anyone asked for them in the first place?

Stommel had stumbled on Howard's show when he was previewing his "Christmas party." She was waiting, her Panasonic tape recorder rolling, when the festivities got under way days later. Her tapes of that one morning in the broadcast life of Howard Stern would lead to further costly battles between the FCC and Infinity Broadcasting over what constitutes legally protected speech on the airwaves. Stommel sent her cassettes to the FCC's Mass Media Bureau. She heard nothing as the agency turned her documented complaint into case 8310-TRW.

The bureau's Complaints and Investigations Branch reviewed Stommel's evidence for weeks. Then, on October 26, 1989, the branch opened an inquiry—one of eight separate actions involving radio stations around the country in the FCC's crackdown on indecency. The investigations branch informed Infinity that it was beginning a formal inquiry, because "it appears that the broadcast of the material in question . . . may have violated [federal law] by including indecent programming aired during daytime hours."

The FCC was back on Howard's case for the first time since it issued its warning to Infinity in 1987. The commission again cited the definition of indecency as "language or material that, in context, depicts or describes, in terms patently offensive as measured by community standards for the broadcast medium, sexual or excretory activities or organs." Such material "may not be broadcast when there is reasonable risk that unsupervised children may be in the audience," Edythe Wise, chief of the Complaints and Investigations Branch, declared.

Among the "Christmas party" excerpts that Wise listed were the following:

"[Gay Choir] I'm dreaming of some light torture, some bruises just to make me moan. . . . Masturbate. Humiliate. Gay sex is fun in the city. Howard Stern is going to learn how great a tuckis [sic] can be."

"When we come back from commercial, we have a young man who wants to play the piano with his, uh, wiener. . . .

"Howard, I'd better go into the other room and, uh, get it ready. I'll come strolling in swinging it. It's bigger than yours."

Infinity responded with legal fervor. In a detailed defense prepared by the Washington law firm of Leventhal, Senter & Lerman, Karmazin argued that the excerpts in question (which included "The big, black lesbian is out of her mind with lust") did not describe sexual or excretory activities or organs. What's more, he said, the "limited amount of description" was not patently offensive under a local community standard or even under a national standard. Karmazin cited the wide popularity of Howard's show among adult listeners in New York, who "typically demonstrate substantially greater tolerance for sexually oriented material." He maintained that the excerpts were consistent with national standards, offering transcripts of recent TV talk shows that focused on racy topics. An edition of *Geraldo* on "breast obsession" featured a Hollywood pinup and a porn star. Host Geraldo Rivera said: "Boobs, zonkers, headlights, watermelons . . . these are just some of the silly and sometimes derogatory words used to describe a woman's breasts." Another broadcast of *Geraldo* that aired without FCC reprimand was titled "Unlocking the Mysteries of Great Sex." It offered frank discussions about "men touching a woman's clitoris," "the angry penis," "angry vaginas," and "problems with firmness and with premature ejaculation," to quote from the dialogue.

Karmazin concluded his defense with compelling research done for Infinity by the Gallup Organization: in calls to 250 households with youngsters six to eleven years of age, only one child, or less than 1 percent of all the children covered by the survey, listened to Stern. Therefore, according to Karmazin, "the excerpts, even if somehow found indecent, are not actionable," because unsupervised youngsters were not listening.

The FCC was unimpressed. On November 29, 1990—nearly two full years after Stommel had isolated but one of Howard's shows designed to shock and titillate—the commission fined Infinity $6,000 for broadcasting indecency. The sum represented $2,000 for each of the company-owned stations that simulcasted the program—New York's "K-Rock," Philadelphia's WYSP-FM, and Washington's WJFK-FM.

Roy J. Stewart, chief of the FCC's Mass Media Bureau, dismissed Infinity's claim that the few references to "penis," "wiener," and "masturbate" were fleeting and isolated, not to mention oblique and innocent. Rather, the bureau concluded that use of these words violated federal law, which prohibits "any obscene, indecent or profane language by means of radio communication." The language was hardly fleeting, Stewart continued, because the excerpts "reflect a dwelling on sexual matters, including sexual intercourse, orgasm, masturbation, lesbianism, homosexuality,* breasts, nudity, and male and female genitalia. Detailed 'descriptions' of those topics are not prerequisites to an indecency finding." In addition, surveys of actual listenership "cannot establish that children will not tune in incidentally or come across the material."

Stommel was delighted by the censure but thought the $6,000 fine ridiculously low. "I would like to see the stations lose their licenses for indecency and obscenity," she said.

Which is exactly what Karmazin was afraid of. He clearly sensed that the FCC ruling could complicate matters when it came time for Infinity to renew the broadcast licenses of the three stations. "We have been a good licensee," he told the author at the time. "When Oprah [Winfrey] says 'penis,' it's okay. When Howard Stern

---

*Stewart's choice of words provoked an angry reaction from the Gay & Lesbian Alliance Against Defamation. It wrote FCC chairman Alfred C. Sikes, stating that Howard Stern's "material is objectionable not *because of* its gay and lesbian content, *but because of the way in which* he maligns and distorts gay and lesbian people and foments violence against our community. Any reasonable person would judge from your statement that the FCC finds gay and lesbian content, per se, obscene."

says 'penis,' it's not okay. That's unfair. Our feeling is that we should have our First Amendment rights."

Karmazin decided to contest the fine. He would go to the courts if the FCC didn't "see the light." He added: "I would have done that show again."

"What's wrong with talking about sex?" Howard said on the air. "Sex is animal."

Perhaps. But in the aftermath of the $6,000 fine, several advertisers reassessed their purchase of commercial time on Howard's show. Spurred by the complaints of Joe DuPont, a New Jersey member of Morality in Media, who was offended by many routines that he heard on the program, Saratoga Springs Mineral Water discontinued its commercials on Stern after spending around $28,000 over two months. "Saratoga has an image to protect and customers, such as yourself, to consider," the company's marketing manager wrote to DuPont. Rickel Home Centers, an advertiser for two years, also pulled out, citing a concern "about 'tasteless comments' made by any broadcast personality, on any show, where we place our advertising." Other companies altered their commercial buys, but some of the fifty-three advertisers initially contacted by DuPont responded with vigorous endorsements of Howard and his right to use the airwaves.

Ken Loderhouse, a vice president of Great Bear Auto Centers, told DuPont: "As to Mr. Stern's style of humor, perhaps you and others 'just don't get it.' The bulk of his insults are 'camp' . . . meaning they are so bad, they are good. In other words, these 'camp' slurs are as antibigot as you can get—so tasteless that no one with any degree of intellectual candlepower can take them seriously. His satiric thrusts are aimed (usually quite accurately) at the simplistic yahoos, whose barnyard philosophies express social and ethnic differentiations in their most ugly form in order to cement their supposed moral superiority." DuPont also received no comfort from former New York City mayor Edward I. Koch, who had been a guest on Howard's program: "You have the right to disapprove or disagree with Mr. Stern's comments, but he has a right to be heard, and you have a right to turn him off."

But the Stommel and DuPont crusades—others would follow them in the years to come—offered striking evidence of how much impact a disgruntled listener could have when channeling his or her anger to the right places.

Howard charged that the $6,000 fine was part of a puritanical conspiracy led by the administration of President George Bush. It was a puritanical conspiracy that the First Amendment champion was eager to exploit. He marketed "Crucified by the FCC," a package of recordings from his radio show that depicted on its cover a Christlike Stern carrying a cross and included an excerpt from the "Christmas party."

Stern hawked the two cassettes through much of 1991 and early 1992. Shamelessly he priced the collection at $29.95, plus shipping and handling of $4.50 and New York sales tax. Total price $37.50, available only through a toll-free number. A guaranteed collector's item sure to grow in value, Howard proclaimed.

And in 1995 collectors would demand $600—and more—and get it—for the two original cassettes.

EIGHTEEN

If Howard Stern was so popular, so good, so funny, why didn't he have his own TV show? That was the question. A fair question, too.

Howard was the first to lament that radio was the basement of show business. *Real* stars worked on the tube or in the movies. "I kinda feel that my career has gotta break out," he said. He also wanted to erase the blemish of the Fox debacle. So he listened when Bob Woodruff, the vice president for program development at WWOR-TV, approached him early in 1990 with an invitation to do a weekly program. What appealed to Woodruff, above and beyond the sophomoric humor, was Howard's skill in getting rock stars and other celebrities to reveal themselves during interviews. Woodruff envisioned a show that would build on Howard's laughs and knack for gab.

Howard agreed, even though WWOR would pay him only a modest sum—around $10,000 a week, or about 10 percent of a weekly $100,000 budget that also had to cover production costs and the salaries of Robin, Fred, Jackie, Gary, and the station's staff. WWOR, based in Secaucus, New Jersey, was a snoozer on the New York dial. It primarily was known for sitcom reruns and broadcasts of New York Mets baseball games. The planned venture offered Howard a chance both to develop his TV talent and to be seen beyond New York. WWOR is a so-called superstation, its signal transmitted by cable systems across the country—to parts unfamiliar with Howard's radio show. The plan to syndicate the program to on-air stations as well held the potential of great financial return. Woodruff, who had been the executive producer of Morton Downey's outlandish show on WWOR, was confident that Howard would remain within the boundaries on controversial material and deliver more than a local product.

WWOR launched *The Howard Stern Show* with four Saturday night pilots. The first aired on July 14, 1990. After a hiatus, the show went into national syndication in January 1991, when WWOR made it an 11:00 P.M. addition to the station's own Saturday lineup. Unlike the Fox pilots, which reflected little creative control on Howard's part, the WWOR show was rude, lewd, disgusting, and hilarious— trademark Stern that pressed against the seams of acceptable television and split them open. Howard Rosenberg, the Pulitzer Prize–winning TV critic of the *Los Angeles Times*, described the show as "at once incredibly funny and incredibly vile."

In blackface and with gigantic lips so that he looked like a grotesque Clarence Thomas, the embattled nominee to the Supreme Court, Howard sipped from a Coke can conspicuously topped with "pubic hair" (recalling an episode alleged in the televised nomination hearings). He presented off-the-wall satires of a suspendered Larry King ogling a trio of female guests and of Johnny Carson ("Johnny Carstern") who socks one of his ex-wives as she sits in the *Tonight* show's guest chair.

Howard used homeless people as contestants in a game of "Howiewood Squares." In an astonishing display, the "Kielbasa Queen" suggestively swallowed a foot-long sausage, then just as easily slid it back out of her throat. The show also brought to candid-camera life the adventures of a roving "field reporter," John Melendez, a long-haired rocker with a staccato stutter and a fearlessness essential to his assignment. "Stuttering John" asked Ted Williams, the revered Hall of Famer: "Did you ever fart in the catcher's face?" He asked CBS anchor Dan Rather: "Do you check after you're done wiping?" Footage of Melendez at work also showed the antijournalist being ignored by just as many celebrities as stood still for his inane questions—or saw him tossed out the door by their handlers. As Melendez proved time and again, many stars have no sense of humor.

Melendez, a former unpaid intern from Long Island, had graduated to a salary of $20,000. He became the talk of the 1992 presidential campaign and the chat-show circuit after he disrupted a "news conference" given by Gennifer Flowers in January 1992 by posing questions that others in the press pack would never have asked. "Did Governor Clinton use a condom?" he wanted to know. "Will you be sleeping with any other presidential candidates?" As captured on videotape, an aide to Flowers threatened to halt the giggling session if there were any more "degrading" questions. But as the segment made clear, Melendez's guerrilla queries were far less degrading than the sight of a supposedly spurned lover venting her scorn on the national stage. Part of Howard's power as a host and a performer was his ability to tweak the famous simply by holding a mirror to their pomposity.

"Ratingswise, the show had phenomenal success," recalled Woodruff, who served as executive producer. In the New York area, Howard often doubled the ratings of NBC's *Saturday Night Live* during the half hour they overlapped. He also outdrew *SNL* among commercially valued segments of the audience, such as men eighteen to thirty-four and women eighteen to forty-nine. However, instead of converting these impressive numbers into commensurate commercial rates of $18,000 to $20,000 per thirty-second spot, WWOR was able to charge advertisers only about half that sum because many sponsors were afraid to associate with Howard.

On the one hand, Howard continued to prove that he was an effective salesman. Accompanied by curvaceous spokesmodels, who freely discussed their measurements while spilling out of bikinis, he repeatedly demonstrated the ease of using the Brother label maker. After the program in which a Brother commercial tested the use of a toll-free number, the company received hundreds of orders. Even when a skit about suicide doctor Jack Kevorkian urged viewers to phone an 800 number for information, an estimated 1,300 callers responded, flooding a legitimate business that happened to have the same toll-free digits. The costly outpouring prompted the proprietor to sue Howard and WWOR. (The case was settled out of court before going to trial in 1995.)

On the other hand, a chain of jewelry stores experienced such a backlash from customers after advertising with Howard and the slinky spokesmodels that the retailer discontinued its spots. "Some beers also wouldn't come on the show—their ad agencies advised against it," Woodruff recalled. Filling many of the commercial slots on WWOR were phone services that suggestively promised fun talk with beautiful women. (Have your credit card ready before dialing.)

Other developments behind the scenes threatened the fiscal health of the program. The syndicator, All American Television, was able to place Howard on about sixty-five stations covering roughly 70 percent of the country, but the figures were below the levels that attracted major advertisers (even if they were comfortable with the program). In addition, WWOR executives found that dealing with Howard became a time-consuming ordeal.

"Having Cheech and Chong as part of the Christmas show [in 1991] wasn't the problem, because we knew the show was in bad taste anyway," Woodruff said. "But Howard wanted to play the Virgin Mary and deliver Jesus with his legs in stirrups. You just don't play around with Jesus like that at Christmastime. There were tantrums and screaming and his agent calling." In the end, Howard's Mary eased her labor pains by smoking marijuana from a bong, as the "shepherds" Cheech and Chong, veterans of stoned comedy, toked up at her side. The final edit omitted the actual "birth" of Jesus, cutting instead to a "baby" whose head was that of the show's producer, Dan Forman. Cheech and Chong noted that the child "made a big dump in the straw, man."

"We [at WWOR] wanted to push the envelope, but we didn't want to kill ourselves doing it," Woodruff said in 1995, explaining why stirrups and a simulated birth were not allowed. "As someone who doesn't like to follow the norm, I loved the show," Woodruff added, "but there was a limit to how far it could go."

The show routinely taped about ninety minutes of material in order to have an hour that would be acceptable to the WWOR lawyer and make it through the editing process. "It was hard to argue with Howard," Woodruff remembered. " Often I had to take the phone from my ear. It was like working with a six-year-old when we wanted to take things out of the show. He'd say, '*You don't know a fucking thing! I'm the creative guy! I'm the guy who's doing it!*' He wasn't mean. He just wanted it his way. The grief factor in dealing with Howard was overwhelming. Between our lawyer, general manager, and me, we would spend half our week dealing with Howard's problems."

In addition, Woodruff and the other WWOR executives had to endure abuse from Howard during his radio show. "We work for idiots," Howard said in one tirade. "They're really pathetic over there."

George Back, president of All American Television, says he was caught in the middle. "The ratings [around the country] were growing," he recalled. "The show didn't take the country by storm overnight, but syndicated shows take time to build. I believe that stations would have upgraded the time periods they were giving the show, and it would have picked up more affiliates."

However, lacking a strong signal from WWOR that it planned to renew the program, a number of affiliates pulled out in order to make other arrangements in time for the fall 1992 season. This left fifty-three stations, covering about half the country. Because the program was producing insufficient revenues to offset the Stern-induced headaches, WWOR announced in July 1992 that it was pulling the plug. "We made this business decision, even though Howard Stern's show had high ratings, because the cost of the show exceeded the revenue," a WWOR spokeswoman said. On the same day, Howard's agent, Don Buchwald, put his own spin on the cancellation: Howard had quit—in order to make movies.

The first movie was supposed to be *The Adventures of Fartman*.

Howard had introduced his gas-blasting character on the radio in Washington, notably as a tool of American foreign policy. Fartman was a superhero; on his TV show, Howard portrayed him wearing a toilet seat around his neck. Howard also amazed—and repulsed—the 1992 MTV Video Music Awards when his designer-costumed Fartman dramatically (and unexpectedly) descended to the stage, exposed fleshy cheeks that poked out of his pants, and wiped out the podium with a smoky boom.

Movie studios had been pitching scripts, but Howard thought they were terrible. Short of a formal contract, he entered into a verbal agreement with New Line Cinema Corp., because the upstart company expressed a willingness to help him bring Fartman to the screen. Jonathan Lawton, a screenwriter whose credits included *Pretty Woman* and *Under Siege*, was hired to prepare a script. It apparently told the story of a New York editor who mutates into Fartman after bad guys fill him with a sludgelike mixture. Fartman then learns to cultivate his colonic powers.

New Line balked at producing a film sure to earn an R rating. It wanted PG-13. This turned off Howard. So did the company's wish to retain the potentially lucrative merchandising rights to *Fartman*. New Line had not secured these rights on two of its earliest pictures, *Teenage Mutant Ninja Turtles* and *Nightmare on Elm Street*, both of which grossed staggering millions of dollars in ticket sales and generated added millions from the sale of souvenir merchandise. Howard complained to *Variety*, "I think they took everything out on me because they blew it with the *Ninja Turtles* and Freddy Krueger [of *Nightmare*], where they didn't have merchandising rights." He said he was being offered only 5 percent of the subsidiary pie.

The disagreements soured the relationship. New Line and Howard drifted apart. *Fartman*, envisioned as a summer draw, sure to do *Wayne's World* kind of business—more than $100 million at the box office—joined Hollywood's pile of unproduced scripts.

* * *

Despite Howard's difficulties in TV and films, there was always radio—and radio was booming.

The fall 1991 ratings, released by Arbitron on January 2, 1992, showed that he had toppled all-news station WINS from first place in New York after a ten-year reign. No longer was he *numero uno* only among a particular age group, or among men, or among city residents. After a decade on the New York dial, he was top gun among all listeners, in the most competitive time period of the day, in the largest radio market in the country. He was reaching more than a million people a week, roughly 7.7 percent of the morning listening audience during an average quarter hour.

A close look at the numbers revealed incredible devotion. His fans were slavish listeners: an average of six and a half hours each week for the men, about four and a half hours for the women, and three and a half or so for teenagers—an average of around five and a half hours a week for the whole audience. On the other hand, WINS—whose familiar pitch, "You give us twenty-two minutes, we'll give you the world," helped pull in many more listeners—held its audience nowhere as long as the new champ of morning radio. WINS's more than 1.7 million morning listeners stayed tuned for an average of only three and a quarter hours a week—perhaps many were getting their twenty-two-minute dose of weather and news, then switching to Howard for outrageous commentary on the news or a frank recap of his lovemaking and/or masturbation of the night before.

If there were ever doubts about Howard's staying power, they were dispelled by the latest numbers. The figures also reflected the wider sea change in programming during his first New York decade. A relic of the 1950s and 1960s—the Top 40 format—had been revived and introduced to a new generation of listeners by WHTZ-FM ("Z-100"), WPLJ-FM, and stations outside New York that wed America's chart-topping hits to a raucous audioscape of satire, song dedications, trivia quizzes, cash giveaways, and silly contests. WHTZ's *Morning Zoo*, launched in 1983, was copied by Top 40 outlets in other markets. But after reaching lofty heights of popularity through the late 1980s (as Howard went from WNBC to "K-Rock"), Top 40 had started a slow fade once more. Ratings slumped, advertisers defected. WHTZ's commercial revenues dropped more than 25 percent, to $15 million, between 1990 and 1991, as Top 40 listening declined by nearly a third in the country's largest radio markets. Fewer pop songs packed the requisite wallop of mass appeal that was the lifeblood of the format. Pop music splintered into ever-evolving sub-genres—such as rap, dance tracks, modern rock, and contemporary jazz—and each sustained its own radio outlets on the increasingly fragmented dial. Programming to a mass of people—*broad*casting, as Top 40 had always done—became increasingly impractical as these niche formats siphoned off listeners, fracturing the mass.

The textbook case of so-called *narrow*casting was New York's WFAN. In 1987, it launched an all-sports format aimed solely at men. After a slow start, and the addition of Don Imus in 1988 (after WNBC went off the air), "the FAN" developed a striking pedigree of young to middle-aged males, many of them earning six figures. The station finished 1992 with estimated commercial billings of $35 million—tops in New York—prompting both Los Angeles' KMPC-AM and Washington's WGMS-AM that same year to drop music formats for sports. Beer makers, car dealers, and other "guy" sponsors had to place spots on WFAN, just as Howard's market-leading appeal to men during the morning hours made his show a must-buy for many of the same advertisers.

Howard's triumph on "K-Rock" also signaled that FM had come of age. He had defeated the entrenched morning powerhouses, such as the news station WINS and WOR-AM's long-running *Rambling with Gambling*, a traditional talk show, and he had done it from an FM base.

Although Howard had purged rock music from his program, he still projected a rock-and-roll sensibility. Like the male listeners whom "K-Rock" wanted to reach, he had grown up with the sounds of the Moody Blues, Joe Walsh, and the other rock veterans who occasionally visited his studio. He could talk and laugh it up with them. With his shaggy hair and black leathers, Howard managed to look every inch the renegade even as he traded in the currency of talk radio.

With the first-place finish declared, he crowned himself "King of New York" (and "King of the Jews") and organized a victory tour around midtown Manhattan for the morning of January 6, 1992. Rising to the occasion with the grace of a sore winner, he made rival station WNEW-FM, on Third Avenue at 42nd Street, one of the first stops during his mobile broadcast. He stepped from the van into the bitter morning cold and screamed into a bullhorn that WNEW-FM was the place "where rock stinks. You say 'rock lives,' we say 'rock stinks!'" He clucked about how "K-Rock" had whipped WNEW-FM in the ratings. He dredged up ancient history by referring to an incident with WNEW-FM's general manager (a former WRNW colleague): "Ted Utz, stop making anonymous calls to my house." Most of his listeners had no idea what he was talking about. (A joke, Utz insisted, that Howard had misinterpreted.)

Minutes later, as Robin Quivers shivered by his side, he broadcast insults outside the *Daily News* because it dared to compare him to Imus the day before. Imus's ratings on WFAN, though good, were nowhere near Stern's commanding 7.7 share. But Imus's newfound importance to New York taste makers threatened to dampen the king's joyful new year. After all, the *News* and other publications were examining Imus and Stern as if they occupied the same stage. It irked Howard. He hated Imus—or so he said.

The published comparisons followed the recent announcement that Infinity Broadcasting planned to buy WFAN for a record-setting $70 million. The two morning men, who had been spitting venom at each other since they both worked at WNBC, were ending up on the same team again. Like it or not, they would become the Mantle and Maris of Infinity.

Had the mighty Howard been involved in the purchase of WFAN? Absolutely not, Karmazin was quick to answer. "When Sony signs a deal with Michael Jackson, they don't ask Bruce Springsteen's advice," he said.

"Well," Howard protested on the air, "if that idiot Imus thinks he's working alongside of me, he's not." He took to calling him "'Anus' . . . because he smells like an anus, because he pees in phone booths." Howard indicated that he would no longer be Infinity's only fair-haired son when the WFAN sale went through. A week after the victory tour, Howard's anger over the pending marriage of his and Imus's stations added heat to the worshipful party broadcast from Tavern on the Green in honor of his thirty-eighth birthday.

"Is it good for me?" the gawky king asked of the WFAN deal. "No."

He said that he resented Imus "as a human being." He was unhappy "that Infinity will be pumping money into a competitor," which employed "this no-talent retard." He added: "By buying WFAN, they publicize my competition, and that can't be beneficial to me. . . . They didn't get my approval to go hire Anus."

So here Howard was, number one in the morning, being feted at Tavern on the Green in New York's Central Park by his colleagues, his parents, Joan Rivers, Jay Leno, Albert Brooks, Jon Bon Jovi, and the black activist Al Sharpton, and he could hardly lay off Imus. It was as if Imus had crashed the breakfast and knocked over the coffee urn.

Stern watchers did not have to look far to learn why his hatred of Imus had intensified. Much of it had to do with envy. He had reached his goal of topping Imus's big bucks with an annual salary believed to exceed $2 million. But Imus still enjoyed far more respectful attention. Twenty years after erupting on the New York airwaves, the original wildman of local radio had survived bouts with booze and cocaine and now was riding a new wave of appreciation for his irreverent bits and jive. He was hotter than ever. Governors and senators were on his program all the time; presidential candidate Bill Clinton would click with the I-Man (and continue to phone his radio show from the White House).

And the wave of appreciation showed no sign of cresting. The year just ended had brought a *New York* magazine cover story on Imus that was reported to have been one of the weekly's biggest sellers. There was a profile on ABC's *Prime Time Live* and a guest appearance on NBC's *Late Night with David Letterman*. Each of these plaudits would have annoyed Howard, who felt chronically shortchanged by high-profile media. "I'd just like a little mainstream recognition," he would complain. But Imus's date on Letterman's nightly bellwether-of-cool, in the summer of 1991, had burned Howard badly. "I don't feel special anymore," Howard told Letterman in his own subsequent appearance. "I thought I was your bitch. Now I feel Imus is your bitch." He asked Letterman to denounce Imus or he would be forced to "resign" as a guest. Letterman refused to do so, and he acted amused. Howard was not. If the ultimate hipster considered Imus as hip and as happening as Howard, then pouting Howard would never go on the show again.

"You know how I feel about one of his [Letterman's] guests," Howard said. "It just kinda ruined everything for me."

But Howard was not so foolish as to kiss off *Late Night* permanently. His nose pressed up against Letterman's bakery window, he later characterized the situation as unresolved. By early 1992, he hinted that there were "informal" talks to bring him back to *Late Night*.

"They won't say they won't have 'Anus' back on," he told his listeners. "It's an awkward situation." But he did eventually return.

Imus was laughing. He dismissed Howard as "a car wreck."

Howard continued to expand his empire, generating huge fees from affiliates that he split with Infinity.

On August 31, 1992, WNCX-FM in Cleveland, the country's twenty-third-largest radio market, added the show. Norman Wain, owner of the classic-rock station, agreed to a deal with agent Buchwald after listening to the program during a vist to New York. "Norman 'got' the humor," an associate explained. The terms: a four-year deal, starting at $400,000 for the first year.

On September 8, 1992, KEGL-FM in Dallas picked up Howard. He introduced himself to the seventh-largest market by mining the assassination of President John F. Kennedy for material. He said that Robin's breasts stuck out as Kennedy's head had stuck out of his limousine in Dallas. He promised to hold a Lee Harvey Oswald look-alike contest in Dallas when his program became number one. The terms: a five-year deal, starting at $700,000 for the first year.

On October 12, 1992, WQBK-FM, licensed to the upstate New York community of Rensselaer, near Albany, became the eighth affiliate. Howard obtained an especially lucrative contract to enter the Albany market, considering that it was only the fifty-fourth largest and his smallest to date. But he chose to characterize his upstate affiliation not as a lucrative business deal, but as a way to fulfill a personal vendetta against Ed Levine, the consultant at rival rock station WPYX-FM, in Albany. Levine had been program director of WJFK-FM for two years after the Washington station began carrying Howard's show. Having seen firsthand that Howard's strategy in new markets began with verbal attacks on all competitors, Levine seized the offensive weeks before the Stern program reached Albany. In published interviews, he fired at Howard as a way to buffer WPYX's new morning team of Mason and Sheehan. "Howard never understood that I was working him the way he works everybody else," Levine recalled in 1995. (After WQBK-FM added Howard's show, Levine started a profitable "Sternbusters" consultancy as a way to continue the feud with Howard while advising stations on how to compete against him.)

Howard's terms with WQBK: a five-year deal, starting at $300,000 for the first year and rising to $350,000. The contract represented a big leap of faith for a station that had estimated commercial billings of only $800,000 the year before. In addition, WQBK-FM was obligated to pay escalating cuts of the station's net advertising and network revenues, starting in the first year with 20 percent of the amount in excess of $1.99 million, 25 percent in excess of $2.28 million, and 30 percent in excess of $2.63 million. (The latter numbers would look like wishful thinking; although WQBK would more than double its annual revenues in three years, in 1994 the station grossed an estimated $1.7 million.)

On top of the fixed annual payments and the slices of revenues owed under the contract, WQBK-FM was obligated to pay $15,269, which was identified as the extra premium that Howard was being charged in 1992–93 to add the station to an insurance policy covering his "liability for certain claims arising out of the broadcast."

Also in October 1992, Howard became the king of Los Angeles radio. Summer ratings showed that he had ousted KLOS-FM's goofy Mark Thompson and Brian Phelps from first place in the morning. The Los Angeles win—a 6.4 share for Howard, a 5.6 for Mark and Brian—was more impressive than his New York crowning, because it had taken him only a year to achieve: Greater Media Inc., the first non-Infinity company to pick up Howard's show, had put him on KLSX-FM in Los Angeles on July 25, 1991. KLSX, a classic-rock station at the time, had been lagging in twelfth place with a 2.8 share of the total listening audience. Its morning show was a ratings embarrassment, claiming only a 1.8 share of the prime-time pie and wallowing in a tie for twenty-first place. "The conventional wisdom was that the market was so big, and it was so extremely difficult to break through, that we had to have someone with atomic energy in the morning," recalled Charles Banta, who was Greater Media's vice president for radio.

Not that it had been easy for Howard to line up a Los Angeles outlet or for Greater Media to sign him. When Howard negotiated his new contract with Infinity in 1990, he insisted that the company allow him to syndicate his show in Los Angeles. He and Buchwald viewed Los Angeles as a potentially grand extension of Howard's market—a way to multiply his radio audience and to increase the potential number of customers for his profitable pay-per-view specials and video sales. However, Karmazin, the Infinity president, was uneasy about exposing the radio company's number one cash cow to Los Angeles' allures of television and films. What if they turned Howard's head away from radio? Buchwald, recognizing that it would be difficult to persuade Howard's boss, told an associate, "L.A. is going to happen over Mel Karmazin's dead body."

When Karmazin finally was persuaded, he came around to the view that syndication into Los Angeles would allow Infinity to increase revenues (from its cut of Howard's deal) without having to purchase a second station in the market. It already owned KROQ-FM.

Even with Karmazin in agreement, negotiations with Greater Media spanned more than six months. The parties sorted through the complexities of liability coverage and other details. What helped ease the process were Howard's warmth and politeness. "I was extremely impressed by how very different he was from his on-air persona," Banta said. "He was shy in some cases and very considerate." At the signing of the contract, a gathering mainly of men, Howard conspicuously crossed the room to greet and act the gentleman toward a female attorney working for Greater Media. "The feeling was, he was no monster," an executive with the company recalled.

According to sources familiar with the KLSX agreement, it was a seven-year deal that called for an annual base fee of slightly less than $1 million—but with no share of the income generated by the show. Only after the Los Angeles arrangement led to the opening of other markets for Stern's show were advertising percentages written into the contracts as precisely as they appeared in the Albany package. Bonuses tied to Howard's ratings performance in Los Angeles boosted KLSX's annual payouts into seven figures. Although the station's mix of advertisers changed dramatically after Howard went on the air—as many blue-chip sponsors originally refused to be part of his show—the addition of local retailers more than made up for the Stern-related increase in the station's overhead. *Duncan's Radio Market Guide*, an annual review of commercial billings, estimated that advertising revenues at KLSX went from $16.2 million in 1990, the year before Howard arrived, to $19 million in 1992, his first full year on the station.

NINETEEN

In the weeks following the Los Angeles victory, Howard's career took two leaps forward with the start of his radio show on the Chicago dial and the announcement that he was joining E! Entertainment Television as host of a weekly cable program, *The Howard Stern "Interview."*

On October 15, 1992, WLUP-AM in Chicago brought Howard to the country's third-largest radio market, advancing his dream to have a national broadcast. The move culminated drawn-out negotiations in which the owner of WLUP-AM, Evergreen Media Corp., demonstrated its repeated willingness to dig deeper into its purse in order to win over Howard. Scrutiny of the Chicago experience reveals the painstaking process of becoming a Stern affiliate and the negotiating acumen of Stern and Buchwald.

Evergreen's Lawrence J. Wert, the vice president and general manager of WLUP-AM and WLUP-FM ("the Loop"), began the romance in January 1992 by telling Buchwald that economic conditions and a desire to grow had prompted the company to consider different programming on its two Chicago stations. Jonathon Brandmeier, the enormously popular morning man heard on both stations, would remain only on WLUP-FM, thereby creating a plum morning opening on WLUP-AM, because Wert predicted that Evergreen's other Chicago stars, midday personality Kevin Matthews and the afternoon team of Steve Dahl and Garry Meier, were unlikely to be moved into the vacant AM slot. Wert wrote to Buchwald, "We determined that nowhere in the country is there a more appropriate proven talent line up [sic] for Howard to be part of. We are familiar with Howard's program, and its broadcast to Los Angeles. We, too, would plan to air it in current form." Wert proposed a five-year deal that would start at $200,000 and rise in $50,000 increments to $400,000 in the fifth year. Wert also offered a bonus plan that would pay Howard $50,000 for every half point he added to WLUP-AM's morning ratings, which then stood at a modest 2.3 share of the listening audience.

Buchwald rejected the proposed package the next day, stating in a letter to Wert: "In my intermittent and brief chats with your associate, I sketched a general form and conditions which would 'make the project work.' Your offer, I'm sure well intentioned, is a far cry from my suggestion."

Four days later, Wert sweetened Evergreen's proposal to $300,000 the first year, $400,000 the second year, and $500,000 in each of the last three years. The bonus, though described differently, was the same as before: $100,000 for each share point added to the ratings.

Buchwald dismissed this plan, too, but encouraged the flirtation. He brought Howard to a meeting with Wert and his Evergreen associates in New York on February 11. Howard and Buchwald said they were concerned that the lesser popularity of the AM dial would work against the success of the show. They wanted an assurance that Evergreen would make the kind of long-term commitment needed to establish the program on AM and that the company would defend against FCC actions that might arise in Chicago. These conceptual matters were easier for Evergreen to finesse than the financial imperatives of doing business with Howard. As the shock jock had made clear several times since his Washington days, he preferred to have most of his money laid out in front of him, not tied to vagaries such as ratings and sales. "Right now the compensation issue looks to be our impasse," Wert explained to Buchwald after their meeting. "You are looking for a significant advance commitment, we want to pay out on performance."

Nevertheless, Evergreen was willing to go higher. Wert proposed a three-year contract with an annual guarantee of $500,000 or 15 percent of the commercial billing on the show, whichever was greater. In addition, every fragment of ratings improvement would be rewarded; Wert offered a $10,000 bonus for each tenth of a share point that Howard added. Translation: If Howard were to add only one full share point in the ratings ($100,000) and draw half the advertising generated by Brandmeier (for a 15 percent share of $813,000), his annual take would reach $913,000, well within reach of seven-figure returns in successive years.

Still no good.

Buchwald and Howard may have doubted that the morning man's performance on WLUP-AM would increase the audience and the commercial billings so quickly as to raise the compensation far beyond the $500,000 guarantee, at least early on. In addition, Buchwald was receiving inquiries about the show from two competing Chicago stations, WCKG-FM and WWBZ-FM. But Evergreen wanted Howard Stern. While expressing a concern that a larger annual guarantee "would leave us vulnerable to a scenario that might not result in a win-win partnership," Wert drafted still another plan on April 24 that increased the guarantees to $750,000, $850,000, and $1 million over three years. This new proposal called for quarterly bonuses equal to 5 percent of the show's net ad revenue (that is, gross revenue minus advertising agency commissions that were not to exceed 15 percent). "That's it . . . clean and without any risk to you or your associate," Wert wrote to Buchwald. "Also no vulnerability to Arbitron [ratings] calculations." Based on projected advertising revenues of $5 million in the first year, the total haul would come to $1 million, Wert explained. But Howard would remain far behind Jonathon Brandmeier's base salary of $2.5 million.

As spring turned to summer, Howard passed the point at which he had predicted his Chicago venture would begin. Negotiations continued as Wert gushed about his station's prospects. "The bottom line is we truly believe that AM1000 is the absolute perfect home for the *Howard Stern Show* in Chicago," he told Buchwald. "There are thousands of morning show/music stations all over the country. There will be only one mega-talent featured [on] AM1000."

The final elements for putting Howard on WLUP-AM involved rejiggering the station's schedule and getting Howard to sign on the dotted line. Wert had expected Brandmeier to continue doing mornings on WLUP-FM. But "Johnny B" chose to give up his early-hours grind of ten years for an afternoon program on WLUP-AM with an eye toward syndication. Dahl and Meier planned to end their long stretch as afternoon personalities and take over the morning show on WLUP-FM (which they had hosted a decade earlier).

On September 29, Wert, Karmazin, and Howard (as president of his own company, One Twelve Inc.—One Twelve for his birthday, January 12) signed a thirteen-page contract. Besides spelling out the annual fees ($750,000, $850,000, $1 million), the 5 percent cut of ad revenue, and the schedule of payments, the document stipulated that Evergreen had to pay a portion of the premium of an insurance policy taken out by One Twelve as protection against "certain claims arising out of the broadcast." Evergreen also agreed to indemnify and hold harmless One Twelve and Infinity Broadcasting against any and all expenses stemming from complaints filed by or with the FCC in connection with the broadcast of the program in Chicago. (Evergreen's liability was not to exceed $500,000 in the first year, $750,000 in the second, and $1 million in the third.)

WLUP-AM could not delete or edit any announcements, "whether live or pre-recorded, promoting products in which Howard Stern has an interest." Chicago listeners would receive the full thrust of Howard's promotions for his videotapes, pay-per-view specials, and other products. But the agreement gave Evergreen the right to delete from the broadcast nine words listed on a separate page—all of George Carlin's "seven dirty words" except piss, which presumably was no longer dirty, plus scumbag, asshole, and douchebag. The banned words also included any "combination or derivative of the foregoing words, excluding the words douche and scum." (It was amusing to imagine attorneys for Infinity and Evergreen considering the merits of various curse words as part of their deliberations.)

Now that Evergreen had a signed deal, the scheduled October 15, 1992, startup on WLUP-AM promised a dandy sideshow. The groundbreaking Howard would be facing the groundbreaking Dahl in an ego-powered morning war—competition that was sure to receive far greater attention in the industry than they had generated during the few months in 1980–81 that their shows were part of a four-way contest for Detroit's rock audience.

Howard was now thirty-eight years old, the happily married father of two girls (with a third child on the way), the owner of a suburban home with a pool, a radio chronicler of his angst and prejudices.

Dahl was thirty-seven, the happily married father of three, the owner of a suburban home with a pool, a radio chronicler of *his* own angst and prejudices.

The two had plenty in common, including spats with the FCC over indecent broadcasts. Now they were working for the same company—and battling for turf.

"Fuck Howard Stern," Dahl told a breakfast meeting of WLUP's advertisers at the Four Seasons in Chicago. "If you spend one penny [advertising] on his show, it's a big mistake. He's a sick, distorted, fucked-up man."

Howard, who had listened in Hartford to tapes of Dahl's early Chicago antics and had gone into radio syndication to pick up where Dahl had stumbled, hammered the market veteran during his October 15 debut. He disputed Dahl's charge that he had pirated the Chicagoan's style.

In striking contrast with Evergreen's initial enthusiasm for Howard's show, the company began to sour on its affiliation by the early summer of 1993. After two ratings periods—not a long span of time, but long enough to detect a pulse of popularity—the program was doing poorly. In Chicago's winter survey, released in April 1993, Howard finished seventeenth overall in the morning. He scored a 2.0 share of the total listening audience, up from a 1.9 that he had attained during his first quarter on the Chicago dial. He was thirteenth among listeners twenty-five to fifty-four years of age. *Chicago Sun-Times* columnist Richard Roeper saw blood in the water: "Stern predicted he'd be No. 1 in Chicago within a year, but it's much more likely he'll go the way of the late Carnegie Deli on Michigan Avenue and the quite dead Nathan's (New York style) Hot Dogs on Rush Street—another wildly successful New York product gone belly-up in Chicago."

A view widely held in Chicago media circles was that the City of the Big Shoulders by nature had little use for New York–style rude and raunch. Los Angeles, on the other hand, may have been more hospitable to Howard's increasing amount of airplay with Hollywood stars and other celebrities; in addition, KLSX, the Los Angeles affiliate, had prepared listeners for Stern's arrival by making generous use of billboards and print advertising.

Evergreen expressed unhappiness about the ratings to Buchwald, who was hearing whispers in the industry that Evergreen planned to switch WLUP-AM to an all-sports format and put Stern, Brandmeier, and the other personalities on WLUP-FM. Evergreen, which was to become a publicly traded company in May 1993, subject to the scrutiny and sensitivities of would-be investors, was indeed having second thoughts about carrying Howard's chutzpah in the showcase position of morning drive. Noting that Boston's WBCN-FM recently had begun to present Howard on a tape delay at night, Evergreen proposed doing the same thing—relocating the Stern show to the so-called safe harbor of evening, where it would be free from the FCC's daytime strictures against indecent programming. Buchwald vetoed the evening idea, calling it an insult, and sought to reassure Evergreen: "We are all agreed this is no easy task to perform but Howard . . . is in it for the long haul—and he & we will win," he wrote to Wert.

Meanwhile, FCC fines had been piling up since two weeks after Howard's Chicago launch. He had become a violation machine.

The commission, which was still seeking $6,000 from Infinity for the 1988 "Christmas party" broadcast, imposed a $105,000 fine on Greater Media in October 1992 for airing indecent material during Howard's show on Los Angeles' KLSX. Speaking with Geraldo Rivera on one of the cited broadcasts, Howard had said: "The closest I came to making love to a black woman was, I masturbated to a picture of Aunt Jemima. . . . I did it right on her kerchief." On another program, reacting to the applause given comedian Pee-wee Herman in an appearance on MTV after he had been charged with exposing himself in a Florida theater, Howard said: "I was sickened. I said I wish that Pee-wee would come out and coat the whole front row with his love juice and really give it to them right in the face. And, as punishment, Pee-wee should be forced to sit in a tub of sperm."

Thomas Milewski, Greater Media's executive vice president, argued that broadcasters were hard-pressed to understand what was permissible under the FCC's indecency rules. The company contested the fines while proceeding with greater caution—the firm quietly took advantage of the time difference between New York and Los Angeles, monitoring Howard's programs and ordering KLSX to delete segments that might be considered actionable by the FCC. The editing process worked this way: Between 3:00 and 6:00 A.M., California time, a period when indecent programming was permissible, KLSX carried the show live and unedited. During the same stretch of time, at Greater Media's headquarters in East Brunswick, New Jersey, junior lawyer Ken Wyker listened to Howard live over New York's "K-Rock," noting those portions that KLSX should omit from the station's taped playback between 6:00 and 11:00 A.M. Wyker made most of the decisions about what should be snipped; other directives came from Milewski. Among the riffs lifted from the tape-delayed playback on KLSX were a few of Howard's graphic fantasies about Cher and other Hollywood beauties. He was annoyed by the censorship, but other nervous Stern affiliates did the same as they sought to show the FCC that they were responsible licensees.

Another indecency violation had been announced by the FCC in December 1992. Citing "the apparent pattern of indecent broadcasting exhibited by Infinity over a substantial period," the commission fined the radio company $600,000, the largest forfeiture order in the agency's history, for airing the same broadcasts singled out in the Greater Media case on the Infinity stations in New York, Philadelphia, and Washington. In August 1993, acting on additional documented complaints about Howard's show, the commission levied a fine of $500,000 against Infinity and a penalty of $73,750 against Americom Las Vegas Ltd. Partnership, the licensee of Stern affiliate KFBI-FM in Las Vegas.

On August 20, 1993, ten months after launching Howard on Chicago radio, WLUP general manager Wert solemnly notified Buchwald and Karmazin that Evergreen was terminating its agreement to carry the show. "We were aware when we signed the contract that there had been past problems with Howard Stern broadcasts, and we could not afford to be exposed to serious FCC violations in the future," Wert wrote. He said "there is no doubt that *The Howard Stern Show* has continued to violate the FCC's present and ongoing conception of indecency. . . . This is not the type of programming which we can or will purchase, nor is it what was contemplated by the express terms of our agreement."

The reasons for the Stern cancellation given by Wert seemed curious in light of Evergreen's vigorous defense against a $6,000 indecency fine levied by the FCC four years earlier in connection with broadcasts made by Dahl and his partner, Garry Meier. Refusing to pay even in the face of a stiffening federal resolve to collect the fine, Evergreen chairman Scott Ginsburg argued that the FCC's policy on indecency was unworkable and unconstitutionally vague. "What gives?" asked *Chicago Sun-Times* broadcasting columnist Robert Feder. "With Evergreen's $28 million purchase of WWBZ-FM (103.5) about to come up for FCC approval, the company didn't want to risk trouble with the feds for airing Stern's show."

Wert insisted to reporters that Dahl and Meier were not indecent on the air. "We're not saying Howard Stern is indecent," Wert told Feder. "But the FCC is. And that's an unacceptable risk for us to take." Wert later claimed that Evergreen had been unaware when it signed the contract with Stern that new complaints about his show were pending before the FCC. Seeking to underscore Evergreen's fear of FCC fines, Wert noted in a 1994 court filing that the newspaper *Electronic Media* had reported that further FCC violations by Infinity might imperil the company's bid to acquire a Los Angeles station. The story was published four days before Evergreen terminated its Stern contract. "At this time [of the report]," Wert recalled, "Evergreen was also considering several acquisitions of radio stations that required FCC approval."

Slow ratings, corporate considerations, and revised programming strategies at WLUP-AM and WLUP-FM had conspired to abort Howard's stay in Chicago. Not for a minute did Howard or Buchwald believe that a fear of fines alone had led to the cancellation. Howard argued that Evergreen's spin was a smokescreen for ratings concerns. Buchwald maintained that good ratings on an AM station would have taken time to build. "I can't tell you what their motivation was," Buchwald complained to a reporter, "but I can tell you they tried to get out of the contract for several months prior without ever mentioning the FCC or giving that as their reason. The first inkling we had that they were going to use the FCC as their excuse for reneging on the contract came twelve hours before we received their termination letter."

After yanking Howard from WLUP-AM's morning slot, Evergreen executives briefly considered rescheduling his show as part of an imminent realignment of its two stations. But on September 23, a few days before the new lineups were unveiled— WLUP-AM became an all-sports station, renamed WMVP-AM— Infinity and Howard struck back. They filed a suit against Evergreen in U.S. District Court in New York that sought $35 million for breach of contract, breach of fiduciary responsibility, fraud, and indemnity, and also asked $10 million in punitive damages. The suit charged that Evergreen knew of the risks involved in carrying Stern and that the company's stated reasons for discontinuing the show were malicious and designed to injure the program.

The suit was quickly dismissed from federal court on a filing technicality and was resubmitted by the plaintiffs in state supreme court, also in New York. Papers filed in the case spelled out the terms of the Chicago deal—no doubt an agony for Stern, who fiercely guarded information about his business affairs. The papers indicated that his WLUP-AM show had been attracting commercials at a modest rate of about $1 million a year.

In the summer of 1994, the court threw out the plaintiffs' claims of fraud and breach of fiduciary duty, trimming the suit to a breach-of-contract and indemnity action.

On March 29, 1995, Howard rebounded on the Chicago dial, when rock station WCKG-FM, owned by Cox Enterprises Inc., picked up his show. WCKG was Howard's twenty-third affiliate (until it grew uncomfortable with his on-air remarks against Chicago competitors, including WRCX-FM's Mancow Muller, and dropped the show six months later. WJJD-AM, an Infinity-owned talk station, stepped in immediately, becoming Stern's third Chicago affiliate in two years). The suit against Evergreen dragged on—the plaintiffs were having difficulty. On June 6, 1995, for the second time, state supreme court justice Beatrice Shainswit denied Infinity and Stern's motion for a summary judgment—this time on their two remaining claims against Evergreen. "Here, there are genuine triable issues arising not only from disputes as to the material facts, but from the numerous defenses which defendant has pleaded," the judge ruled. "The record presented to the court indicates that plaintiffs have failed to cooperate with discovery [proceedings], and have sought to capitalize on the obstacles they interposed to cut off access to evidence that could bolster the defenses. Evergreen has had no opportunity to conduct discovery on disputed material facts."

Justice Shainswit noted that Infinity and Stern had twice rejected Evergreen's proposal to move Howard's show into a late-night slot free from indecency regulations: "We thus have a record whereby plaintiffs were unyielding in continuing indecent broadcasts, and were risking forfeiture, not only of their own broadcasting privileges, but defendant's as well."

She concluded: "The parties fundamentally disagree on every relevant fact at issue."

A trial loomed. Howard escalated his war of words against Evergreen's executives. One summer morning he addressed Wert: "I wish AIDS on you, and I wish AIDS on your family."

An outside lawyer was appointed to referee discovery proceedings, which Justice Shainswit ordered completed by February 1, 1996.

Just as the viewer response to Howard's first pay-per-view special helped him overcome his Fox strikeout, the overwhelming success of his first book—*Private Parts*—in the fall of 1993 obscured the Chicago washout. However, the book was conceived for a different purpose. In the fall of 1992, when Buchwald started to sound out New York publishers about an autobiography, one of the agent's main objectives was to uproot the impression in the entertainment industry that the shock jock somehow had failed in the movie business when the *Fartman* deal with New Line fell through. "There was a perception that he had taken a hit," Buchwald told a reporter in an unguarded moment. "So we thought of the book as something that would both produce income and suggest to people that Howard had economic clout."

Howard was loath to admit it, but the publishing market had been softened for him by fellow radio broadcaster Rush Limbaugh. When Buchwald was shopping Howard's book, Limbaugh's *The Way Things Ought to Be* reigned as the stunning hit of the fall 1992 publishing season. Signed by Pocket Books, a unit of Simon & Schuster, the collection of Limbaugh's conservative political views had gone back to press so many times that there were 1.9 million hardcover copies in print after three months. Limbaugh's nation-wide radio popularity and the verve with which he promoted the book on his radio and TV shows translated into gargantuan profits—hardcover sales alone earned Limbaugh $3 million. Limbaugh enlightened New York book publishers as to the potential mass appeal of the radio medium.

"Well, you're going to find a lot of similarity between me and Rush Limbaugh, because he got his entire fucking show from me," Howard would later grouse to *Rolling Stone*. "Rush Limbaugh was a failed disc jockey until he heard my radio show and said, 'Oh, that's what you do.' And what I resent about that fat cock is that he—just like so many other pricks in our industry—rather than saying, 'Hey, I give Howard some credit for opening things up for me,' every chance he gets, he says, 'I don't want to be pumped in with Howard Stern.'"

In early 1993, Howard signed a contract with Simon & Schuster, the parent company of Limbaugh's publisher, to write a book that would be edited by Judith Regan, who had shepherded Limbaugh's volume into print. His advance was around $1 million, more than four times what Pocket, with modest expectations, had given Limbaugh. Because Simon & Schuster wanted to bring out the book in the fall, Howard absorbed himself in the project through the spring and early summer to meet the short deadline. He drew from a large computerized archive of articles that had been written about him and of discussions heard on his show to produce an unwieldy manuscript that he then brilliantly shaped into *Private Parts* with the assistance of writer Larry (Ratso) Sloman, a cigar-smoking hippie type known for a book about Bob Dylan's Rolling Thunder Revue tour of the 1970s and his work on alternative publications such as the magazine *National Lampoon*.

Publication in October triggered rapid sales that recalled Limbaugh's print debut—as well as a fanatical outpouring unique to Howard's legions. Sales were so swift that Simon & Schuster had to more than double its initial printing, distributing a total of 750,000 copies within the first week, then adding 250,000 more by the first month's end. An author signing at a Barnes & Noble store on Fifth Avenue in New York City shut down the thoroughfare near St. Patrick's Cathedral as an estimated ten thousand fans angled for peeks and autographs. They chanted: "Howard! Howard! Howard!" An executive at the bookstore chain described it as a far bigger turnout than those for General Norman Schwarzkopf and basketball star Magic Johnson. Four days later, the crowd at a signing in the Wall Street area stretched for four blocks.

"This is, like, the biggest thing I've ever done," Howard said. "Since I wrote this book, I'm a near deity."

Private Parts debuted on *Publishers Weekly*'s national bestseller list at number one. The book led *USA Today*'s newly inaugurated best-seller list on October 28 as it outsold the second and third titles combined, Robert James Waller's *The Bridges of Madison County* and Waller's new novel, *Slow Waltz in Cedar Bend*. An autographing in Pasadena, California, drew ten thousand people in December.

Less an autobiography than a book-length comedy routine about his life and politically incorrect opinions, *Private Parts* was vintage Stern—self-loathing and self-congratulatory, hateful of his enemies and loving toward his wife, putridly rank and wickedly funny—a 448-page exercise in anti-Establishment freedom that shrewdly cloned his outrageous radio persona. Some stores and libraries declined to stock the book. Among them was the Rockville Centre Public Library. No hometown hero was he.

As the $23 title went on to sell a million copies in hardcover, promising Howard a payoff of about $3.5 million, the response revealed a wider mainstream acceptance of the shock jock than was conveyed by radio ratings alone. Until the book was published, sending autograph-seeking men and women running into the streets of New York City's midtown and financial district, Stern loyalists easiest to spot were the truck drivers who lumbered through Manhattan's clogged avenues while listening to his show cranked up to maximum volume. Now, it could be seen all too clearly that his following included white-collar professionals, young and middle-aged, who shortened train commutes to the Connecticut, New Jersey, and Long Island suburbs by reading the book and laughing, sometimes not only to themselves. Unlike Limbaugh, whose *Way Things Ought to Be* was panned by many book critics who did not appreciate his chest-thumping humor or faulted his rigidly conservative approach, Howard drew noticeably respectful media attention. The book was funny.

He had had a taste of respectful attention earlier, when the E! cable channel's launch on November 27, 1992, of *The Howard Stern "Interview"* warmed critics to his probing style. In this third stab at television, Howard's weekly one-on-ones with Garry Shandling, Donald Trump, James Brown, Boy George, and other celebrities who shared the couch with him went well beyond the fawning chit-chat that marked talk shows featuring actors and singers with products to plug. He did not interview his guests so much as he needled and nudged them for information. He persisted in asking an amused Moon Unit Zappa, a performer of little achievement, exactly how she spent her time and if she was sponging off her famous father, musician Frank Zappa. Howard Rosenberg, the *Los Angeles Times* critic, had liked Stern's syndicated TV show, and he liked this one, too, writing that it "yielded more information than what's available from traditional talk shows. There may not be a better half hour on television." As the antihost confessed, "I was expecting everyone to give me negative reviews."

For all of the costly fines levied against his radio employers for broadcast indecency, for all of the moralizing against him by Morality in Media and other organizations, the huge sales of his book and the accompanying media reaction indicated that Howard had pressed so hard against the walls separating acceptable from unacceptable humor that he'd toppled them.

"Howard Stern is the most brilliant—and misunderstood— comic artist in America," gushed Owen Gleiberman in his B+ review of the book in *Entertainment Weekly*. "He is also the Lenny Bruce of the information age: a kamikaze hipster with a machine-gun brain, a slash-and-burn rock & roll nihilist who, in his hostility and wit, his dazzlingly intuitive observational powers, his savage compulsion to smash every taboo that middle-class society places in his path, is probably the only professional entertainer in the country who answers to no one but himself." He was given celebrity treatment by David Letterman and *People*, and by *Donahue*, *Dateline NBC*, and *CBS This Morning*. After writing off Howard's pay-per-view work and noting that the syndicated show "was longer on cruelty than effort," *Daily News* critic David Bianculli observed: "It's pretty clear, after watching Stern on the tube this week, that things have been reversed. Stern has learned how to handle himself better in a visual medium, and now knows what to do with television. . . . Stern has matured as a TV personality—and trust me when I say that I never expected to write a sentence containing both the words 'Stern' and 'mature.'"

Judging from his next move, one could presume that raves such as these, confirming Howard's belief in his own economic clout and comedic appeal, also unsettled him. Perhaps they clashed with the bad-boy persona that he had cultivated for nearly fifteen years outside the media mainstream. He would not disappoint his hardcore fans. On *The Miss Howard Stern New Year's Eve Pageant*, a pay-per-view special produced by Main Events Television and transmitted from Symphony Hall in Newark, New Jersey, a scantily clad woman put previously chewed food into the mouth of her "slave" girl and another woman sang a tune calling for the anal rape of the president, his wife, and the pope. After a topless woman fainted, Howard said, "I can't believe that nobody fucked her while she was passed out."

New York Post TV editor Adam Buckman, called the end-of-1993 special "the most disgusting two hours in the history of television." Free in pay-per-view territory from FCC restraints, he "turns out to be more nasty and hateful than he ever seemed to be on radio."

The bottom line? It was the most popular nonsports event in the history of pay-per-view. It attracted around four hundred thousand households, at $39.95 each, for gross revenues of nearly $16 million. In topping the previous record, held by the singing group New Kids on the Block, which in 1990 had drawn about 270,000 subscribers, Howard himself pocketed as much as $4 million.

In announcing ahead of time that some would consider the TV special raunchy, Howard put the entertainment industry on notice that he did not care about its reaction. According to Buchwald, the show was aimed at fans—and their response was "very rewarding." Predictably, the media backlash, and reports that Fox owner Rupert Murdoch was horrified by what he saw, were cited in the collapse of discussions to try yet another late-night show on the fourth network, this time as Chevy Chase's successor. Talks with Paramount Pictures for a low-budget movie version of *Private Parts* also broke off around this time; it was likely that the studio lost out by denying Howard's standing request for big money up front. *Variety* columnist Michael Fleming detailed a Paramount proposal giving Howard a cut of gross receipts in lieu of a big payment for the film rights and an acting fee. It wasn't Howard's kind of deal.

Paramount's withdrawal cleared the way for a seven-figure agreement, in March 1994, with Rysher Entertainment Inc., a TV production company eager to expand into movies. But as months passed, the snail-like pace of the project recalled the *Fartman* fizzle with New Line. Shooting was to begin in the fall—but did not. Rysher confirmed that John Avildsen, of *Rocky* fame, was going to direct; weeks later, he backed out. There were disagreements over the script. The chances of producing a summer 1995 release faded. It would be two years before a movie version of *Private Parts* went into production.

Between the book royalties and the pay-per-view profits, Howard's earnings in the final months of 1993 totaled around $7.5 million (exclusive of the riches that awaited him in 1994 from the paperback edition of *Private Parts* and the video of his New Year's Eve show). He held commanding positions in radio, book publishing, and on cable TV. But the self-proclaimed "King of All Media" still awaited his star turn on the wide screen.

TWENTY

Howard revealed in several interviews that he had practiced Transcendental Meditation since the early 1970s. But few knew the level of his commitment to the technique or that his wife and his parents also were serious about TM.

A major goal of meditation is to get in touch with the true self. As defined by the Indian guru Maharishi Mahesh Yogi, who developed the Transcendental Meditation program in 1957, in TM "the conscious mind comes to a state of self-referral awareness, which is the simplest form of human awareness where consciousness is open to itself." Repeating one's mantra for fifteen to twenty minutes in the morning and evening, while sitting comfortably with eyes closed, the individual is supposed to experience a state of restful alertness, or transcendental consciousness. TM is said to produce many benefits, including clearer thinking, because, the maharishi says, transcendental consciousness is the fundamental field of existence—and one of infinite creativity.

TM was first popularized in the West in 1967, when the Beatles listened to the maharishi in Britain and stayed with the spiritual leader at his ashram in India. In the United States, the growth period for the TM movement occurred during the mid-1970s—spurred, many practitioners say, by Merv Griffin's long television interview in 1976 with the maharishi and the broadcaster's revelation to the audience that he, too, meditated. Several meditation centers opened on Long Island around this time, but the Sterns of Rockville Centre were years along in their enthusiasm.

By the 1980s, Ray Stern was taking advanced courses at a TM center in the Long Island community of Huntington, about a half hour's drive from her Rockville Centre home. "She realized there was more to life than what she saw on the surface—and she wanted to tap into it," said Jennine Fellmer, an instructor at the center. "She was dedicated to TM and taking care of herself and refining her nervous system."

Ben Stern, who for years had encouraged work-weary friends and business associates to learn TM as a way to relax and energize themselves, also progressed in the technique. "Ben was a fun-loving type of individual who was very awake," Fellmer recalled. "He liked to challenge things, so we challenged his challenging." Ben accepted the challenge of taking a thirty-three-lesson course, the Science of Creative Intelligence, taught by Fellmer. The course, which met for two and a half hours two nights a week and on weekends, posits that the nature of life is to grow and evolve toward fulfillment. The course aims to impart a broader perspective of the environment useful in an individual's personal and professional life.

As his parents used some of their leisure time to pursue greater balance through TM and related instruction, Howard took the unusual step of seeking a consultation from an Ayurvedic doctor visiting the TM center. Ayurveda, which means "science of life," is India's traditional medicine. Ayurvedic physicians, many of whom are MDs, grasp a person's wrist to read not only the standard pulse, but also various other pulses recognized by these trained practitioners. After using this kind of tactile CAT scan, Ayurvedic doctors may advise a patient to avoid spicy foods, to exercise more, or to undergo a tonsillectomy. Specific diets also may be recommended.

The nature of Howard's consultation remained a private matter. However, his submission to such an unorthodox form of medicine (since popularized in the United States by Deepak Chopra, M.D., author of the best-seller *Ageless Body, Timeless Mind*), combined with twice daily meditation, dramatically illustrated that the off-air Howard bore little resemblance to the shock jock who urged shapely women to disrobe in his studio. Although the particulars of Howard's off-air lifestyle were not known to most of his colleagues and listeners, the difference between his public and private selves was greater than they imagined.

"TM gives Howard enormous energy, clarity of mind, and creativity," said Janet Hoffman, a TM instructor and director of the Maharishi Vedic School in Manhattan, where Robin Quivers took advanced courses. "Howard is a very nice person, very kind. But he's also an entertainer, so people don't necessarily see that kind side of him."

Hoffman points out that the 1.5 million Americans who have learned TM range from generals in the military to murderers who were taught the technique in prison. In considering whether there was a contradiction between Howard's ardent embrace of the serene practice of TM and his wild actions on the radio, Hoffman said: "That's like saying about a person who loves children so much, why does he cheat on his taxes? Not all qualities are the same. You grow from where you are."

In other words, TM does not turn people into angels.

"People are surprised I meditate," Howard acknowledged to a reporter, "because they think, Well, how come he's such a maniac? But the thing is, when you meditate, you're a better maniac."

Howard privately demonstrated his belief in TM's benefits by supporting a curious—some would say wacky—candidate for high office.

During the 1992 presidential campaign, Howard frequently called for the defeat of George Bush largely because of the president's antiabortion position and the indecency charges that the FCC was pursuing against Infinity Broadcasting. "Any woman who votes for Bush is an imbecile, with that abortion thing," Howard said. "I don't know what party I'm affiliated with, but this time I'm affiliated with—anybody who is in power, I'm not affiliated with. I want them voted out, especially the president, because I think he's set a mood in this country of conservatism. I'm talking about moral conservatism, you know, that whole *religioso* thing. I just think it's way out of hand."

And he added: "I'd like a conservative president fiscally and a liberal president when it comes to free speech and abortion."

He first warmed to Democratic candidate Jerry Brown, impressed by the former California governor's anti-Washington views during phone-ins to the show. He later told listeners that the Democratic nominee, Bill Clinton, was his choice. However, despite these public pronouncements, Federal Election Commission records show that Howard and Alison each put their money, $250 donations, behind the 1992 presidential campaign of John S. Hagelin.

John *who?*

The thirty-eight-year-old Hagelin, a soft-spoken TM practitioner and a Harvard-educated physics professor, was on leave from Maharishi International University, an accredited school founded by the Maharishi Mahesh Yogi in the farm country of Fairfield, Iowa. His Natural Law Party was formed in Fairfield in April 1992. The party's slogan was: "Only a new seed will yield a new crop." Hagelin espoused the widely accepted belief in TM circles that greater use of meditation could reduce stress levels and thereby head off costly health problems. He wanted all presidential candidates to undergo what he called a "brain-mapping" test, an electroencephalogram, to determine their "moral fiber, creativity, and stability in a crisis." Hagelin said he would not disclose the results of his own electroencephalogram unless Bush and Clinton submitted to the procedure, but his wife, Margaret, assured people that her husband measured "in the top 1 percent," whatever that meant.

Hagelin maintained that the peaceful aura, or so-called unified field, produced by widespread meditation would help him cut taxes, balance the budget, and curb inner-city crime. He proposed releasing negative energy through techniques such as TM, because "unless one can dissolve the deep-seated accumulated stress and tension and frustration in the nation's urban areas, then all of the other well-

230

meaning programs—job training, et cetera—cannot work." (Trying to achieve this "maharishi effect" in 1993, Hagelin became scientific adviser to a Washington gathering of a few thousand people who meditated hours a day for eight weeks. The group took credit for a concurrent reduction in local crime, an improvement in President Clinton's relations with Congress, and an increase in global harmony.)

Unlike the on-, off-, and on-again presidential campaign of billionaire H. Ross Perot, the Natural Law Party was one of many fringe organizations that had only a slim chance of stealing attention from the Republicans and Democrats. Nevertheless, Hagelin was as eligible as Bush and Clinton for federal matching funds if he raised $5,000 in contributions of $250 or less in each of twenty states. Alison Stern made her $250 donation in August 1992. Howard contributed $250 to the Dr. John Hagelin for President Committee of New York less than a month before Election Day.

Raising nearly $1.2 million from around nine hundred individuals, Hagelin received $350,000 in taxpayer funds, was on the ballot in twenty-nine states, campaigned around the nation—and pulled in 37,137 votes. Hagelin said in 1995* that he did not know Howard Stern, had never met him, but was pleasantly surprised to learn that the famed broadcaster had been among his contributors.

If Howard voted for Hagelin, he kept the news to himself. On the air he claimed to have backed Clinton.

The private Howard, the one who meditated and contributed to a "brain-mapping" candidate, did not host the morning radio show. The other Howard, the naughty one did.

Two years later, the question was: Howard Stern for governor?

Why not!

Despite Howard's widespread popularity, the growing influence of talk radio in the political culture, and the anti-incumbent battle cry reverberating across the United States, the notion that

---

*On July 20, 1995, Hagelin announced that he was a candidate for president in 1996. He hoped to appear on the ballot in all fifty states.

America's notorious shock jock wanted to succeed Mario M. Cuomo as governor of New York had the double whiffs of publicity stunt and sideshow distraction. On close examination, however, Stern's venture into Empire State politics in 1994 reflected his love for theatrical gestures and the earnest wishes of a fringe party to capitalize on his popularity. He was able to play politics as intensely and effectively—and as slyly—as a seasoned candidate, until the rules clashed with his desperate need for control.

For several years, devoted members of New York State's Libertarian Party who tuned in Howard's broadcasts felt a philosophical kinship when, for example, he supported the privatization of government services and decried high taxes. In 1990, a party member, Robert Goodman of the Bronx, sent Howard literature about the Libertarians and urged him to consider a run for governor in that year's election. Howard declined, but he endorsed the Libertarian candidate, W. Gary Johnson, who garnered 24,611 votes statewide, as Cuomo was reelected to a third four-year term.

It was Johnson's respectable showing that set the stage for the Libertarians' embrace of Howard four years later. Short of fifty thousand votes in the most recent (1990) quadrennial balloting, the party once again was forced under New York law to carry out a tedious petition drive in order to put its candidates on the ballot. Fifteen thousand valid signatures, including one hundred from each of sixteen congressional districts, were mandatory. If the Libertarians fielded a candidate who netted fifty thousand votes in the November election, they would lose their fringe-party status and automatically place party candidates on the statewide ballots during the next four years. The fifty thousand votes would free the faithful from having to wield petition-toting clipboards on street corners in the August heat.

In March 1994, Howard threatened to challenge Cuomo for reelection, largely in opposition to the governor's stand against reinstitution of the death penalty. Goodman again pitched Howard the Libertarian Party's virtues. "I don't know exactly how much of the credit or the blame I deserve for what happened next," Goodman said.

On March 21, a Monday, Howard broadcast the faxed correspondence from Goodman and began a public flirtation with the
Libertarian Party. One of the party's vice chairmen, Joseph
Brennan, a longtime listener who had tried to enlist Howard's
backing when he had run for mayor of New York City in 1993,
was surprised by Howard's gubernatorial interest, then sought
to channel the broadcaster in an organized fashion. As Howard continued to do his March 21 program, Brennan left a message for
him at "K-Rock." He was phoned back by Stern's producer, Gary
Dell'Abate, three times off the air to answer questions, such as
Would support of the death penalty conflict with Libertarian Party
views? As Brennan explained to Dell'Abate, the absence of a platform plank on the death penalty meant that Howard's approval of
capital punishment would not disqualify him from running as a
Libertarian. Before the Monday show ended, Howard spoke on the
air directly to Brennan, who told him about the party's nominating
convention, scheduled for the following month in Albany, the state
capital. Later in the day, Brennan alerted Libertarian officers
around the state and in Washington, assuring them that Howard's
interest was not a hoax and preparing them for the inquiries that
were sure to come from newspeople.

Howard became the best-known challenger to Cuomo when he
announced on March 22 that he would be a candidate. Libertarian
state chairman Ludwig B. Vogel phoned the show and encouraged
the radio star to seek the party's nomination. In a gesture that in-
curred the wrath of others in the party hierarchy, Vogel informed
Howard that it would be easy enough for him to gain the Libertarian
nod: all Howard had to do was pack the April convention with his
supporters, have them sign up for party membership, and win two-
thirds of the votes cast at the gathering. Simple as that. "We didn't
have a lot of bargaining strength with Howard to give the nomination away like that," Brennan lamented a year later. "By giving it
away on the second day of our involvement with him, he basically
could do what he wanted from then on. The length to which he included us after that was by his own choice."

"I don't know what the hell a Libertarian is," Howard said on the air. Vogel himself was unsure if Stern was a Libertarian or a libertine. Howard, however, stressed that he wanted the Libertarian nomination, because the party's workers would gather the signatures needed to put him on the ballot, sparing his supporters from having to write in his name upon entering the voting booth. Howard vowed to bring back the death penalty. He also promised to quicken traffic flow by improving the collection of highway tolls and to see to it that road construction occurred only at night. After fulfilling this three-point platform, he would step down and cede the office to the lieutenant governor, whoever that might be.

Political consultant Jay Severin, who counted Republican candidates among his clients, speculated that Howard could become "the Ross Perot of New York" because he had the potential to spoil a two-man race between Cuomo, the Democrat, and the Republican nominee. It was unclear whether Cuomo or the GOP would lose more votes to Howard's candidacy. Pundits noted that Howard's reach on radio stations throughout the state—in New York, Rochester, Albany, and Buffalo—gave him a large soapbox from which to attack the other candidates. Howard's support of the death penalty threatened to siphon votes from the declared Republican candidates, all of whom favored the return of capital punishment. "Given the intensity of the anger and frustration among the voters, I'm not entirely certain that Pee-wee Herman couldn't mount a viable campaign," Severin added. "A lot of people have a threshold definition of politicians that Howard Stern meets."

Day three, March 23: Howard formalized his gubernatorial intentions during an on-air press conference with the Libertarians Vogel and Brennan. "I swear to you this is no disc jockey shtick," he declared from a podium lined with copies of his latest video, which was on sale. "I swear to you I am a serious candidate for the governor of New York"—so serious that he admitted: "I am not perfect. I masturbate. I am forty years old, and maybe I talk about sex too much. But I am honest to a fault. Who else would reveal that the size of his genitals is under two inches?" He agreed with the Libertarian Party's call for "less government in our lives."

Bill Winter, the communications director at the party's national headquarters in Washington, expressed wariness: "Mr. Stern is a professional entertainer, and we're sure his campaign will be entertaining. We just hope that it won't detract from the serious positions the Libertarian Party advocates—reducing the size, cost, and power of government."

At his home in upstate Buffalo, attorney James Ostrowski, who had heard Howard press his candidacy on March 21, was horrified by the unexpected turn of events. Months earlier, Ostrowski had edged into the lead for the Libertarians' gubernatorial nomination by defeating Brennan and two other hopefuls in a straw poll among members of the party's biggest chapter—in New York City. He called Vogel's appearance on the Stern show "unauthorized" and threatened to challenge at the convention those party applicants who did not "in all sincerity" adopt the Libertarians' fundamental principle: the absolute right of the individual to enjoy his life, liberty, and property without interference from big government. Ostrowski charged: "If Howard Stern thinks he has the nomination sewn up, he is living in a dream world. The rank and file of the Libertarian Party are not going to allow their party to be taken over by a 'shock jock' who supported virtual socialist Bill Clinton in the last election."

Ostrowski's misgivings were drowned out by the Stern-driven buzz. The party, which had only about four hundred members, received hundreds of phone calls from people seeking applications for membership, the first step leading to participation in the April convention in Albany. An on-line survey of computer users conducted by Prodigy Services Company found that 51 percent of the three thousand respondents living in the state backed Stern's candidacy, compared with 21 percent for Cuomo and 22 percent for the Republican nominee, still to be named. A New York *Daily News/* WNBC-TV/Harris Poll, taken within days of Howard's announcement, showed that 9 percent of New York City voters would vote for Stern—71 percent figured that his candidacy was a publicity stunt.

Among those suggesting that the Stern-for-governor effort amounted to little more than a bid for attention was Howard's employer, Infinity Broadcasting. It wrote to the New York State Board of Elections for a ruling as to whether Howard's daily promotion of his campaign constituted an in-kind contribution from the radio stations broadcasting his show. Infinity's attorney, Bruce P. Keller, argued that "Mr. Stern is not a candidate as that term is defined . . . and that the provision of airtime for the broadcast of his show is not a contribution." Keller added: "In fact, the slight 'noise' created by Mr. Stern's pronouncements is probably most consistent with his ongoing—and successful—efforts to expand the market for his show."

In response to Infinity's inquiry, the board of elections ruled on April 25 that Howard's radio show did not represent a donation to his Libertarian campaign, because the program stemmed solely from an "employer-employee relationship . . . that predates the host's announced candidacy by several years." Therefore the show was not subject to regulations on political contributions. The board added: "If during the normal course of business, the talk show host is authorized to exercise his discretion as to matters that will be the subject of discussion and decides to discuss and promote his candidacy, the Board is of the opinion that it would not be an in-kind contribution by the radio station to the host-candidate."

The ruling offered relief to an anxious Infinity, which, Keller explained, sought "to maintain its normal operating practices, including the daily broadcast of Mr. Stern's show on several radio stations throughout the State." Coupled with an FCC determination that Howard did not have to provide equal-time access to other office seekers until the board of elections certified his candidacy (on completion of the summer petition drive), the ruling allowed him over several months to promote his campaign and views without fear of intervention by the state or the FCC.

The board's decision provided an upbeat Monday postscript to Howard's tumultuous convention weekend in Albany. Traveling from New York by chartered bus, which stopped en route at a strip club, Howard had been welcomed in the state capital on Saturday by dozens of tailgate-partying fans intent on legally overwhelming the Libertarians' gathering and supplying the ballots needed to give their candidate the party's nomination. Besides paying a $15 membership fee, the party crashers had to sign an application stating that they were "in substantial agreement" with the party's five governing principles, which included "Each individual possesses the inalienable right to life, liberty and justly acquired property" and "The voluntary exchange of goods and services is fundamental to any socioeconomic system which provides for the harmonious integration of divergent value systems." As *New York Newsday* columnist Gail Collins observed the scene, "The Libertarians are proudly and gloriously nerdy to the core, and so the convention produced an interesting clash of cultures—as if a high school motorcycle gang had crashed an Audio-Visual Club meeting."

"Do we want the death penalty?" Howard asked the crowd.

"Yes!"

"Are you ready to vote for the death penalty?"

"Yes!"

Predictably, Howard won the required two-thirds majority on the first ballot, receiving 287 of the 381 votes cast. Ostrowski finished second with 34 votes. Howard learned of his nomination while he was meeting with Ostrowski and other party officials in an upstairs room, away from the raucous scene in the main hall of the Italian-American Community Center. Robin Quivers and Don Buchwald, Howard's agent, also were on hand.

Howard now had to solidify his hold on the nomination by making sure that his choice as the candidate for lieutenant governor, Stanley H. Dworkin, was approved by the convention. Time was running out: the convention was supposed to clear out of the community center by 4:00 P.M., less than an hour later. "I want to get this done today," Howard said. He urged Ostrowski and the others to fall in line behind Dworkin, suggesting that it would be embarrassing if his pick of a running mate turned into a fight in front of the many reporters covering the convention. In a display of newfound political muscle, Buchwald indicated that unless the Dworkin matter was decided in Howard's favor, his client would ask supporters to stay in Albany overnight to ensure the choice of running mate. The only element missing from the display of political arm twisting was a thick fog of cigar smoke.

Dworkin, who had been recommended to Howard by a bookkeeper in his manufacturing business, had spoken to the broadcaster earlier in the week and met him for the first time in Albany. Dworkin saw the campaign as an opportunity to present his proposals for legalized gambling and an end to the sales tax on clothing purchases. To old guard Libertarians, Dworkin was alien to the party—for nine years he had been a Democratic legislator in Rockland County.

"I definitely had hard feelings about Dworkin being forced on us," recalled vice chairman Brennan, who attended the upstairs meeting with Howard. "The Democratic Party was one of our arch enemies." But Brennan agreed not to challenge Dworkin's nomination: "By that time, what was the point in fighting?"

Ostrowski, weary and embittered, also decided not to contest Dworkin's candidacy on the convention floor. "I washed my hands of it," he said. "But afterward, it was amazing that I was grilled by angry members who claimed that I was part of a secret meeting to get Dworkin on the ticket. After all I had done to prevent the party from being turned over to Stern, it was a little like criticizing Robert E. Lee for surrendering to Ulysses Grant by saying to him, 'Didn't you do anything to stop these people?'"

The mood among committed Libertarians soured further when Vogel, the state chairman and a Stern partisan, sought to push through the nomination of Dworkin before the 4:00 P.M. curfew. Vogel called for the waiving of parliamentary rules that allowed other candidates for lieutenant governor to be placed in nomination and to address the convention—a lengthy process that would have required a second day of convention business and possibly cost

Dworkin the nomination if most of Stern's backers did not stick around.

According to the party bylaws, a waiver of the rules could be approved only by unanimous consent, which was lacking. The clamor that went up from the Stern supporters overwhelmed the dissents. "Point of order!" and "You can't do this!" were shouted by party members who wanted to follow the rules and hear from other candidates. Once the waiver was declared approved, Dworkin's name was put to a voice vote. Most of the voters screamed for their man Stan.

"The voice vote for Stan Dworkin was where Howard lost the support of the old-timers," said Sean Dougherty, a party member and the media coordinator. "I think that none of them came back after that—and some of them were our best petitioners."

Nevertheless, it was mission accomplished for Howard. He went home to Long Island with a weekend's worth of audiotape and war stories to share with his radio listeners. Camera crews had amassed plenty of videotape in case Howard wanted to sell a memento of the campaign. About eighty party members convened at an Albany hotel on Sunday for the final day of convention business. They completed the Libertarian ticket, nominating candidates for the United States Senate, state attorney general, and comptroller. They displayed their ire at Howard's triumph by ousting Vogel as chairman. An angry member exclaimed, "This is not the Howard Stern Party."

Still, it was clear that Howard had enriched the Libertarians— by more than doubling the state party's enrollment, to about seven hundred members, and by attracting unaccustomed media attention. "Even if the newspapers ran fourteen inches on Stern and only one inch on the party, that was one more inch that we got in the past," Dougherty conceded.

On paper, at least, the Stern candidacy looked serious enough to gather support among voters. After George E. Pataki, a state senator from Putnam County, had emerged as the likely Republican rival to Governor Cuomo, a New York *Daily News* poll in early June revealed that Howard was tapping into the undecided vote. In a three-way race, he would capture 7 percent of the votes cast, compared with 47 percent for Cuomo and 40 percent for Pataki.

The results reflected Howard's electronic power; off the air, he did little to further his candidacy. "We did not campaign," Dworkin recalled. "No appearances, no dinners, no press releases. Because of Howard's concerns about equal time, we also agreed not to spend or raise money."

Ostrowski viewed the Albany aftermath in a harsh light: "After the convention, Stern and his people had no contact with the party." At a state committee meeting in June, Ostrowski proposed that the Libertarians forgo a petition drive on Howard's behalf unless he campaigned actively and made himself available to party officials. The committee rejected Ostrowski's resolution, partly in the belief that the former candidate's proposal was rooted in self-interest.

Howard could bypass the Libertarians' internal misgivings simply by speaking on the radio directly to voters, but his indifference toward the party and his independent style did not free him from two especially onerous campaign requirements. The intensely private candidate was obliged to state his home address on the petitions used to place his name on the November ballot. Also, he had to complete a financial-disclosure form that would offer an unprecedented listing of his assets. The manner in which he addressed both requirements appeared to reveal cynical underpinnings in his candidacy.

"It was bizarre—we needed his address to put on the petitions and he wouldn't give it to us," Ostrowski recalled.

Judging from Howard's security concerns, he had reasons for withholding his home address, in Nassau County, from a public document. In 1989, he had received his first licenses to carry a handgun, a Smith & Wesson .38-caliber revolver, from Nassau County and from New York City. (By 1994 he also was licensed to carry a second weapon, a .32-caliber.) In seeking the original New York City permit, police sources said, he had reported several death threats. "I'm telling you, we're under siege," he said one day on the air. "Put a gun in your buttocks, if you have no place to put it. . . . Be armed at all times in your home."

Rather than fight the address requirement on security grounds, or withdraw from the race, Howard proceeded in a questionable manner to get around the problem. On July 11, 1994, as the petition-gathering period neared, he filed a change in his voting address with the Nassau County Board of Elections, stating that he had moved from Old Westbury, where he indeed had been living for six years, to Plainview, which was several miles to the east. If the information was to be believed, Howard Stern had moved into a forty-year-old, six-room, brick-frame house on Sylvia Road, where most of the dwellings seemed to have been shaped by the same cookie cutter. Plain Plainview. But in signing the change-of-address card, he had affirmed that "the information provided herein is true and I under-stand that this application will be accepted for all purposes as the equivalent of an affidavit, and if it contains a material false state-ment, shall subject me to the same penalties for perjury as if I had been duly sworn."

When Howard submitted the change of address, one of his friends, Michael F. Rakosi, a real estate developer who held a mort-gage on the Plainview home, was foreclosing the loan. According to court papers, the mortgage on the Sylvia Road property had been taken out eight years earlier by a woman who failed to make the monthly payments and owed around $100,000 in principal alone. Howard listed the house as his place of residence shortly before the court ordered it sold at auction. (It was acquired at auction by the agent who had serviced Rakosi's mortgage.)

If Howard was living in the Plainview house—his wife did not change her voting address from Old Westbury—he had little regard for appearances. The property became an eyesore: the windows were bare of curtains, the front lawn tall and scraggly for want of a mower. A for-sale sign standing amid the weeds added to the look of abandonment.

Although Howard's use of the Plainview address on Libertarian petitions went unnoticed while he was a gubernatorial candidate, he would have exposed the party to potentially disastrous consequences if the petitions had been challenged over a question of residency. New York State election law defined residence as "that place where a person maintains a fixed, permanent, and principal home and to which he, wherever temporarily located, always intends to return." One way that the board of elections confirmed a person's place of residence was by checking if his spouse and children also lived at the address in question.

"I was told by Buchwald or Gary [Dell'Abate] that Howard was finalizing a lease agreement at that address," Brennan, the Libertarian vice chairman, remembered. "I didn't know if he was living in the place or not."

Completing a financial disclosure statement also bugged Howard. Administered by the New York State Ethics Commission, under the Ethics in Government Act of 1987, the statement was designed to root out conflicts of interest and to encourage ethical behavior among state employees, elected officials, and political candidates. Among the particulars that an individual had to list on the eleven-page form were sources of income, properties in which the person held an interest, and the types of securities that he owned. Contrary to Howard's repeated complaint that he would have to lay out his finances in unnecessary detail, the form did not call for precise dollar amounts of income or the exact market value of his holdings. An individual had to note only a category of values and amounts—from A (under $5,000) to F ($250,000 or over). If Howard was earning $2 million or $10 million from Infinity Broadcasting, he could get away with listing F as the amount of his compensation. The world knew that he was receiving at least $250,000 from his radio show—why was the form a problem? The New York State Ethics Commission made the stated sources of income available for public inspection, but *not* the categories (A to F) listed by those completing the form.

Howard, nevertheless, bristled over the disclosure requirement, just as he dodged reporters' requests and a court order to disclose his finances. Asked by *Playboy* how much he was paid to write *Private Parts*, he replied: "I don't talk about the figures. Never do, never have. Never talk about my salary." Was this hypocritical? After all, he pressed his celebrity guests about their wealth. "No, not so far as I'm concerned," he added. "Some people have a need to talk about that kind of shit. Their place in show business goes up when they talk about how much money they have. . . . But I don't have a need to brag about how much money I make. I don't think it's healthy." (A negligence suit filed against Howard in 1993 by a woman whose toll-free business phone number had been used accidentally as part of a skit on his syndicated TV show was settled out of court after the judge hearing the case ordered him to stand trial and provide financial documents because he might be liable for punitive damages.)

Seeing no way around financial disclosure in the gubernatorial race, Howard ordered his lawyers to state supreme court in hopes of blocking the ethics commission from enforcing the requirement while he sought to overturn it. He argued that the disclosure law violated his constitutional rights to privacy, freedom of speech, and freedom of association. Had he won a temporary injunction, it would have given him time to stay in the race without listing his sources of income. An injunction might have allowed him to continue his candidacy through Election Day, at which point a loss at the polls would have removed the need to divulge his finances.

But on August 2, state supreme court justice Harold J. Hughes denied him an injunction. He upheld the ethics commission's opinion that the public needed the disclosure law in order to know if a candidate had a "hidden agenda" related to his financial interests. Hughes noted that forty states and the federal government had similar rules. The jurist held out little hope that Howard could succeed in overturning the New York law.

Hughes's decision left Howard with a deadline of three weeks to fill out the disclosure form or face penalties that included a maximum fine of $10,000 and a year in jail. Suddenly his candidacy, which in four months had generated far more publicity than most three-issue campaigns, looked like a giant hassle for the "King of All Media." Besides, there were embarrassing reports that the Libertarian Party stood far short of the fifteen thousand signatures needed to put his name on the ballot. There also loomed the inevitable need to give opposing candidates equal radio time in the event that the board of elections validated his candidacy. For Infinity Broadcasting and the owners of Howard's three upstate affiliates, compliance with equal-time provisions could prove disruptive, burdensome, and costly.

On August 4, Howard announced during another on-air press conference that he was withdrawing from the race. He blamed the "ridiculous" disclosure rule for his decision. He had been ignorant about financial disclosure, he said, and thought it was necessary only to declare stock in companies that did business with New York State.

"They wanted me to disclose my entire income to everybody," he told the assembled reporters. "The reason I never told you how much money I have in the bank is because it's none of your business. It'll never be any of your business. It has nothing to do with me running for government—and that's for sure. . . . So if you want to know how much money I make, screw you. I am never going to tell you how much money I make. I'm not going to tell anybody."

But as the lawyers whom he had retained to seek the injunction surely told him, the state law did not require him to disclose his "entire income." The reporters covering the press conference, perhaps unfamiliar with the instructions on the disclosure form, did not press him on the issue. Howard would have had to identify the sources of his income, but the form allowed him to leave everyone guessing—and guessing wildly—as to exactly how much he earned, because it called only for the broadly descriptive categories of his wealth. The completed form would have become available to the public, but the categories that Howard wrote down (such as "Category F—$250,000 or over") would have been edited out.

"I am the most honest person in the world today," he said. "Anybody who admits to having a one-inch penis is honest."

He denied that he had entered the race for publicity. He took credit for giving the Libertarians "a higher profile than they ever had." He declared: "I am still a political force, and I will become an even bigger political force."

Daily News columnist David Hinckley called it "a four-handkerchief moment for the Republic." He wrote that "it remains hard to believe, despite his insistence to the contrary, that he ever had much more in mind for his 'race' than shtick."

Pundits viewed Howard's withdrawal as a blow to Cuomo, because several polls showed that the Stern candidacy was pulling about five percentage points from the total held by Pataki. The exit left the Libertarians with mixed feelings. The move threw chaos into the party's petition drive, because Stern partisans quit the effort. "It left us in a bind, to say the least," Brennan recalled. "He dropped out at the worst possible time." Others, such as Goodman, whose faxed entreaty had stirred Howard to seek the party's nomination, saw the Stern chapter as a media bonanza for the Libertarians: "Even if I thought the episode was horrible, I'd have to go along with the idea that there's no such thing as bad publicity. You have to get people's attention."

A committee on vacancies that had been formed by the Libertarians at the Albany convention replaced Howard as the party's gubernatorial candidate with Robert L. Schulz of Glens Falls, the founder of the All County Taxpayers Association. He had been contesting the power of state and local governments through the courts for years. Party stalwarts stepped in to help salvage the petition drive; the national headquarters of the party contributed funds to hire petitioners. The national office also held on to the hope that the new gubernatorial candidate would collect fifty thousand votes and thereby automatically reserve a ballot position in New York State for the party's presidential choice in 1996.*

Howard pulled away from the Libertarian Party, but quietly at first. In a September conversation with U.S. Senator Alfonse D'Amato, the New York Republican and Pataki's biggest booster, Howard revealed that he would support Pataki. This was great news for D'Amato, who had been a guest on Howard's radio show, received his on-air support for re-election, and repeatedly defended him in Washington. (D'Amato called on the FCC "to reject these narrow-minded calls for punitive actions" against Howard's employer, Infinity Broadcasting.)

With the election twelve days off, Stern officially endorsed Pataki during a twenty-minute phone conversation with the candidate on the air. Howard was one of the few politically vocal celebrities to reject Cuomo. Pataki, like Howard, favored a return of the death penalty, and he seconded Stern's concerns about traffic tie-ups on Long Island.

On November 8, the underdog Pataki defeated Cuomo by four percentage points—such a slim margin that Howard's endorsement appeared to have had an impact. "Small things do have a large impact in a close race," said Lee Miringoff, director of the Marist Institute for Public Opinion, in Poughkeepsie, New York. "Stern was part of the noise at the end. He may have been 'credentializing' for Pataki, reinforcing the support of those leaning toward him and re-

---

*In response to challenges filed by Republicans, who feared that the Libertarians would siphon votes from Pataki, the board of elections invalidated so many of the petition signatures submitted by the Libertarians that the party fell short of the fifteen thousand needed to put Schulz and the rest of the party's ticket on the ballot. But Schulz, a crafty litigator, and the party sued in federal court and obtained injunctive relief that enabled the party to place its candidates on the ballot after all. On December 27, 1994, in a significant decision stemming from the case, a federal appeals court ordered New York State to give minor parties such as the Libertarians "an equal opportunity to win the votes of the electorate" by providing access to lists of registered voters at no cost—access that had been routinely granted only to the major parties. Howard's withdrawal had caused the Libertarian campaign to stumble, but in his absence the party went on to win serious electoral reform.

inforcing the concerns of some people that Cuomo was arrogant and maybe had been governor too long."

The Schulz-Dworkin ticket had a dismal showing; the 9,506 votes was the lowest total in the twenty years that the Libertarians had fielded candidates for governor. As Ostrowski saw it, "We are left in the end with the depressing facts: more publicity than ever before and the lowest vote total ever." Even Johnson, the party's dimly remembered 1990 nominee, had pulled in 24,611 votes with far less media attention (but with Howard's putative backing).

Howard received sixty-nine write-in votes.

"I couldn't be happier," Howard told his listeners on the morning after. "We got a strong voting bloc behind us [to elect Pataki]." He brushed off a caller who argued that the best man won and that it had nothing to do with Howard's support. "You suck," Howard told the caller. "Don't rain on my parade, you bastard, you SOB."

When Pataki phoned the show minutes later, the governor-elect lavished praise: "I tell you, you guys are the best. . . . You did get the word out. It was just great, Howard, and I gotta thank you."

"No, no, no," Howard replied. "Thank *you.*"

Pataki's wife, Libby, also checked in to express appreciation. Asked if she had slept with her husband the night before, she said: "I slept with him about twenty-five minutes."

"How was it?"

"I don't know. We were dead."

"You're a very sexy woman," Howard told her, before adding, in a Groucho-like leer: "So tonight's the night where you can really appreciate each other and bask in each other's glow, am I correct?"

Mrs. Pataki giggled.

"Will that be happening?" he wanted to know.

"Hopefully."

"Oh, God bless you. Take pictures and send me one."

On January 1, 1995, Pataki was sworn as New York's fifty-third governor. Howard and Alison Stern occupied two of the best seats on the stage in Albany's Knickerbocker Arena. They were in the third row, so close to the podium that they appeared in most of the photos and television footage shot as Pataki took the oath and delivered his inaugural address. "We just met face to face for the first time," Howard told a reporter afterward while signing programs for others on stage. "It was quite exciting." Later, he and Alison, as well as Howard's parents, were guests of the Patakis at the governor's mansion.

The new governor publicly and generously acknowledged Howard's enthusiastic radio support. Political commentators covering the inaugural festivities suggested that Howard's leaving the race and backing Pataki in the clutch had helped the Republican's campaign in a big way.

Pataki probably did not know that, as the Nassau County election records showed, Howard himself had not voted in November.

TWENTY-ONE

After Governor Pataki thanked Howard for his support by giving him first-class treatment at the inauguration, Governor Christine Todd Whitman of New Jersey belatedly showed appreciation for Howard's backing in her 1993 upset win over the incumbent, James Florio. On the autumn morning that Howard had promised to endorse the first New Jersey gubernatorial candidate to call him, Whitman won the phone race and profited afterward from the favorable exposure on Howard's show, which reached Garden State voters via radio stations in New York and Philadelphia. Whitman now told Howard on his broadcast that she planned to fulfill a promise made in 1993 by naming a highway rest stop after him.

Unlike Clara Barton, Walt Whitman, Woodrow Wilson, Thomas A. Edison, and other figures whose names were affixed to rest areas on the busy New Jersey Turnpike, Howard would be memorialized at a smaller stop with picnic tables located off Interstate 295, in the rural south Jersey community of Springfield Township, population 3,028. An aluminum plaque showing Howard poking his head from an old-fashioned outhouse was to be mounted at a cost to the Republican State Committee of about $1,000.*

---

*The plaque was installed on March 21, 1995, and stolen four days later. "That's that," Whitman said. "We are not going to replace it. We'd be replacing it every week." The thieves mailed the plaque to Howard. The rest stop continued to attract his fans.

Howard thanked the governor and said he was touched: "I've always dreamt of a rest stop that I would drive by with my family and people could relieve themselves while they see my name."

Not everyone rejoiced in Whitman's lighthearted gesture. Myra Terry, president of the state chapter of the National Organization for Women, declared: "Howard Stern promotes women as sex objects for his own amusement and promotes the stereotype of women being whores, lesbians, and bitches. I think it's in really bad taste." Walter Fields, Jr., political director of the New Jersey chapter of the National Association for the Advancement of Colored People, said: "I think women and racial minorities in this state should be outraged. We are insulted." Diana McCague, the leader of a gay rights group called the Lesbian Avengers, said she was upset because "I don't get the governor of this state endorsing someone who makes jokes at the expense of oppressed people." SHOCKER, *The Trentonian*, a tabloid published in the state capital, screamed in huge type on page one. "Jersey rest stop named for (gasp!) Howard Stern."

Asked by reporters if her action might be viewed as support for Howard's controversial remarks, the governor replied: "Let's not get ridiculous. He's always been very polite when I've been on with him. . . . I am not giving Howard Stern my imprimatur."

Coming in the aftermath of Pataki's homage, Whitman's humorous nod on January 26 did go a long way to illustrate an increasing, oh-well acceptance of Howard's rogue antics among a wider audience and a tacit recognition among politicians willing to play along that he commanded the powerful devotion of his fans. Whitman was a rising star in her party. She had been chosen by the Republican National Committee to give the nationally televised rebuttal to President Bill Clinton's State of the Union address two days before she honored Howard—the same Howard who said that he found her an attractive woman. "I would 'do' her in a second," he told his listeners, because she had a "tight ass" and "big cans."

At the end of the week, the long-haired champion of two governors was draped in a towel in his studio as he was treated to a Super Bowl rubdown given by a mother and daughter.

"Girls, are you disgusted by me?" he asked the scantily clad duo.

"I love your feet, Howard," the mother replied.

"Rub my feet, rub her, rub me, rub everybody," he instructed the women, who also sought to please Jackie Martling and the rest of Howard's on-air crew.

The week in January 1995 had encapsulated the contradictions that were Howard Stern. He was a friend of leading politicians (a presidential candidate, Senator Arlen Specter of Pennsylvania, would drop by before long), yet his own political incorrectness inflamed many others; a free-speech firebrand whose willingness to talk about almost anything, and to do so in an often hilarious manner, incensed those who regarded his satirical swipes and sexual obsessions as wicked and raunchy crud; a mainstream success, as evidenced by the ratings he earned around the country and by the sales of *Private Parts*, who insisted time and again on aiming bra-and-panties jollies at the male listeners making up the core of his lucrative radio franchise.

One question remained unanswered: Who was the *real* Howard Stern?

The answer: All of the above.

He now had three young daughters—Emily, Debra, and a baby, Ashley. He made it perfectly clear that the older girls did not listen to his radio confessions. What's more, he wanted all three to achieve greater dignity in life than the women who routinely came to show off their curves in his studio. (Since June 1994, his fans were able to see the spankers and strippers during half-hour segments of the radio show televised each night on cable's E! network.)

Despite the public displays of affection and respect, despite the throngs that turned out for his book signings, despite the prominent seat on Pataki's dais, Howard preferred and indeed craved the security and anonymity of home. Since reaching the New York radio dial in 1982, he and Alison had moved several times—from an apartment in a Queens high-rise to a series of homes on the North Shore of Long Island—mainly to escape nosy fans who learned where they lived. In the fall of 1988, they bought a large, secluded house in the well-to-do community of Old Westbury for $1.24 million, taking out an $850,000 mortgage from Boston Safe Deposit and Trust Company to complete the transaction. After renovation in 1990, the twenty-year-old dwelling and its full basement totaled thirteen rooms and four and a half baths. It was a sunny, gable-roofed home set on nearly three acres, which included a tennis court, a heated pool, and a cabana. Lavish by the standards of most listeners, the house and its amenities, secured behind an electronic gate, hardly filled the potential reach of the extremely wealthy owner. Other properties along the North Shore, the countrified choice of the Vanderbilts and F. Scott Fitzgerald's Jay Gatsby, offered more land, more panorama, and more cachet. Howard appeared to have placed a higher priority on convenience and isolation.

Here, at the address he withheld from his nominating petitions for governor, he could turn off the outrageous broadcast personality and not have to show off for the neighbors. He could shut down the motor mouth and lose himself in hours of television and home videos—thrillers and horror flicks were among his more frequent selections. Or he could unwind by noodling on his home computer or working on the media projects that helped to make him a very rich man. To leave the wooded sanctuary and mingle in public was a chore, typically requiring advanced planning. For example, his staff parties at Scores, discussed at length on the radio, took place during the day, when the upscale Manhattan topless club was usually closed to other ogling customers and he could enter and exit with few fans waiting for him at the door.

Except for these naughty forays among beautiful women—the parties at Scores helped Howard fortify his bonds with the tight-lipped and loyal group of men who worked with him on the radio show—the off-air Howard Stern bore little resemblance to the foul-tongued morning man and scourge of the FCC. "That's Howard's act," Ben Stern assured a radio personality who hated being ridiculed on the air by his son. The real Howard was a nice Jewish boy from Long Island, a devoted family man who solicitously asked friends about their own families, a health nut who scorned drink and drugs—and followed the more elusive Ayurvedic prescriptions for a healthy life, which include a sound home environment and workaday routines.

Then again, it was simplistic to say that the often crude persona he presented for more than four hours each weekday morning was entirely an act. Because it was not an act. It was *the other Howard*, the one that Transcendental Meditation helped him tap into. As his friends and associates observed, Howard had an unusual ability to reach this other side of himself on the radio—the sex-driven, go-scratch-yourself Howard. The radio personality was not the warm and quiet Howard familiar to those who knew him off the air.

"The Howard you hear on the radio is a different side of Howard," said Randall Bongarten, the general manager who allowed him to unleash his act at WNBC-AM. "And, okay, it's an act that sells and he knows how to use it. But the thing that makes him popular is that he asks the questions that are on people's minds. That's truth. That's what communicates truth, the fact that he does that. It's the big draw of Howard."

In an interview with *Rolling Stone*, Howard, however, insisted that on the radio he could be "exactly who I am and say exactly what I feel." He added: "I really feel I'm role-playing in real life. But I can get on the radio and be who I feel I am inside. In real life, I sit and hold back all the time. I hate that. But you can't function in real life if you go around telling people what you think."

Even those broadcasters who recoiled at Howard's outspoken contempt for his foes and at his prurient interests agreed that, in the words of talk-radio pioneer Bill Mazer, now the morning man on New York's WEVD-AM, "he widened the room for all of us." In the wake of Howard's extraordinary ratings success, almost every topic became grist for discussion on the nation's airwaves, from the sexual transgression of actor Hugh Grant with a Hollywood streetwalker to the carnal adventures graphically described by teenagers and adults calling "Love Phones," a popular nighttime broadcast being syndicated by WHTZ-FM.

When *Radio & Records* put out its twentieth-anniversary issue, in 1993, it was no surprise that the industry publication named Howard Stern the most influential air personality of the previous two decades.

TWENTY-TWO

Since the autumn of 1985, when Howard Stern was lured by Mel Karmazin to New York's "K-Rock," the two men had become giants in broadcasting and helped build Infinity into the dominant force in radio.

From a total of ten stations in 1985, Infinity by the summer of 1995 had grown to twenty-seven. The lineup included solid producers of ratings and revenue, what Karmazin called "oceanfront properties," in the ten largest radio markets, such as the Boston rocker WBCN-FM and New York's all-sports WFAN. As the largest American company devoted exclusively to radio, Infinity posted revenues in 1995 of $325.7 million, an increase of $52 million over the year before (Howard generated up to $22 million of the annual revenue, a diminishing percentage amid expansion). And, the corporation did plan to expand. Karmazin and his team lobbied in Washington to have Congress lift the cap that prevented companies from owning more than twenty AM and twenty FM stations.

In a printed assessment of Infinity prepared in the spring of 1995, media analyst John S. Reidy of the Smith Barney brokerage firm lauded the corporation's management as being "without peer in acquiring, promoting, and improving cash flow generation of local radio properties." Among the wide variety of respected institutions owning stock in Infinity—and, by extension, in Howard Stern—were Lehman Brothers Holdings, Equitable Companies Inc., Bankers Trust New York Corp., Bessemer Trust Company, Bank of Boston

Corp., Citicorp, California State Teachers Retirement System, New York State Teachers Retirement System, Chase Manhattan Corp., Bank of Tokyo Ltd, Prudential Insurance Company, and many others.

Karmazin, who joined Infinity in 1981 as president of the company's radio division at a salary of $125,000 a year, had total pay in 1994 of $2.4 million. Although the industry's intense interest in his business activities clashed with his wish to avoid the spotlight— Howard did not mention Karmazin's name on the air—the executive unavoidably enlarged his profile by becoming one of the more active contributors to political candidates. Among them was a large bipartisan mix of United States senators, such as Bill Bradley, Bob Packwood, Connie Mack, John H. Chafee, Trent Lott, Kay Bailey Hutchison, Daniel K. Inouye, Ernest F. Hollings, and Daniel Patrick Moynihan. In addition, Karmazin reigned over a mammoth chunk of the network radio business as a result of a complex deal finalized in 1994 that linked Infinity to two large distributors of radio programming, Unistar Communications and Westwood One, and installed him as chief executive officer of the newly formed colossus. Besides Stern, who had a total of twenty-six stations in twenty-four markets* airing his show, and Don Imus, whose program on WFAN was being distributed by Westwood One to dozens of stations, the enlarged pool of national talent working for the various Karmazin-led companies included the syndicated air personalities Casey Kasem, Bruce Williams, Jim Bohannon, and G. Gordon Liddy.

---

*Besides WXRK-FM in New York and KLSX-FM in Los Angeles, the stations carrying *The Howard Stern Show* as of December 1995 were WYSP-FM in Philadelphia, WJFK-FM in Washington, WJFK-AM in Baltimore, KEGL-FM in Dallas, WNCX-FM in Cleveland, WQBK-FM and WQBJ-FM in Albany, KFBI-FM in Las Vegas, WEZB-FM in New Orleans, WNVE-FM in Rochester, New York, KOME-FM in San Jose, California, WBCN-FM in Boston, KROD-AM in El Paso, Texas, WYAV-FM in Myrtle Beach, South Carolina, WTKS-FM in Orlando, Florida, WBGG-FM in Miami, XTRA-FM in San Diego, California, KEDJ-FM and KHOT-FM in Phoenix, Arizona, WJJD-AM in Chicago, WKOC-FM in Norfolk, Virginia, WVGO-FM in Richmond, Virginia, and WXDX-FM in Pittsburgh. WWKB-AM in Buffalo would drop the show in January 1996 because of a change in its format.

In the ten years since Howard had joined Infinity and expanded into other markets, it remained difficult to explain the exact reason for his outsize appeal. Was he the class clown of the airwaves or the successor to Lenny Bruce, who decades ago daringly found comedy in religion, politics, and sex? Was Howard a dirty middle-aged man or an actor simply playing the part (and laughing all the way to the bank)? A spitball shooter or a social commentator?

A 1994 analysis by The Interep Radio Store, the nation's largest radio-sales company, revealed that in New York, Los Angeles, Philadelphia, and Washington the highest percentage of Howard's listeners were twenty-five to thirty-four years of age and that seven out of ten were male. Qualitative data showed that his listeners twenty-five to fifty-four ranked above the market average in such categories as $75,000 household income and ownership of homes over $300,000.

Ratings released by The Arbitron Company in January 1996 reflected Howard's extraordinary success. Besides drawing around four million listeners a week, his show was number one in New York, number one in Dallas, number two in Philadelphia, and ranked among the top five in Los Angeles and other markets. These Arbitron report cards, which also showed Howard's prodigious popularity among men and high-income households, explained why advertisers not deterred by his remarks flocked to buy time on his program.

In 1995, "K-Rock" took in an estimated $30 million in commercial revenue; Howard generated around half that amount. Sponsors that wanted Howard to read and personalize a live, one-minute commercial on "K-Rock" were being charged $5,000, a fourfold increase since 1990 and the highest sum in New York radio. That so many advertisers were willing to pay such rates underscored Howard's proven ability to create product awareness and put people in stores.

The "K-Rock" sales force typically sought a minimum commitment from a sponsor of three commercials a week. However, the station's strategy was to avoid long-term contracts. "We want long-term clients, but we try not to lock them into long-term contracts because we then have the freedom to raise the rates around the holidays and at other times when Howard's show is sold out," a "K-Rock" salesperson explained. To help develop lucrative relationships, the sales department usually scheduled one client meeting a week in which Howard calmly and attentively asked the advertiser about his product or service and how it differed from others on the market. Since his days at WNBC, he made time for those sponsors who wanted to meet with him.

"Howard knows that sales are the bread and butter of the station," the salesperson said. "Howard also wants to get the guy to believe in Howard. He's his own best asset in the meetings, because most people only know him from what they hear about him or read in the papers."

What people read in the papers sometimes involved his caustic commentary. After the Tejano music star Selena had been shot to death by the president of her fan club in the spring of 1995, Howard aired one of her songs and added the sound of gunfire. Speaking in a broad Mexican accent, he said: "*Sí*, let's dance to happy, Madonna-like music . . . and big, chubby girls in thongs. . . . Let's eat spicy food." He said that "Spanish people have the worst taste in music." Mexican Americans and other Hispanic groups were outraged—especially those in Texas. They wrote letters of protest to the FCC and called for boycotts against advertisers on the show and his Dallas affiliate, KEGL-FM. In a striking turnaround, Howard seemed to apologize—and in Spanish: "As you know, I am a satirist. . . . My comments about the tragic death of Selena were certainly not intended to cause any further pain to her family, friends, or fans."

What generated even greater media attention—and no doubt prompted unfamiliar listeners to sample Howard's show time and again—was his seemingly ceaseless war with the FCC over on-air comments that the commission considered indecent. The FCC levied its first fine against Infinity Broadcasting ($6,000) for Stern material in 1990. By September 1994, when the penalties against the company had burgeoned to $1,706,000,† Karmazin disclosed at an industry seminar that Infinity already had spent more than $3 million on legal expenses. At the same time, Karmazin emphasized that the corporation would not pay the fines, because the FCC was "not clarifying the [indecency] rules for us or telling us exactly what we did wrong." Infinity was prepared to incur even higher legal fees in its fight against the FCC, because, Karmazin added, "we think that it's wrong to take the cheaper way out [and pay the fines]."

Meanwhile, the tedious, perhaps even pointless, task of monitoring his show dragged on. If Infinity Broadcasting had spent more than $3 million to defend its most valuable broadcaster, it was possible that American taxpayers, like it or not, had paid much more to restrain and explain him. At the FCC's M Street headquarters in Washington, the offices and the records room in the Complaints and Investigations Branch were inundated with audiotapes, correspondence, and legal briefs pertaining to Howard and his show. Thousands of letters, faxes, postcards, telephone messages, and mass-produced petitions were indexed, numbered, and affixed to copies of correspondence mailed by the FCC in response. Members of Congress who received complaints and other comments about Stern from their constituents typically forwarded copies to the FCC, generating still more responses from the agency. In one such exchange, Representative Robert S. Walker of Pennsylvania expressed a voter's concern that the FCC was "unjustly harassing Howard Stern. Accordingly, I would like to take this opportunity to express my interest on behalf of my constituent and to request that this matter be reviewed as expeditiously as possible." As the files showed, high-level agency officials or one of the FCC's ranking commissioners usually replied to the lawmakers, who dutifully forwarded the letters to their constituents. To examine the thick sheafs

---

†The owner-operators of Stern's affiliates in Las Vegas and Los Angeles also were fighting a total of $216,250 in show-related FCC fines for indecency. More than a dozen other indecency fines unrelated to Stern's show also had been levied against still other stations around the country.

of correspondence in the threadbare records room was to realize that freedom of speech and freedom to dissent were costly rights to exercise and honor. The letters reflected an incalculable expenditure of manpower and clerical hours. They also offered rare insights into Stern's vast audience of detractors and admirers.

A woman from Port Orange, Florida, urged FCC commissioner James Quello to take "quick and decisive action on the pending complaints against this show. What we need is our minds filled with positive thoughts and not sick and negative ones."

From Cerritos, California, came an unsigned complaint "about the most revolting monster ever to hit the airwaves: Howard Stern. . . . The New Years [sic] 'show' which he offered for $40 (and which one of our neighbors taped), even grossed out the men. The show was vile, disgusting, repulsive, and repugnant. Nothing could have been worse. We only watched it a few minutes before we all excused ourselves. . . . Are there no laws to bar freaks such as he is from broadcasting such utter filth? . . . *Please, please* do something for the good of all humanity and keep this vile monster off the air and TV for good. He really ought to, in my opinion, be in jail for what he says and does."

A man from Rehoboth, Massachusetts, recalled driving home from a meeting in Boston and discovering Howard's show on WBCN-FM while switching between stations. Howard apparently was talking in detail about a video "involving multiple lesbian partners, one of which was an amputee. The discussion was graphic in nature and went into significant detail about the sexual acts performed. . . . I was unable to listen to this program for more than one minute, at which time I changed the dial." The man continued: "Be advised that while I do not consider myself to be a prude, nor do I normally take the time to address complaints regarding things that I hear on the radio, I do believe that this specific incident and the information that was being disseminated over the airwaves was going far beyond the boundaries of bad taste and well into what can be construed as obscene material. . . . Therefore, I am asking that you investigate this specific program." He concluded: "I recognize that I control the radio dial as well as the radio dial for my children; however, it is my concern that when material of this nature is broadcast over a free market we are doing significant damage to our culture and specifically our youth."

Among the letters from Howard's fans and defenders was one forwarded to the FCC by Senator Dianne Feinstein, of California. A man in Los Angeles had argued: "I have never written a political leader before, but an injustice currently being carried out by the Government in the form of selective punishment and an attempt to circumvent the right to free speech has prompted me to ask for your intervention. As you may know, the FCC has been fining the employer of Howard Stern hundreds of thousands of dollars for comments made on his radio show. Regardless of how we feel about Mr. Stern's show and its contents, clearly it is no more obscene or pornographic than many television and radio shows which have not be[en] the target of fines or penalties. This is obviously a misuse of the powers of the FCC and an attempt at blatent [sic] and illegal censorship."

A New York photographer called on Vice President Albert Gore to look into why the FCC was dogging Stern: "Rude, crude, in bad taste, Howard is hardly the type of person one might immediately stand for. However, we here in America have a thing called the First Amendment, which protects Mr. Stern as much as it protects fundamentalist Christians, whom I find to be much more offensive. I would no more suggest they be muzzled than that they be killed. America is built on diversity and opposing viewpoints, and capitalistic free market principles."

A woman from Plano, Texas, wrote that she had attended her first Christians in Action meeting and was "very disturbed at the process that took place." The guest speaker "gave virtually no information except we had to get this 'Potty Mouth' off the air and then about 100 people started writing letters furiously" to the FCC and Dallas affiliate KEGL-FM. The woman said she was bothered that "uninformed people are influencing what should or should not be on the radio." She also said: "I must share with you that I am a fan of

Howard. He has a bawdy sense of humor and most of the time I find it relaxing to listen to him. Howard's show is just part of my radio routine. I also listen to National Public Radio, Christian Music, other talk shows and good old rock-and-roll. Although I would not go so far as to call Howard a role model, I find that he is basically an honest man and seems to have a lot of integrity." She cited Howard's respect for the institution of marriage and his belief that "all children should receive parental guidance. An unhappy listener called in one day and told him she thought he was disgusting and that she would never allow her child to listen to him. [His] response was 'good, that means you are a good mother. . . .' When Howard occasionally gets too intense for me, I simply switch the station. . . . In summary, I am in favor of *The Howard Stern Show* remaining on the air. For those who find it offensive, simply turn the dial."

As letters such as these continued to reach the FCC, the standoff between the two adversaries—the FCC trying to purge the airwaves of indecency and Infinity refusing to pay $1.7 million in fines—inched toward a potentially decisive arena, as a result of a major court decision. On June 30, 1995, the United States Court of Appeals for the District of Columbia Circuit upheld FCC policy by approving the agency's rules that ban indecent programs between 6:00 A.M. and 10:00 P.M. The court dismissed broadcasters' contention that the FCC's regulations were too broad.

The court's ruling strengthened the Justice Department in the event that it decided to act on behalf of the FCC and sue Infinity to collect the fines. At first glance, it appeared that nothing would please Karmazin more; for years he had called on the FCC to give Infinity its day in court to challenge the commission's actions. Although the latest turn in the enforcement of directives on indecency applied to all radio and television programming, there arose the distinct possibility that Howard Stern might stand at the center of a landmark case heard by the Supreme Court of the United States. The Republic in all its seriousness would learn once and for all if the bad boy of the airwaves had the right to discuss his masturbatory fantasies and bowel movements at eight in the morning.

Or so it seemed. Two months later, in a stunning development, Infinity agreed to pay the federal government every penny that it owed, plus an additional $9,000, to settle all indecency complaints pending against the company. The timing of the announcement—on September 1, 1995, the Friday of Labor Day weekend, which meant that the story would appear in the little-read newspapers of the following day—suggested that Infinity was embarrassed by its capitulation. Nevertheless, it was page one news in New York: "PAY UP," the *Daily News* screamed in letters three inches tall. "Howard Stern's bosses to shell out 1.7M for his dirty talkin'."

For years Howard had expressed nothing but contempt for the FCC and its commissioners. For years Karmazin had presented himself as a stalwart champion of the radio industry's need for clearer FCC guidelines on indecency. He had vowed to spend as much as it would take to fight what he considered the FCC's vague definition of indecency because "I don't know how you can be involved as a leader in the radio industry and not fight for the things that you believe are right."

Now there would be no Supreme Court test. Infinity finally blinked, because the FCC's ire over Howard Stern—additional indecency complaints reportedly were under review—threatened to slow the commission's approval of the radio company's expansion plans. Howard Stern was good for business, but Infinity decided not to allow his big mouth to interfere with the acquisition of more stations, now that Congress might increase the number of outlets that a company could own. According to a knowledgeable source, Infinity's attorney, Steven A. Lerman, who through the years had filed the stacks of legal briefs in defense of Stern, persuaded the adamant Karmazin to set aside his ego and clear the company's slate with the FCC instead of allowing the matter to impede acquisitions. Infinity admitted no wrongdoing or liability and vowed to continue its support for a fight being waged by a coalition of broadcasters against the FCC's indecency regulations. However, Infinity essentially surrendered in its battle over principle and sought to hide behind the transparent text of an FCC statement, which said that the company's payment of $1,715,000 was "a voluntary contribution to the U.S. Treasury." As Karmazin bluntly advertised in his own prepared statement, resolution of the proceedings with the FCC "will enhance our opportunity to further expand the Howard Stern program into additional markets."

Returning from vacation days later, Howard argued that government harassment "finally got to" Infinity. It sounded as if he understood and accepted the company's wish to pay the fines and get on with business, but, after years of viciously attacking the FCC, he emphasized that he himself had played no role in the capitulation. "I was not in on this decision, nor did I know about it, how's that?" he claimed. "And I was plenty upset." Had he been fined directly, he wanted his listeners to know, he would have let the government put him in jail instead of paying penalties issued in violation of his First Amendment rights.

Infinity was quick to take advantage of its newly cleansed record with the FCC. On September 22, the company announced that it planned to pay $275 million for the seven major-market radio stations owned by Alliance Broadcasting Inc., expanding Infinity's portfolio to thirty-four outlets. (In an ironic twist, the big winner in the deal was one of Howard's old nemeses, former WNBC general manager John P. Hayes, Jr., who had founded Alliance in 1990 and had assembled the group of stations piecemeal for only $77 million.) Before long, Infinity also would take its first step outside radio, agreeing to pay $300 million for TDI Worldwide Inc., a leader in outdoor advertising on buses and in transit locations.

As 1995 slipped into history, Howard's rewards for drawing around four million listeners a week and generating up to $22 million of Infinity's annual revenues were breathtakingly rich. His gross earnings in 1995 from radio work would total around $8 million, based on the author's knowledge of Stern's contract with New York's "K-Rock" and the fees from affiliate stations that he split with Infinity. In addition, industry observers estimated that, as the marquee name of E! Entertainment Television, he was receiving around

$1.5 million a year—roughly $30,000 for each radio broadcast video-taped at "K-Rock" by the cable channel, which nightly played back separate half hours of him and his gang doing radio. A contract with ReganBooks, a division of Rupert Murdoch's News Corp., to write a second book paid him an advance of around $3 million.

Bottom line: Howard Stern was expected to earn about $12.5 million in 1995.

The response to his new book indicated that the future held the potential for even greater riches. Called *Miss America*, despite the protests of lawyers representing the Miss America Beauty Pageant, the book showed Howard in trampy drag on the cover (and photographed alongside former Infinity board member O.J. Simpson, the recently acquitted murder defendant, on the back). Between the covers were 482 pages of perverse fantasies (such as "My Fantasy Fuck List"), hateful recriminations (against Rush Limbaugh and others), bizarre confessions (including an apparently successful bout with obsessive-compulsive disorder), and many salacious photographs. In other words, *Miss America* was not too different from *Private Parts*, published two years earlier (and due to be filmed for Paramount Pictures after all, in 1996). "Reading *Miss America* might also put you through several stages of reactions that cover the spectrum from pleasure to revulsion," *New York Times* reviewer Richard Bernstein wrote. *Entertainment Weekly* gave the book a B+, saying that Stern's shtick "can still be pretty darn funny."

The new book was released on November 7 and immediately sold 33,000 copies at Barnes & Noble stores—a first-day record for the giant chain—and another 17,000 at Waldenbooks outlets. Discussed at length by the author, whose radio shows sounded like infomercials for the book, *Miss America* went on to sell a total of 120,000 copies in its first week. This awesome sum exceeded the initial figures for recent novels by the popular John Grisham and Michael Crichton. Naturally, the book bumped Colin Powell's *My American Journey* from the top spot on national bestseller lists (although, despite continued strong sales, within a few weeks it was displaced from the lead position on lists appearing in *The New York*

Times and *USA Today* by computer guru Bill Gates's *The Road Ahead* and a holiday favorite, Richard Paul Evans's *The Christmas Box*).

But no other personality was able to attract such crowds to book signings. Not Powell, not Magic Johnson, not Norman Schwarzkopf. An estimated four thousand fans kept Stern autographing books for seven and a half hours at the Barnes & Noble superstore in Carle Place, Long Island. He signed thousands more in San Francisco. The fifteen thousand fans drawn to his appearance at a Borders outlet in Los Angeles shut down several blocks of Westwood Boulevard.

On a cold Thursday afternoon in November, he arrived at Brentano's Bookstore on Fifth Avenue in Midtown Manhattan dressed like a honky-tonk beauty queen. Waiting for him were thousands of fans, lined up east on 48th Street and then north on Madison Avenue for five more blocks. Most were men between eighteen and thirty years old who had skipped work or classes and waited hours for the chance to share the few seconds it would take Stern to scrawl his name in their copies.

Brentano's ornate, black iron building originally had housed the elegant Scribner's bookstore. On the upper floors, the genteel publishing firm of Charles Scribner's Sons had welcomed Ernest Hemingway, Thomas Wolfe, F. Scott Fitzgerald, and other great writers who helped define American literature in the Twentieth Century.

Who could have imagined that one of the most popular authors to follow them into this cathedral of letters would be a gawky and bejeweled "Miss America" for the masses?

INDEX

ABOUT THE AUTHOR

Paul D. Colford, a native of Jersey City, New Jersey, joined *Newsday* in 1980 and was among the first reporters assigned three years later to the paper's New York City edition, which became *New York Newsday* (discontinued in 1995). He also wrote a weekly column about the radio industry for eight years. Still based in *Newsday's* Manhattan offices, he now covers the publishing industry; his column on books, magazines, and newspapers also appears in the *Los Angeles Times*. He is the author of *The Rush Limbaugh Story*, published by St. Martin's Press in 1993, and has worked as an on-air host over WOR-AM, the New York news/talk station.